Employment Termination
Source Book

HR Source Book Series

Employment Termination
Source Book

A Collection of Practical Samples

Wendy Bliss, J.D., SPHR
and
Gene R. Thornton, Esq., PHR

Society for Human Resource Management
Alexandria, Virginia
USA
www.shrm.org

This book is published by the Society for Human Resource Management (SHRM®). The interpretations, conclusions, and recommendations in this book are those of the author and do not necessarily represent those of SHRM.

The Society for Human Resource Management (SHRM) is the world's largest association devoted to human resource management. Representing more than 200,000 individual members, the Society serves the needs of HR professionals by providing the most essential and comprehensive set of resources available. As an influential voice, SHRM is committed to advancing the human resource profession to ensure that HR is an essential and effective partner in developing and executing organizational strategy. Visit SHRM Online at www.shrm.org.

Library of Congress Cataloguing-in-Publication Data

Bliss, Wendy, 1955-
  Employment termination source book : a collection of practical samples / by Wendy Bliss and
      Gene R. Thornton.
    p. cm.
  ISBN 1-58644-066-7
  1. Employees—Dismissal of—Handbooks, manuals, etc. I. Thornton, Gene R. II. Title.

HF5549.5.D55B55 2006
658.3'13—dc22

                                        2006016010

Cover design and layout: Shirley Raybuck
Interior design and layout: Carol Levie
Editorial: EEI Communications
Index: Sharon Johnson
Printing: Central Plains Book Mfg.
CD-ROM: Automated Graphic Systems

Printed in the United States of America.
10 9 8 7 6 5 4 3 2 1

This book is dedicated to these dear, departed family members,
now gone but not forgotten:

Our fathers, Bill Bliss and Norm Thornton;
Aunt Edith, Uncle Al, and Aunt Gertrude;
stepfather Frank Pope;
cousins Bobby and Nancy;
nephew Jeremy;
and Foster and Kiki.

Contents

Figures

Acknowledgments

We are grateful to many people and organizations for their contributions to the publication of this book.

Our editor, Laura Lawson, knows when to work closely with her authors and when to leave them alone at their computers! Laura provided useful insights on the book's concept and content at the outset, then paved the way for the collection of the SHRM member samples used in the book. She stepped back for several months as we immersed ourselves in drafting the text and selecting and preparing forms for publication, then she carefully shepherded our manuscript through editing and printing.

Several other individuals played important roles in the editorial process. Sharon Koss, SPHR, CCP, president of Koss Management Consulting, and Gary Kushner, SPHR, CBP, president and CEO of Kushner & Company, reviewed the manuscript and offered valuable feedback. Nicole Gauvin, SHRM's editorial coordinator/permissions editor, obtained the necessary consents to use the forms provided by SHRM members and assisted with marketing efforts.

The response to SHRM's call for samples for the book was immediate, enthusiastic, and generous from members and the SHRM Employee Relations Special Expertise Panel. We offer our sincere thanks to the following organizations and their HR professionals and consultants for the diverse array of high-quality samples considered for inclusion: Ace Communications Group; Adelphi, Inc.; Axiom Consulting Group, Inc., Behr America, Inc.; Burke Porter Machinery; Center for Health Care Strategies, Inc.; City of Phoenix, Arizona; City of Richardson, Texas; Computer Automation Systems, Inc.; Dash Multi-Corp., Inc.; Emergent Genetics; Florida Insurance Guaranty Association; Four Winds Hospital; General Fire & Casualty Company; Glen Ivy Hot Springs; Harper's Restaurants; Henry Ford Health System; Hondros College; Hunter Douglas, Inc.; Internet 2; JVM Realty Corporation; John Knapp; LBX Company LLC; Microdyne Outsourcing, Inc.; Milbank Manufacturing Co.; MIT; Mutual Benefit Group; Northpointe Bank; Northwestern College; Peopleopolis; PGHR Consulting; Pharmagraphics; Silgan Closures LLC; Tennessee One-Call System, Inc.; United Natural Foods, Inc.; and Yusen Air & Service (USA). We commend these persons and organizations for their willingness to share best practices experiences and materials.

Finally, we are grateful to our not-so-silent partners—our families—for a lifetime of encouragement and support of our professional endeavors, and for their obvious pride in our joint authorship of this book.

Preface

The goal of the Employment Termination Source Book is to provide users with a practical tool for handling the challenges posed by all types of termination situations, whether voluntary (resignation, job abandonment, retirement) or involuntary (discharge, reduction-in-force, job elimination).

Who Should Read This Book?

Four groups will benefit from the Employment Termination Source Book:

- Human resource professionals. HR professionals are typically responsible for the processes associated with the involuntary or voluntary termination of employment. The Employment Termination Source Book provides HR professionals with 97 customizable samples covering every aspect of the termination process. Additionally, the book contains ample discussion of the wide-ranging challenges faced by HR professionals relating to termination of employment and offers numerous recommendations and tips to help them succeed in their tasks.

- Non-HR managers and supervisors. Although these managers and supervisors work outside the HR field, they often must deal with various legal and practical issues arising out of the termination of employment. They play a critical role in the termination process but all too often are insufficiently educated about the law and inadequately prepared for their role in the process. Managers and supervisors have the ability to "sink the ship" or "save the day" before an HR professional ever gets involved. Increasingly, non-HR managers and supervisors are being targeted for individual liability by employment law statutes and lawsuits brought under the common law. A manager or supervisor who reads this book and applies its advice will be well prepared to deal with every aspect of the termination process and will be able to say with confidence, "Not on my watch."

- CEOs, presidents, and vice presidents. Why would senior executives need to be steeped in the particulars of employment termination? Precisely because employment, and the termination of employment, goes to the very heart of what organizations do. For HR professionals and non-HR managers and supervisors to be successful in their roles in this area, senior management must be not only on board but at the helm. They must drive the formulation of a corporate philosophy on termination (see Chapter 1) and the creation of a corporate infrastructure to deal proactively with termination challenges (see Chapter 3). In the event of class action lawsuits or alleged violations of the Sarbanes-Oxley Act of 2002, senior management will be held accountable, whether by law or in the corporate arena. They should be fully aware of the risks of getting it wrong—risks that include legal liability, loss of trade secrets and other valuable assets, criminal liability, and even loss of life. The Source Book provides corporate executives with the big picture on termination of employment so they can steer their companies safely past the shoals and into the profitable waters of commerce.

■ Lawyers, both in-house and outside. For in-house lawyers and outside counsel who don't specialize in employment law and litigation, the legal issues surrounding the termination of employment may be only a narrow section of the areas in which they are expected to render competent legal advice. The discussion of federal and state statutes and common law theories of recovery in the Employment Termination Source Book provides a good starting point for legal counsel to spot hazards that may confront their organizations in this area. Clients rarely ask lawyers, "What does the law say?" Instead, they ask, "What do you think we should do?" To competently answer that question, the lawyer needs to understand the termination process from the inside out, not only as it exists at the particular organization but also in terms of best practices. A lawyer who advises the client in every instance to take the course that is least likely to result in liability is doing only half the job. The Source Book provides best practices advice in all areas of concern pertaining to the termination of employment.

What Is in the Source Book?

The Source Book consists of five chapters of text followed by 97 samples of termination policies, forms, checklists, worksheets, and notices. The CD-ROM accompanying the book contains all the samples in a fully customizable format. The chapters include numerous tables that summarize important information about the various laws that affect termination of employment, as well as tips for handling specific situations.

Chapter 1 lists and defines the ways in which the employment relationship can be brought to an end, and discusses the risks and challenges posed by each termination scenario. The major steps on the path to voluntary and involuntary separations are outlined, and the chapter offers a model for safe, legal, professional, and ethical handling of all types of terminations.

Chapter 2 contains an overview of the common law claims that may arise in the context of termination of employment and offers guidance on how employers can avoid incurring common law liability. This chapter also highlights the many applicable federal statutes and alerts employers to numerous areas in which state governments have passed laws that go far beyond the federal laws.

Chapter 3 offers extensive practical advice on how organizations can be proactive in addressing termination challenges through advance planning. Chapter 4 tells how to conduct termination meetings and exit interviews in ways that are safe, sensitive, legal, professional, and ethical.

Chapter 5 addresses the reality that the employment relationship doesn't usually end when the employee walks out the door and cashes the final paycheck. This chapter provides strategies for skillfully handling common post-termination challenges.

A Word about the Samples

The samples in Part 2 include a wide variety of documents for various types of terminations. The reader will find policies, forms, checklists, worksheets, records, notices, certificates, letters, agreements, questionnaires, and separation packet materials for use before, during, and after employee separations.

Most of these samples were solicited from SHRM's more than 200,000 members; some were developed by the authors. We received many more samples than we could include in the book. Those ultimately selected for inclusion are from large and small companies in many industries, and they vary in content, format, complexity, and formality. They were chosen to provide readers with a diverse collection of termination materials used in the real world.

The samples are easily customizable using the accompanying CD-ROM. They come in two formats: Portable Document Format (PDF) and Rich Text Format (RTF). See "Using the Accompanying CD-ROM" at the back of the book for more information.

Each sample was developed by the contributing organization to meet its own particular termination objectives and requirements in the states in which it operates. Before adapting or using any of these materials, you may want to have them reviewed by legal counsel.

Discussion of Law in This Book

The authors have attempted to give the reader a basic understanding of federal and state laws that affect the termination of employment. However, laws do change. The Employment Termination Source Book is a great starting point, but not the final word on the topics covered. The Source Book should not be considered legal advice, which requires the consideration of all relevant facts pertaining to a particular situation. Employers are encouraged to retain qualified and experienced attorneys about specific termination issues.

PART 1

THE EMPLOYMENT TERMINATION PROCESS

Chapter 1
Fundamentals

Parting is such sweet sorrow . . .

—William Shakespeare, *Romeo and Juliet*

Termination: Your Toughest Task

The employment relationship is exactly that: a relationship. Like any other relationship, it has a beginning, middle, and end. This book in the SHRM *Source Book* series deals with the end: voluntary or involuntary termination of the employment relationship.

For most people, losing a job ranks among the toughest experiences in their lives. It is difficult if the reason for termination is lack of work; it is worse if the reason is substandard performance or violation of company policy. But what about the other side of the relationship? The task of discharging or laying off an employee can be one of the least pleasant and most stressful aspects of a manager's job. Even resignations can be difficult for managers, as valued employees are lost to competitors, other life priorities, or retirement.

The termination of employment affects the organization as well. A layoff may signal the failure of management to anticipate organizational needs and economic conditions. A disciplinary termination is a sign of failure in hiring and supervision. Resignations may reflect deficiencies in a company's compensation, training, supervision, or culture.

Types of Termination

Employees and employers part company for a variety of reasons. In most cases, when an employee voluntarily ends the employment relationship, the employee exerts control over the circumstances under which he or she leaves but has limited avenues to pursue legal action against the former employer at a later date. Conversely, when the employer terminates the employment, the employer exerts control over how and when the employee will go but, in doing so, may open the door to a plethora of legal claims based on the discharge.

Voluntary Termination: "I Quit!"

A voluntary termination occurs when the employee decides to leave and initiates the separation process. Most voluntary terminations involve an employee *resignation*. Some employees leave to take a position offering them something that is not available in their current position, such as a promotion, better pay and benefits, or a more flexible schedule. Others resign for purely personal reasons, such as to raise a family, relocate, or retire. Sometimes employees quit without having another job to go to, because they are dissatisfied with their job, their supervisor, or the company's policies and procedures. Whatever the reason, resignations can create immediate problems for the individual's supervisor and the organization in getting work done until a replacement has been hired and trained. Moreover, resigning employees often succumb to short-timer's syndrome, slacking off after giving notice.

Occasionally, employees initiate their departures by taking the path of least resistance and least communication. Rather than announcing his or her intention to leave a job, the employee simply doesn't show up at work for several consecutive days or fails to return to work after a leave of absence or a vacation. When such *job abandonment* occurs, the organization is left to solve the mystery of the employee's absence and to determine when and how to officially terminate the relationship.

Involuntary Termination: "You're Fired!"

Although voluntary separations pose challenges for managers and human resource professionals, they are minor compared with the issues that can arise when the organization initiates the termination. When an employee is dismissed, the company must walk a legal tightrope and be ready to address potential workforce morale, productivity, and security issues.

A *discharge* occurs when an employer terminates a single employee "for cause" because of things the employee has done wrong. The four most common reasons for discharge are (1) poor performance; (2) attendance problems; (3) violations of company policies, standards, or work rules; and (4) serious misconduct.

A second type of involuntary termination involves the "no fault" dismissal of one or more employees. In such situations, the employer terminates a group of employees because of the organization's weakening financial condition or in furtherance of its business strategy. Sometimes these terminations result in a *temporary layoff* (or *furlough*), in which the affected employees may have recall rights to their jobs for a certain period. In other cases, the terminations are final and without recall rights. No-fault terminations may occur as part of a *restructuring* to make the organization more efficient or through a *reduction in force* (RIF; also known as downsizing or rightsizing) that is accomplished by closing plants or offices, eliminating departments and business units, or implementing a mass layoff of a given number of employees throughout the organization. (Note: The term *layoff* is often used generically, including in this book, to describe any involuntary group termination, regardless of the reason for it or its temporary or permanent nature.)

The Employment Termination Journey

Voluntary and involuntary separations begin very differently but end up in the same place: the organizational exit ramp. Along every termination trek are four major checkpoints that HR professionals and managers should prepare for by completing key tasks and documentation. These checkpoints are (1) pre-termination planning; (2) notification of the termination decision; (3) the post-notification exit process; and (4) post-termination interactions with former employees.

Figure 1-1 lists key tasks and documents for voluntary departures at each of the checkpoints, and Figure 1-2 lists tasks and documents for involuntary departures. Chapters 3, 4, and 5 cover steps to take while on these two different paths to the exit ramp to ensure the smoothest journey possible for the departing employee and the organization.

Figure 1.1 The Voluntary Termination Path

STEP 1	STEP 2	STEP 3	STEP 4
Pre-Termination Planning	**Notice of Employee Departure**	**Exit Process**	**Post-Termination Activities**

Key HR and Management Tasks:
- Create an infrastructure to protect against disclosure of confidential information or unfair competition, and to prevent other losses resulting from terminations.
- Stay current on federal, state, and local laws pertaining to voluntary terminations.
- Establish an "early warning system" to identify potential voluntary separations.
- *For resignations:*
  - Decide how to respond to resignation-specific issues (e.g., requested notice, pay in lieu of notice, rescission of resignation, and retaining key employees after they have given notice).
- *For job abandonment:*
  - Define job abandonment, and determine appropriate investigation and response mechanisms.

Key Documents:
- Resignation and job abandonment policies
- Non-compete, non-solicitation, and non-disclosure agreements
- Policy on severance pay
- Policy on rehire
- Reference policies
- Policy on access to personnel file

Key HR and Management Tasks:
For resignations:
- Determine reason employee is resigning.
- Establish what tasks resigning employee will complete before last day.
- *For job abandonment:* Investigate absence without notice and attempt to contact employee before implementing a job abandonment termination.

Key Documents:
- Resignation letter or confirmation
- Job abandonment letter

Key HR and Management Tasks:
- Notify management, staff and customers of employee's departure.
- Plan for timely replacement of employee.
- Provide departing employee with post-termination benefits information.
- *For resignations:*
  - Complete all items on exit checklist.
  - Conduct exit interview.
  - Schedule appropriate farewell activities.

Key Documents:
- Exit checklist
- Exit survey or questionnaire
- Departure announcement
- Termination certificate
- Reference authorization
- COBRA and benefits forms
- Record of termination

Key HR and Management Tasks:
- Take necessary steps to prevent loss of company property or disclosure of proprietary information by former employee.
- Administer COBRA and other post-termination benefits.
- Respond to unemployment insurance claims.
- Respond to reference requests.
- Retain personnel records as required by law and company policy.
- Destroy personnel records in accordance with legal requirements.

Key Documents:
- Documentation of reference requests
- COBRA and benefits forms

Figure 1.2 **The Involuntary Termination Path**

STEP 1
Pre-Termination Planning

Key HR and Management Tasks:
- Create an infrastructure to protect against disclosure of confidential information or unfair competition and to prevent other losses to the organization resulting from terminations.
- Stay current on federal, state, and local laws pertaining to involuntary terminations.
- Take steps to preserve the organization's status as an at-will employer (if applicable).
- Contact employment attorneys or HR professionals to review and advise on termination decisions and procedures before implementing them.
- Plan termination meeting and exit process logistics.
- Develop termination package and packet.
- *For individual discharges:*
  - Establish and follow consistent disciplinary procedures.
  - Conduct a thorough pre-termination review before making a discharge decision.

For group terminations:
  - Consider viable options in lieu of group terminations.
  - If other options to group terminations are not viable, decide whom to terminate and when.
  - As necessary, send WARN notices and any other legally required documents prior to termination.

STEP 1
(continued)

Key Documents:
- Employment-at-will policy and disclaimer
- Work rules
- Discipline policy
- Corrective action forms
- Discharge policy
- Non-compete, non-solicitation, non-disclosure agreements
- Policy on severance pay
- Policy on rehire
- Reference policies
- Policy on access to personnel file
- WARN notices

STEP 2
Termination Meeting

Key HR and Management Tasks:
- Develop and follow termination script or outline.
- Anticipate employee reactions and respond appropriately.
- Implement necessary and appropriate security measures for termination meeting, gathering personal belongings, and departure from the premises.

Key Documents:
- Termination notice
- Separation agreement

STEP 3
Exit Process

Key HR and Management Tasks:
- Provide departing employee with post-termination benefits information.
- Notify management, staff, and customers of employee's departure.
- Complete all items on exit checklist.
- If appropriate, conduct exit interview.
- Take steps to ensure workplace safety and to protect company property and proprietary information.
- If applicable, plan for timely replacement of employee.

Key Documents:
- Exit checklist
- Exit survey or questionnaire
- Departure announcement
- Reference authorization
- COBRA and benefits forms

STEP 4
Post-Termination Activities

Key HR and Management Tasks:
- Take necessary steps to protect against harm to human, tangible, and intangible assets by former employee.
- Administer COBRA and other post-termination benefits.
- Respond to unemployment insurance claims.
- Respond to reference requests.
- Retain personnel records as required by law and company policy.
- Destroy personnel records in accordance with legal requirements.

Key Documents:
- Documentation of reference requests
- COBRA and benefits forms

Perspectives on Termination: The Good, the Bad, and the Ugly

If handled correctly, employee exits, whether voluntary or involuntary, can lead to a professional parting of the ways with minimal or no negative feelings between the employee and the company. For this to occur, managers and HR professionals must anticipate and address the legitimate issues and needs of departing employees. Unfortunately, the path to termination is fraught with potential pitfalls.

Employer Goals: The Good Things about Termination

Employers have much more good to gain in terminations than just "good-bye" to resigning employees, "good luck" to laid-off workers, and "good riddance" to discharged employees. In responding to voluntary terminations, an employer's main objectives should be to minimize work disruptions before and after the employee's last day, to ensure proper outprocessing of the employee, and to end the relationship on a positive note. In rare instances, the employer may want to persuade the employee to change his or her mind and not leave the organization.

When a discharge occurs, one primary objective should be to minimize exposure to legal claims. In addition, the employer should strive to conduct the termination in a way that is respectful and fair, and that minimizes false rumors and bad will among the rest of the workforce.

In layoffs, a critical employer goal should be to select individuals for termination on the basis of legitimate criteria and, in so doing, decrease the likelihood of individual or class action lawsuits. Additionally, employers should aim to administer group terminations as effectively, efficiently, and consistently as possible, with due regard for the impact on the remaining employees, as well as the communities in which the employers operate.

By focusing on these goals for voluntary and involuntary separations, employers have the opportunity to

- improve the quality of the workforce by discharging unproductive or problem employees, or replacing resigning employees with even more capable workers;

- keep legal expenses down by avoiding claims and lawsuits by former employees; and

- establish a reputation inside and outside the company as a responsible and professional employer.

Chapters 3, 4, and 5 will show you how to capitalize on these opportunities by taking the correct steps before, during, and after the termination.

Employee Concerns: Good Things to Keep in Mind

A separation, whether voluntary or involuntary, tends to be a time of major uncertainty and daunting transition for employees. From before the termination decision is made until an employee leaves the organization and moves on to the next phase professionally and personally, he or she is likely to have feelings of insecurity and anxiety in one or more areas.

Most involuntarily terminated employees have immediate and significant concerns about loss of income. They will want to know how much future compensation is available to them through severance payments and unemployment benefits they might receive. All terminated employees will want information and assurances about the nature and extent of post-employment compensation, including earned but unpaid commissions, accrued vacation pay, vested retirement funds, and options for continuation of health insurance or other benefits. Employers must understand that financial issues will be foremost in an employee's mind during the termination process. The failure to accurately and immediately address a departing employee's questions about compensation and benefits, or to timely pay any amounts due the employee in connection with the termination, is a sure way to inject conflict and calamity into the termination process.

Employment terminations are emotionally charged events. Involuntarily terminated employees may experience a range of negative feelings about being let go, including anger, embarrassment, and loss of self-esteem. Although many resigning employees look forward to their departure, they also may feel keenly the impending loss of daily interactions with co-workers. They may fear that they will be treated insensitively by their supervisor, human resource staff, or other company personnel before or after they leave, or worry that derogatory comments will be made about them after they're gone. Uncertainty over the employment references they will or will not receive is perhaps one of longest-lasting concerns employees have after a separation.

These concerns can be substantially reduced for departing employees if the company develops a strategy and takes proactive steps in four areas—philosophy, processes, paper and people—described later in this chapter.

What Can Go Wrong: The Bad and Ugly Possibilities

Many dangers surround the employment termination process. The mishandling of any one of an array of sensitive separation activities or the misreading of the emotional state and likely reactions of affected employees can have disastrous consequences. Legions of employers, supervisors, and HR professionals have experienced firsthand some of the awful results of a termination gone wrong.

If you are unprepared and unlucky, your nightmare separation scenario could include the following:

- **Lawsuits.** More employment lawsuits occur after termination than at any other phase of the employment life cycle. According to a survey by SHRM in the late 1990s, 80 percent of employment lawsuits were initiated by former employees, whereas only 3 percent were initiated by job applicants. Such lawsuits can be very costly. According to Jury Verdict Research in Horsham, Pennsylvania, the median jury verdict awarded in wrongful termination lawsuits from 1994 to 2000 was $157,000.[1] In some cases, an individual employee may be awarded millions of dollars for an employer's wrongful conduct in a termination. For example, in 2005, a Los Angeles jury awarded $20 million to an 85-year-old doctor who claimed that he was forced to retire (at age 81) as chief physician at a California state prison.[2] An employer's potential legal and financial liability increases dramatically in group terminations, because terminated employees may band together in a class action lawsuit. Chapter 2 will review the many bases for legal claims by former employees and provide guidance on minimizing exposure to such claims.

- **Injury to competitive position.** When employees leave, they may take some of your organization's most valuable assets: customers, trade secrets, confidential financial information, intellectual property, or co-workers. The loss of any of these assets to competitors can weaken and even destroy your organization. For example, in one recent case, two attorneys who left a law firm to establish a competing firm intentionally printed out confidential client information, encouraged employee dissatisfaction months before their departure, erased computer files, and personally contacted clients before leaving. The departure of these two attorneys resulted in the loss of six attorneys and 144 clients to the new law firm.[3] In another case, the general manager of a branch of a freight forwarding business engaged in direct competition while still employed by supplying his next employer with confidential information about customers and freight rates and causing the lapse of his current employer's facility lease so he could negotiate a lease for the same facility for his next employer.[4] Employers can defend against these situations after the fact (as both employers in these examples did successfully) with lawsuits alleging unfair competition, breach of a noncompete agreement, breach of the duty of loyalty, misappropriation of trade secrets, or copyright infringement. However, such litigation tends to be expensive and disruptive; a better strategy is to prevent employee misappropriation of intangible assets in the first place. Proactive measures to protect these valuable assets should be implemented long before an employee resigns or is terminated. Chapter 3 discusses pretermination policies and documentation that provide such protection.

- **Whistle-blowing.** An employee who has knowledge of illegal or unethical business practices may view a termination as an ideal time to report such activities to law enforcement officials, the press, or others.

- **Theft or destruction of property.** A discharged or laid-off employee may decide to compensate him- or herself by stealing computers or peripherals, books, software, or other valuable company property. Or the employee may take revenge by, for example, introducing a computer virus, deleting computer files, or sabotaging data or equipment.

- **Workplace violence.** Giving an unstable employee a pink slip may make him or her see red. Fired or laid-off employees sometimes respond with workplace assault, homicide, and suicide. Even mere threats of this nature can be very distressing to employees who have knowledge of them. According to a *USA Today* study of 224 fatal workplace violence incidents from 1975 through 2003, the most common motivator behind workplace homicides was a firing, which preceded 26 percent of these fatal attacks.[5] Often, the violence is directed toward particular management representatives or co-workers whom the former employee blames for the termination; but innocent bystanders—co-workers and managers who just happen to be in the wrong place at the wrong time—can also be victims. A 2004 SHRM workplace violence survey revealed that in 9 percent of responding organizations, HR professionals were sometimes the target of workplace violence.[6] These facts make it obvious that terminations are a deadly serious business for all involved and that employers must assess the potential for, and respond appropriately to, incidents of workplace violence in connection with employee terminations. Chapters 4 and 5 offer practical advice on handling terminations with, and post-termination security against, potentially violent individuals.

In addition to these worst-case scenarios, employers routinely face garden-variety problems. Decreased productivity may occur after the announcement of any type of termination, as departing employees get short-timer's syndrome, or as the organization scrambles to fill a vacant position. In group terminations, employers not only must handle multiple terminations, but also must address the needs of shell-shocked RIF survivors.

A Strategy for Successful Terminations

Terminations are tough—tough for employees, who face major life changes when leaving a job either by choice or by surprise, and tough for employers, who may face significant legal, physical, and economic repercussions for any missteps. Because lives, livelihoods, and your organization's reputation and financial well-being hang in the balance, it is essential to devise a legal, effective, and humane strategy for both voluntary and involuntary employment terminations. Like a completed puzzle, this strategy should integrate four key "*p*"ieces: *p*hilosophy, *p*rocess, *p*aper, and *p*eople.

- **Philosophy.** Well-managed companies have a philosophy about the way they do business and how they approach the human resource function. A company's philosophy should extend to its handling of termination of employment. The company's termination philosophy should provide the foundation for the development of termination policies and practices that are aligned with the company's vision, values, and business strategy. For example, an organization might decide, in the interests of operational efficiency, to adopt a strict zero-tolerance stance toward terminations. This philosophy could be supported through firm adherence to company disciplinary polices regardless of mitigating or extenuating factors, limited or no severance benefits to exiting employees, and a practice of never rehiring a former employee. On the other hand, an organization might decide, in the interest of creating a reputation as an employer of choice, to take a more lenient, soft-landing stance. This philosophy could be supported by a progressive discipline policy that includes a last-chance decision-making leave prior to discharge; a formal, standardized company severance program; and a willingness to rehire former employees who leave the company in good standing. The following are some of the philosophical issues related to various aspects of employment termination:

  - Are we willing to say that we will terminate employment only for cause, or do we want to take the position that we can terminate employment for any reason, or no reason at all, as long as it isn't an illegal reason?

  - Will we adopt a progressive discipline policy, including appeal procedures, or will we maximize our discretion to act in any way we see fit under the circumstances?

- If we discover that an employee is not really qualified to do the job we hired him or her to do, or if we have a manager with some rough edges, are we willing to expend more resources on training or executive coaching, or are we just going to throw them back into the pond and hope for a better catch next time?

- How will we respond to an employee resigning to take a better job? Will we celebrate the employee's success or act like a jilted lover?

- To what extent will we attempt to avoid layoffs by using other cost-cutting measures?

- If a layoff becomes necessary, will we merely say, "Sorry, goodbye," or will we offer the departing employees severance pay, benefit continuation, or other measures to ease the pain?

- Will we aggressively oppose unmeritorious claims for unemployment insurance benefits or view unemployment insurance as a sort of severance benefit payable to everyone, regardless of the reason for termination?

- Are we going to adopt a "name, rank, and serial number" reference policy, or are we willing to offer truthful, objective information about former employees' performance and work behaviors, thereby rewarding our good former employees, being a responsible citizen of the community in which we do business, and making it tougher for our bad former employees to become repeat offenders?

- What reputation do we want to have among plaintiff employment lawyers? A company with such good HR practices that if a former employee is looking to sue, that employee probably doesn't have a very good case? A company that, if sued, will quickly settle? A company that will fight employment lawsuits to the bitter end?

Philosophical issues such as these are an undercurrent throughout this book.

- **Processes.** Terminations should not be improvised. Savvy employers create an infrastructure, develop procedures, and follow practices that facilitate smooth and professional handling of all types of terminations. These formalized processes should be based on careful consideration of the *who, what, when, where and how* issues of job separations, including these:

- How do we anticipate and respond to employee-initiated departures?

- How do we make discharge and layoff decisions?

- How do we comply with applicable laws during employee separations? When do we notify an employee who is being discharged?

- In what circumstances do we ask a resigning employee to leave before his or her stated last day?

- When do we deem an employee who fails to report to have abandoned his or her job?

- When and where do we hold termination notification meetings?

- Who will conduct termination meetings and exit interviews?

- When and where do we conduct exit interviews?

- When and how do we retain and destroy personnel records of former employees?

In developing processes, employers should cover activities that occur before, during, and after the separation. Chapter 3 focuses on the issues to be considered and steps to be taken before termination. Chapter 4 addresses the two main events of termination: the termination meeting and the exit interview. Chapter 5 describes several common challenges faced after termination, along with strategies for maintaining professional interactions with terminated employees.

■ **Paper.** In real estate, it's location, location, location; in HR, it's documentation, documentation, documentation. Documentation provides a history of employee departures long after the employees are gone. It can be the strongest evidence in your favor if a former employee sues your organization. On the other hand, lack of documentation or inaccurate, incomplete, or inflammatory documentation can be the deciding factor against you in litigation. Employers need to take care when creating a paper trail about what documents to use, how long to keep them, and when to get rid of them. Part 2 of this book and the accompanying CD contain 97 customizable forms, checklists, policies, letters, notices, agreements, worksheets, and other documents that you can use as a starting point in your quest to make your company's termination infrastructure the best it can be. Chapter 5 takes up the issues of retaining and destroying employment records.

■ **People.** At its core, employment termination is about people—their decisions, actions, and attitudes at the end of an employment relationship. An employer may have done an excellent job putting together the other three "*p*"ieces of its termination puzzle by defining a termination philosophy, implementing effective separation processes, and maintaining accurate and complete paperwork. But without the *people* piece, the puzzle isn't complete. Employers can't control the attitudes and reactions of departing employees; however, they *can* set behavioral expectations and ground rules for the company representatives who play a role in employee separations. When employers treat departing employees humanely, honestly, and fairly, employees are less likely to sue or otherwise cause harm. Chapters 3 through 5 contain suggestions for managing the interpersonal aspects of terminations in a positive and professional manner.

By bringing together the four "*p*"ieces—*p*hilosophy, *p*rocesses, *p*aper, and *p*eople—your organization will lay the foundation for safety and success in the area of employment termination.

Chapter 2
Legal Issues

No man is above the law, and no man is below it;
nor do we ask any man's permission when we require him to obey it.

—Theodore Roosevelt

Termination: The Riskiest Phase of the Employment Relationship

Of the three phases of the employment relationship—beginning, middle, and end—the last is by far the riskiest in terms of an employer's exposure to lawsuits. Though it is disappointing not to be offered a job or not to get a raise or promotion, those situations are very different from losing a job one already has.

Lawsuits arising out of the hiring process are relatively rare. They are more common in the middle of the employment relationship (e.g., charges of sexual harassment, equal pay claims, glass-ceiling allegations, and reasonable accommodation complaints). But nothing compares with being discharged to jumpstarting thoughts about suing an employer.

Why is this so? For one thing, the loss of a regular paycheck puts most individuals in a desperate race to find new work—before the vacation must be cancelled, before the COBRA insurance runs out, before the house goes into foreclosure. Most people fail to save enough money for such a rainy day. Even for those who do, the economic pressure can be very great.

But the experience of job loss isn't just a matter of dollars. Involuntary termination is a blow to one's mental health. In her groundbreaking book *On Death and Dying*, Elisabeth Kübler-Ross identified five phases of the grieving process: (1) denial and isolation, (2) anger, (3) bargaining, (4) depression, and (5) acceptance.[7] Other scholars have noted that these phases are not limited to the loss of a loved one but occur with virtually every kind of major loss one can experience. The phases are not necessarily sequential or even distinct. Thus, upon losing a job, an employee may simultaneously experience (in varying degrees) denial, isolation, anger, bargaining, and depression—everything but acceptance. In such an atmosphere, a lawsuit may offer a terminated employee the promise of being made financially whole, saving face, regaining equilibrium, or just getting even with the former employer.

Managing the risk of termination-related lawsuits requires an understanding of the numerous laws involved, a sincere commitment to obey the law, and the consistent application of established procedures designed to accomplish that end.

Legal Bases for Termination Lawsuits: Two Kinds of Law

Broadly speaking, two kinds of law apply to the termination of employment: common law and statutory law. This chapter first covers legal issues in termination that arise under common law, then focuses on the impact of numerous federal and state statutes on employment termination.

Judges create *common law* through written opinions based on the application of legal precedents; legislative bodies create *statutory law* through legislation. By *legislative bodies* we mean not only Congress and the legislatures of the various states but also bodies such as city councils and boards of county commissioners, who also may write laws affecting the termination of employment. We also mean regulatory agencies that have been authorized to promulgate rules and procedures for implementing a statute.

Common Law Claims

Some common law claims arise directly out of the act of discharge. These claims include *wrongful discharge* and *constructive discharge*. Other common law claims are *torts* (civil, as opposed to criminal, wrongful behavior) that may arise in connection with a discharge.

Wrongful Discharge and the Growing List of Exceptions to Employment-at-Will

Historically, *employment-at-will* meant the right of an employer or employee to terminate employment at any time, without prior notice, for any reason (whether good or ill) or for no reason at all. The doctrine of employment-at-will has experienced a great deal of erosion and is best defined today as the right of the employer and employee to terminate employment at any time, without notice, and for any reason—except an illegal reason. It is the illegal reasons that make a discharge wrongful (also sometimes referred to as *wrongful termination* or *unjust dismissal*).

Today, more than 40 years after the passage of Title VII of the Civil Rights Act of 1964, it is clearly a form of wrongful discharge to terminate someone's employment simply on the basis of race, national origin, color, gender, or religion. More recently, with the passage of the Age Discrimination in Employment Act and the Americans with Disabilities Act, it became illegal to terminate an employee on the basis of the employee's age (40 or older) or disability. Still more recently, prohibitions against discrimination have been extended in some states and municipalities to parental status, sexual orientation, and other protected characteristics.

For the most part, the exceptions to employment-at-will have been the result of legislation. But judges got into the act too, creating, most notably, the *public policy* exception and the implied contract or *promissory estoppel* exception.

The courts of almost all states now permit a discharged employee to sue for wrongful discharge on the basis of the public policy exception. Public policy violations arise where termination was based on the employee exercising an important statutory right (such as filing a workers' compensation claim), fulfilling an important public obligation (such as performing jury duty), refusing to engage in illegal conduct (such as overbilling on a government contract), or whistle-blowing (reporting an employer's illegal conduct to appropriate authorities or, in some instances, to the press).

Wrongful discharge claims based on promissory estoppel exceptions typically arise when a judge determines that promises contained in an employee handbook have created an implied contract between employer and employee (e.g., a promise to impose discipline progressively). And, in a handful of states, judges hold that in every employment relationship, the employer owes the employee an implied duty of "good faith and fair dealing."

Additionally, the employer and the employee may make a written contract specifying under what conditions employment termination will be deemed wrongful. For example, they might agree that employment can be terminated only for "good cause" and then define those circumstances. Or they might state that employment will be for a minimum number of years, in which case it would be a breach of contract for either the employee or employer to terminate the relationship earlier. Or they might alter only the "without notice" aspect of employment-at-will, agreeing instead to provide no less than two weeks' notice of any voluntary or involuntary termination.

These are all examples of wrongful discharge in a purely legal sense. A discharge could also be deemed wrongful if it is handled in a way that causes unnecessary hurt to the employee or defeats objectives of the employer. Here, *wrongful* is used in a cultural sense. A prime example is an instance in which a boss, upon learning of an employee's alleged infraction of a company rule, storms into the employee's office, loudly accuses the employee of the infraction, and then yells within earshot of other employees, "You're fired! Pack up your stuff and get out of here!" Handling a termination in this way unnecessarily publicizes the termination and is calculated to anger and humiliate the employee. Additionally, it is counterproductive to the employer's interests of reducing the risk of exposure to lawsuits and fostering high morale.

Much will be said throughout this book on how to conduct "rightful" terminations, that is, those that are not wrongful in either the legal or cultural sense. For now, consider the tips in Figure 2-1. Following these suggestions can help minimize your organization's potential exposure to wrongful discharge claims.

Constructive Discharge: The Nondischarge Discharge?

Substantial legal risks are associated with firing or laying off employees. Some managers respond to this situation by saying to themselves, "If I just make work so miserable for the employee that he or she decides to quit, then I won't have to worry about being sued." In addition to being unethical, this reasoning is mistaken.

An employer that uses this approach to employee terminations is deliberately engaging in *constructive discharge*. Not only is constructive discharge just as legally actionable as an outright firing or layoff, it can actually give the employee a better lawsuit: The employee may be able to show a pattern of arbitrary and capricious abuse as evidence of intentional discrimination or malice, which could cause the court to impose punitive damages.

Just because an employer refrains from the deliberate strategy of constructive discharge doesn't mean the employer won't be accused of it. Claims that an employee was constructively discharged arise most often in the context of discrimination claims, but they can arise in other contexts as well. In most jurisdictions, the fact that an employer tolerated abusive conditions can support a claim for constructive discharge, even without the intent to force the employee to resign. For example, an employee's resignation because the company has uncorrected Occupational Safety and Health Act (OSHA) violations that make the work hazardous may be deemed a constructive discharge.

Figure 2.1   Conducting "Rightful" Terminations

- Consider whether a lesser form of discipline is adequate to correct the problem.

- Fire only for "good cause," even if employment-at-will applies, but don't promise to fire only for good cause.

- Be fair, but don't promise to be fair.

- Never fire in anger.

- Review performance and disciplinary documents in the employee's personnel file before making the decision to terminate. If these documents cast doubt on the fairness of a proposed termination (for example, years of excellent performance appraisals and no written disciplinary write-ups or warnings), consult with an attorney regarding appropriate corrective actions to take in the situation.

- Run the termination decision by an impartial observer, either a human resource staff representative or a manager outside the employee's chain of command.

- Make sure the termination is not based in part on an employee's protected status, such as race, national origin, color, gender, age, religion, or disability.

- Don't fire the employee for refusing to perform an illegal or unethical act.

- Make sure the termination is not retaliation against the employee for exercising important rights or performing public duties.

- If the employee has a written contract, adhere to it. If procedures are outlined in an employee handbook, follow them.

- If verbal promises were made to the employee, keep them.

- Tell the employee the reason(s) for the termination without sugarcoating or piling on extra reasons.

- Document the reason(s) for the termination in a termination memo.

- Respect the employee's dignity and privacy during the termination process.

- Have two company representatives attend the termination meeting, one to run the meeting and one to serve as a witness.

- Deliver the final paycheck, including any required vacation pay, in a timely manner.

- Deliver all required notices (for example, COBRA) in a timely manner.

An employee who claims constructive discharge must clear one more hurdle than does an employee suing for an actual discharge: Did the employer make working conditions so intolerable that a reasonable person in the employee's position would have felt compelled to resign? This test can be very difficult for employees to satisfy.

Constructive discharge actions tend to fall into four broad fact patterns. First are the cases in which the employee is subjected to a continuous barrage of derogatory comments about performance, appearance, attitude, or morality. Second are the cases in which an employee reasonably expected opportunities for advancement, but discriminatory actions or policies effectively locked him or her into a particular job. Third, an employee may resign in the face of a sexually or racially hostile work environment and may assert that the employer failed to take prompt and effective remedial action. Fourth, employers sometimes give employees the option to resign in lieu of being fired. This circumstance is frequently seen in unemployment insurance cases in which the employer hopes to avoid responsibility for the termination on the basis that the employee resigned. State labor departments usually see such a circumstance as a de facto firing and require the employer to prove that the employee was discharged for good cause to avoid having the employer's account charged with a valid claim for benefits.

In themselves, garden-variety bad working conditions are generally insufficient to support a claim for constructive discharge. The claim is stronger if the employee can point to a tangible employment action such as a demotion, reduction in salary, reduction in job responsibilities, reassignment to menial or degrading work, reassignment to work under a younger supervisor or one with less seniority, badgering, public humiliation, harassment, threats of violence, or suggestions that the employee should resign

Other Tort Claims

So far, we have discussed legal claims that arise out of the act of discharge itself. Employers should also be aware of several other tort claims, described in Figure 2-2, that may arise in conjunction with a discharge but do not necessarily pertain to the discharge per se.

Several important observations can be made about the tort claims described in Figure 2-2. First, many of the claims can be asserted not only against the employer but also against an individual (including managers, supervisors, and HR representatives). Second, in some cases, persons other than the discharged employee—such as an accused harasser, a witness, or a spouse—may assert the claim. Third, some situations may give rise to more than one type of claim.

Many diverse legal claims can arise out of the termination of employment. What can managers and HR professionals do to protect their companies and themselves from such lawsuits? Here are a few basic rules:

- Treat termination information on a strict need-to-know basis.

- Tell the truth.

- Be prepared, deliberate, and self-controlled.

- Show compassion, not animosity, during discharges.

- Respect the dignity and privacy of terminating employees.

Following the advice in Chapters 3 through 5 can help those involved with the termination process stay within appropriate behavioral boundaries during this most legally risky phase of the employment relationship.

Figure 2.2 Torts and Terminations: Potential Legal Claims

Legal Claim	Gist of Claim	Danger Zone
Defamation: Libel (written) or Slander (spoken)	The employer or a co-worker makes a false, derogatory statement of fact about an employee	This claim typically arises when responding to reference requests or notifying other employees about a terminated employee's departure. It may also arise in the course of an internal investigation.
Invasion of Privacy: False Light	This type of privacy violation occurs when an employer or co-worker places an employee in a false light before the public. This tort is very similar to defamation and is not recognized in all jurisdictions.	This tort also typically arises in the context of reference requests or explaining to other employees why someone is no longer with the company. The twist here is that the defendant may be saying something that is neither false nor even a clear statement of fact, but rather the statement leaves a false impression in the mind of the recipient.
Invasion of Privacy: Intrusion	A second type of privacy violation occurs when the employer or a co-worker improperly intrudes into an employee's legally protected zone of privacy.	This claim typically arises in an internal investigation when an employee's desk, purse, or locker is searched for drugs or other evidence of misconduct. Searches of computer records can also give rise to this claim. Occasionally, employers are so foolish as to illegally tap telephones or otherwise record conversations.
Intentional Interference with Contract or Employment	A manager or other co-worker, out of personal animosity rather than legitimate business interests, causes an employee to be fired.	This claim often comes up when an accused harasser is fired and alleges that the complaining party lied about the alleged harassment.
Intentional Interference with Prospective Contract or Employment	A manager or other co-worker, without legitimate business justification, prevents a discharged employee from obtaining a new job.	The situation described immediately above sometimes extends to the discharged employee's attempts to find a new job. Accordingly, caution is advised when responding to reference requests or informing customers about the termination of an employee.
Intentional (or Negligent) Infliction of Emotional Distress, a/k/a Outrageous Conduct	The employer does something outrageous or malicious in the termination process, causing emotional distress to the discharged employee.	This claim can be made against an employer who fires an employee in anger, publicly, without due investigation or deliberation, or with the intent of hurting the employee rather than simply remedying a problem.

Another Basis for Termination Lawsuits: Statutory Law

In addition to common law claims, a number of laws have been enacted by federal and state legislatures that regulate the termination of employment in various ways. Employers should also make themselves aware of any applicable local ordinances.

Federal Statutes Regulating Termination Practices

The following are several broad categories of federal statutes that in some way affect the termination of employment.

Nondiscrimination and Equal Employment Opportunity Laws

A collection of federal laws makes it illegal to discriminate in the termination of employment on the basis of race, color, national origin, sex, pregnancy, religion, age, and disability. These laws are (a) Title VII of the Civil Rights Act of 1964 (Title VII); (b) the Age Discrimination in Employment Act of 1967; (c) the Older Workers Benefits Protection Act of 1990; (d) the Pregnancy Discrimination Act of 1978; (e) the Rehabilitation Act of 1973; and (f) the Americans with Disabilities Act of 1990. The applicability of these statutes to a particular employer depends on the size of the employer and whether the employer is the federal government, a federal contractor, or a company or organization receiving federal financial assistance.

Title VII prohibits two distinct types of discrimination: (1) *disparate treatment* discrimination and (2) *disparate impact* discrimination, also known as *adverse impact* discrimination.

Disparate Treatment Discrimination—Disparate treatment discrimination occurs in terminations when an employer consciously takes the employee's protected status into consideration when making a discharge or layoff decision. An example of this intentional form of discrimination is an employer who learns that an employee is pregnant and, on the basis of that fact, selects the pregnant employee for layoff rather than a less-qualified employee who is not pregnant. An employee who quits or is fired as a result of being the victim of sexual harassment also may have a claim for disparate treatment discrimination.

Disparate Impact Discrimination—Disparate impact discrimination occurs when an employer adopts a policy or practice that seems neutral and non-discriminatory on its face but that has a disproportionately negative impact on members of a protected class. This legal claim is based, in part, on the reality that people can discriminate without intending to do so. Once a disparate impact is shown, the employer has the burden of demonstrating that the requirement is job-related for the position in question and consistent with business necessity. If the employee can point to a less discriminatory way to satisfy business needs, the employer may be obligated to adopt that alternative.

For example, suppose an employer needed to lay off employees in a particular job classification. Suppose further that the employer didn't want to go through the difficult process of selecting employees for layoff according to work performance and, therefore, decided to make one of the layoff criteria whether the employee had a high school diploma. That may seem a rather innocuous way to upgrade an employer's remaining workforce, but it probably wouldn't fare very well in the courts. Studies have shown that some minority groups are less likely than the general population to obtain a high school diploma. Because the employees without high school diplomas had previously held the positions, the employer would not be able to show that the diploma criterion was job-related and consistent with business necessity. The employer would be required to adopt selection criteria that did not have such a disparate impact on protected classes.

Federal Antiretaliation Statutes

Lawsuits based on unlawful retaliation can be even more difficult for employers to defeat than those based on direct discrimination. Employers must not attempt, or appear to attempt, to get even when conducting disciplinary terminations or layoffs when the affected employees have participated in protected activities.

The various federal equal employment opportunity (EEO) laws prohibit retaliation because the employee has exercised his or her rights under the statute at issue. For example, Title VII makes it illegal for an employer to discriminate against an employee because that employee opposed any discriminatory practice; made a charge of discrimination; or testified, assisted, or participated in any manner in an investigation, proceeding, or hearing. Consequently, an employer's exposure to claims of unlawful retaliation is even broader than its exposure to claims for the underlying type of discrimination. The employee who claims to be the victim of discrimination can additionally claim to be the victim of retaliation for complaining about such discrimination. Meanwhile, if 10 other employees participate in the investigation of that claim and all 11 are subsequently selected for layoff, while others who did not participate in the investigation are not selected for layoff, a discharged employee, a plaintiff's lawyer, and a jury might well believe that unlawful retaliation has occurred.

Many other federal statutes regulating the employer-employee relationship make it illegal to terminate an employee in retaliation for the employee exercising his or her rights under the statute. The following are some of these statutes:

- The **Occupational Safety and Health Act of 1970** gives employees the right to seek safe and healthful job conditions without fear of punishment. Covered activities include voicing concerns to an employer, participating in OSHA inspections, and refusing to work when a dangerous situation threatens serious injury or death. OSHA prohibits an employer from firing an employee in retaliation for taking these actions.

- The **National Labor Relations Act** (NLRA) gives employees the right to organize and join unions, to bargain collectively, and to engage in other concerted activities for the purpose of collective bargaining or other mutual aid or protection. The NLRA prohibits retaliation, including firing or threatening to fire, against employees who have exercised such rights.

- The **Fair Labor Standards Act of 1938** guarantees employees minimum wages and overtime pay, and prohibits retaliation based on the exercise of those rights.

- Similar protection is afforded to whistle-blowers under the **Sarbanes-Oxley Act**. This law is discussed at some length later in this chapter.

Federal Statutes That Provide Job Protection during a Leave of Absence

Two federal statutes—the Family and Medical Leave Act and the Uniformed Services Employment and Reemployment Rights Act—expressly regulate the ability of an employer to terminate an employee in connection with a qualifying leave of absence.

The Family and Medical Leave Act—Not all employers are subject to the Family and Medical Leave Act (FMLA), and even if the employer is covered, not all employees are eligible for

FMLA leave. Nor is FMLA leave available in every instance related to "family" or "medical" reasons. The legal details of such matters are beyond the scope of this book.

The FMLA prohibits an employer from *terminating the employee* while he or she is on FMLA-qualified leave, except in the case of (a) bona fide job elimination; (b) termination for reasons not related to the employee's medical condition or use of leave; or (c) the employee's inability to return to work upon the expiration of all available leave. Apart from these circumstances, an employee is entitled to be reinstated to the same position—or an equivalent position with equivalent pay, benefits, and other terms and conditions of employment—he or she held before the FMLA leave began. Applying these rules in real life is often more challenging than the straightforward language may suggest.

First, if an employer implements a bona fide reorganization that results in an employee's job being eliminated, an employee on FMLA leave may be terminated just as though he or she were not on leave. In other words, in such a situation, a person on FMLA leave is not given special rights compared with the rights of workers not on leave. Nevertheless, employers should be careful to ensure that if the reason given for termination is "job elimination," the job (and not just the person holding it) has truly been eliminated. Sometimes, fulfilling that obligation requires more than merely taking the responsible manager's statements at face value. This is especially true as many courts hold that the FMLA provides for individual liability against managers, including HR managers. An employer, supervisor, or HR manager who calls a termination a job elimination when it really isn't is courting danger.

Second, employees on FMLA leave are not given special rights if they have violated company policies or failed to meet expected performance levels. Such employees can be fired just as employees would be who are not on FMLA leave. However, as important as maintaining adequate documentation of performance problems always is, it is even more critical if the discharged employee is on FMLA leave.

Finally, even if an employee is unable, upon expiration of all available leave, to return to full-time work performing all regular duties, the employer cannot assume, in all situations, that employment may be terminated. Suppose the reason for the leave was the employee's disability. If that is the case, the Americans with Disabilities Act (ADA) may require the employer to extend a reasonable accommodation to the employee. A "serious health condition" under the FMLA may also be a "disability" under the ADA. So don't fall into the trap of failing to consider the ADA when the reason for FMLA leave relates to the employee's serious health condition.

The Uniformed Services Employment and Reemployment Rights Act of 1994—The Uniformed Services Employment and Reemployment Rights Act (USERRA) applies to all employers, regardless of size, and all regular employees, regardless of position or full- or part-time status. It regulates leaves of absence taken by members of the uniformed services, including Reservists, and by National Guard members for training, periods of active military service (whether voluntary or involuntary), and funeral honors duty, as well as time spent being examined to determine fitness to perform such service.

USERRA provides three important benefits with respect to termination: (1) protection from discrimination on the basis of military service; (2) protection from termination for a period of time after return from service; and (3) the right to re-employment upon conclusion of military service.

First, as with other federal employment laws, USERRA contains a broad antidiscrimination and antiretaliation component. Accordingly, employment cannot be terminated just because the employee is a member of or applies to be a member of a uniformed service, or performs, has performed, applies to perform, or has an obligation to perform service in a uniformed service.

Second, covered employees have a right not to be discharged except for cause for up to one year following re-employment.

Third, USERRA provides re-employment rights. The nature of the position the returning employee is entitled to depends on the length of service. Generally, if service has been less than 91 days, the employee is entitled to return to the same position, or the position he or she would have attained but for taking leave. In other words, if the employee would have been promoted if not for the military leave, he or she is entitled to the promotion upon return. The returning employee is entitled to all pay increases, seniority increases, and other benefits that would have been obtained but for being absent on leave. This is sometimes referred to as the *escalator principle*.

There are three exceptions to the re-employment obligations: (1) the employer's circumstances have so changed as to make such re-employment impossible or unreasonable; (2) re-employment would impose an undue hardship on the employer; or (3) the employment from which the person leaves to serve in the uniformed services is for a brief, nonrecurrent period, and there is no reasonable expectation that such employment will continue indefinitely or for a significant period. In these situations, the burden of proof is on the employer to show that the exception applies.

Subject to certain exceptions, there are several eligibility requirements for an employee to attain these rights:

- The employee must give notice of the need to leave for military service. The notice may be oral; employers are not permitted to demand written notice.

- The employee must be released from service under honorable conditions.

- The employee must not exceed five years of military leave with any particular employer. Annual training and monthly drills do not count against the cumulative total.

Figure 2-3 summarizes re-employment and job protection rights under USERRA. Employers should be aware that numerous exceptions might be applicable under particular circumstances. Additional guidance on compliance with USERRA is available from the National Committee for Employer Support for the Guard and Reserve by calling (800) 336-4590 and on the Internet at www.esgr.com. The U.S. Department of Labor publishes a list of frequently asked questions for reservists who are called to active duty (www.dol.gov/ebsa/faqs/faq_911_2.html).

Figure 2.3   Summary of USERRA Re-employment and Job-Protection Provisions

Length of Service	Deadline to Return to Work or Apply for Re-employment	Post-Return Job Protection (Discharge Only for Cause)	Position Entitled To	Employer's Obligation to Help Qualify
30 or fewer days	Return to work by the first regularly scheduled workday following completion of service.	None, except as provided by 38 U.S.C. § 4311		
31–180 days	Apply for re-employment within 14 days after completing service.	180 days		
More than 180 days	Apply for re-employment within 90 days following completion of service.	One year		
Less than 91 days			The job left or that would have been attained but for the leave.	Regardless of the length of service, if the returning employee is not qualified for the better job, the employer must make a reasonable effort to help the returning employee become qualified for the better job.
91 or more days			At the employer's option, either (1) the job left or that would have been attained but for the leave, or (2) a position of like seniority, status, and pay.	

Federal Statutes Regulating Notices in the Termination Context

Under some statutes, the act of terminating employment triggers the obligation of the employer to send out certain notices. The termination of employment triggers notice requirements under the Worker Adjustment and Retraining Notification Act, the Consolidated Omnibus Budget Reconciliation Act, and the Health Insurance Portability and Accountability Act.

Worker Adjustment and Retraining Notification Act—The goal of the aptly named WARN Act (Worker Adjustment and Retraining Notification Act) is to minimize harm to workers and communities by requiring employers under certain circumstances to provide them with warning of a mass layoff or plant closing. The WARN Act generally requires covered employers who are planning a plant closing or a mass layoff to give affected employees at least 60 days' notice. Sixty days is the minimum; the provision is not intended to discourage employers from giving employees even more advance notice. Not all plant closings and layoffs are subject to WARN, and certain employment thresholds must be reached before WARN applies. The WARN Act sets out specific exemptions and provides for a reduction in the notification period in certain circumstances. Damages and civil penalties can be assessed against employers who violate the Act; however, courts do not have the power to enjoin a plant closing or mass layoff.

When notice is required, it is given to four distinct groups:

(1) to each representative of the affected employees;

(2) in the absence of a representative, to each affected employee;

(3) to the state or entity designated by the state to receive such notice; and

(4) to the chief elected official of the local government where the mass layoff or plant closing will occur.

As summarized in Figure 2-4, the required content of the notice depends on which group is receiving it. Sample WARN notices for each of these four groups appear in Part 2, Section L.

Figure 2.4 **Information to Include in WARN Notices**

Who Is Entitled to Notice	Content of Required Notice for Each Type of Recipient
Each representative of the affected employees.	(1) The name and address of the site where the mass layoff or plant closing will occur. (2) The name and telephone number of a company official to contact for further information. (3) A statement as to whether the planned action is expected to be permanent or temporary, and whether the entire plant is to be closed. (4) The expected date of the first separation and the anticipated schedule for making separations. (5) The job titles and positions to be affected, and the names of the workers currently holding affected jobs.
In the absence of a representative, each affected employee.	(1) The name and telephone number of a company official to contact for further information. (2) A statement as to whether the planned action is expected to be permanent or temporary, and whether the entire plant is to be closed. (3) The expected date when the plant closing or mass layoff will commence and the expected date when the individual employee will be separated. (4) An indication of whether bumping rights exist.
The state or entity designated by the state to receive such notice.	(1) The name and address of the site where the mass layoff or plant closing will occur. (2) The name and telephone number of a company official to contact for further information. (3) A statement as to whether the planned action is expected to be permanent or temporary, and whether the entire plant is to be closed. (4) The expected date of the first separation and the anticipated schedule for making separations. (5) The job titles of positions to be affected, and the number of affected employees in each job classification. (6) An indication of whether bumping rights exist. (7) The name of each union representing affected employees. (8) The name and address of the chief elected officer of each union.
The chief elected official of the local government where the action will occur.	Same requirements as for notice to state above.

The WARN Act does not apply to all employers. It applies only to those that have (a) 100 or more employees, excluding part-time employees, or (b) 100 or more employees, including part-time employees, who, in the aggregate, work at least 4,000 hours per week (not including overtime). Workers on temporary layoff or on leave who have a reasonable expectation of recall are counted as employees. An employee has a "reasonable expectation of recall" if the employee understands, through notification or industry practice, that the employment has been temporarily interrupted and that he or she will be recalled to the same or a similar job. In most cases, government entities are not covered by WARN, but most other entities are covered.

The WARN Act applies to *plant closings* and *mass layoffs* as those terms are defined in the statute:

- **Plant closing:** The term means the permanent or temporary shutdown of a "single site of employment" or one or more "facilities or operating units" within a single site of employment if the shutdown results in an "employment loss" during any 30-day period at the single site of employment for 50 or more employees, excluding any part-time employees. An employment action that results in the effective cessation of production or the work performed by a unit, even if a few employees remain, is a "shutdown." A "temporary shutdown" triggers the notice requirement only if there are a sufficient number of terminations, layoffs exceeding six months, or reductions in hours of work as specified under the definition of "employment loss." (The phrases in quotation marks are defined terms in the WARN Act, and must be studied carefully to be correctly applied.)

- **Mass layoff.** If at least 500 employees, excluding part-time employees, lose employment during any 30-day period, the action qualifies as a "mass layoff." Additionally, if at least 33 percent of the employees at a single site of employment lose employment during any 30-day period, the action qualifies as a "mass layoff" unless that percentage amounts to fewer than 50 workers. In other words, a layoff of 50 workers will not be deemed a "mass layoff" if those workers comprise less than 33 percent of the workforce.

The WARN Act recognizes that a layoff may occur over a period of weeks or even months and that what starts out as a small layoff may, over the course of time, become sufficiently large that the affected parties should be given notice. The purpose of the WARN Act would be defeated if employers could structure a large layoff as a series of smaller layoffs to avoid notice requirements. As discussed below, the Act includes two rules to address this situation.

The WARN Act recognizes that, over a period of time, an employer may be faced with separate and distinct situations necessitating layoffs. In such situations, employers are not penalized for failing to anticipate the need for additional layoffs caused by separate and distinct circumstances. For example, say that an employer initiates a layoff because of a sluggish market for its products. Two months later, its supplier of critical components suffers a fire, rendering the employer unable to fill even the orders it has. The layoff resulting from the supplier's fire would not be considered part of the earlier layoff in determining whether, over the span of several months, the total layoffs were large enough to trigger the notice requirements.

The WARN regulations say that, in deciding whether notice is required, the employer should

(a) look ahead 30 days and behind 30 days to determine whether employment actions both taken and planned will, in the aggregate for any 30-day period, reach the minimum number for a plant closing or a mass layoff and thus trigger the notice requirement; and

(b) look ahead 90 days and behind 90 days to determine whether employment actions both taken and planned that separately are not of sufficient size to trigger WARN coverage, will, in the aggregate for any 90-day period, reach the minimum number for a plant closing or a mass layoff and thus trigger the notice requirement.

An employer is not required to give notice if it can demonstrate that the separate employment losses are the result of separate and distinct actions and causes, and are not an attempt to evade the requirements of WARN.

Thus, in determining whether WARN notice is required, the employer must look back as well as forward to see whether the conditions requiring a WARN notice have been met. Because of the complexity of this determination and the potentially severe consequences of failing to provide notice when required, it is highly advisable to consult experienced employment lawyers whenever it appears that WARN might be applicable.

With certain exceptions, notice must be given at least 60 calendar days before any planned plant closing or mass layoff. When not all employees are terminated on the same date, the date of the first individual termination within the statutory 30-day or 90-day period triggers the 60-day notice requirement. A worker's last day of employment is considered the date of that worker's layoff. The first and each subsequent group of terminated employees are entitled to a full 60 days' notice.

Where WARN notification is required, any reasonable method of delivery that is designed to ensure receipt of the notice at least 60 days before separation is acceptable (e.g., first class mail or personal delivery with optional signed receipt). Inserting the notice into pay envelopes is another viable option. A ticketed notice (i.e., a preprinted notice *regularly* included in each employee's pay envelope) does not meet the requirements of WARN.

Consolidated Omnibus Budget Reconciliation Act of 1985—Most employees are aware that the Consolidated Omnibus Budget Reconciliation Act of 1985 (COBRA) refers to the right of an employee to continue certain employer-provided insurance benefits after the termination of employment. COBRA also provides for continuation of benefits to children who have lost their dependent status and spouses who become divorced or legally separated.

Most states provide for continuation coverage that is applicable to employer benefit plans that do not fall within COBRA's eligibility parameters. These state requirements are often referred to generically as *COBRA*, although *state continuation coverage* is a more accurate term.

COBRA requires group health plans to allow "qualified beneficiaries" to continue group health insurance coverage for up to 18 months (29 or 36 months in certain circumstances) after a specified "qualifying event." Qualifying events include the following:

- Termination of employment (except in the case of gross misconduct).

- Reduction in hours worked, resulting in loss of coverage.

- Death of the covered employee.

- Divorce or legal separation from the covered employee.

- Employer's filing of Chapter 11 bankruptcy.

- Loss of status as a dependent under a group health plan.

- Employee's entitlement to Medicare.

Qualified beneficiaries may elect to continue coverage, at a cost of up to 102 percent of the cost to the plan (150% for the 19th through 29th months of coverage for disabled qualified beneficiaries or their covered dependents). The percentages above 100 are to compensate the employer for administering the benefit after the employee has left.

COBRA requires various notices to be provided at various times and under various circumstances. Employers, plan administrators, and employees or other qualified beneficiaries are required to provide the notices. Some notices are triggered by the termination of employment (see Figure 2-5); samples of those notices are included in Part 2, Section J. The U.S. Department of Labor publishes a list of frequently asked questions about COBRA (www.dol.gov/ebsa/faqs/faq_consumer_cobra.html).

The Health Insurance Portability and Accountability Act of 1996—The Health Insurance Portability and Accountability Act of 1996 (HIPAA) brought sweeping changes to the health care industry.[8] HIPAA also affects employers that provide health insurance benefits to employees.

A key goal of HIPAA was to make it easier for an employee to change jobs without losing health care coverage. HIPAA limits exclusions based on pre-existing conditions, prohibits exclusion on the basis of health status, and guarantees the ability to renew health insurance coverage. Another key goal of HIPAA was to ensure the privacy of health-related information.

With regard to termination of employment, two aspects of HIPAA are important. First, an employer should not release medical information about a former employee or any other covered individual in any instance without the consent of that person or a court order. In some instances, a self-insured employer may be deemed a "covered entity" for purposes of HIPAA. In this case, the employer would need a HIPAA-compliant consent from the former employee. This requirement addresses HIPAA's accountability goal. Second, HIPAA requires employers to give employees and/or qualified beneficiaries

| Figure 2.5 | COBRA Notices and Forms Applicable to Termination of Employment | | |

Type of Form	Deadline	From → To	Sample No.
General Notice of Continuation Coverage Rights	Within 90 days after new participant is first covered under plan	Employer → Employee and Spouse	J.1.1
Employer's Notice to Plan Administrator of Occurrence of COBRA Qualifying Event	Within 30 days of qualifying event	Employer → Plan Administrator	J.2.1
Qualified Beneficiary's Notice to Plan Administrator of Occurrence of COBRA Qualifying Event	Within 60 days of qualifying event	Qualified Beneficiary → Plan Administrator	J.2.2
Model COBRA Continuation Coverage Election Notice (with Election Form)	(If no outside Plan Administrator) within 44 days of receipt of Notice of Qualifying Event (when triggered by termination, reduction in hours, death, employer's bankruptcy)	Employer (if no outside Plan Administrator) → Qualified Beneficiary	J.3.1
Model COBRA Continuation Coverage Election Notice (with Election Form)	Within 14 days of receipt of Notice of Qualifying Event	Plan Administrator → Qualified Beneficiary	J.3.1
Election of Coverage	Within 60 days of COBRA Election Notice or date of loss of group health plan coverage, whichever is later	Qualified Beneficiary → Plan Administrator or Employer (if no outside administrator is used)	J.3.1
Notice of Unavailability of COBRA Coverage	Within 14 days of COBRA Election Notice or date of loss of group health plan coverage, whichever is later	Plan Administrator → Applicant for COBRA coverage	J.4.1
Notice to COBRA Beneficiary of Early Termination of COBRA Continuation Coverage	As soon as practicable once it has been determined that coverage will be (or has been) terminated	Plan Administrator → Qualified Beneficiary	J.5.1

written certification of coverage, outlining the coverage the employee had during the 24-month period before coverage terminated. This requirement addresses HIPAA's portability goal.

The employer must provide certification of coverage on three occasions:

- when coverage ends (usually at the same time COBRA notification is required);

- when COBRA coverage (if elected) ends, or at the end of the grace period for payment of a COBRA premium; and

- upon request by an employee at any time within 24 months of the end of coverage.

Employers must provide the names of dependents on the certification statement. If the dependents had different types of benefits, employers must provide separate certificates indicating which beneficiaries received which benefits. The certificate(s) must reflect all periods of creditable coverage. *Creditable coverage* is defined broadly to include coverage under (a) a group health plan, including a government or church plan; (b) individual health insurance; (c) Medicare or Medicaid; (d) military-sponsored health care; (e) the Federal Employee Health Benefits Program; (f) the Indian Health Service program;

(g) a state health benefits risk pool; (h) any health benefit plan under Section 5(e) of the Peace Corps Act; and (i) a public health plan, as defined in the HIPAA regulations. The certificate may be provided by the health insurance carrier instead of the employer. Failure to provide a certificate when required may subject the employer to a penalty of $100 per individual for each day of noncompliance, up to 10 percent of the plan sponsor's annual health care payments or $500,000, whichever is less.

A HIPAA-compliant certification of coverage is reproduced in Part 2, Section K.

Federal Statutes Regulating Separation Agreements

Depending on the circumstances, three statutes may affect an employer's policies and practices with respect to providing severance pay to departing employees: the Older Worker Benefit Protection Act, the American Jobs Creation Act, and the Employee Retirement Income Security Act.

The Older Worker Benefit Protection Act of 1990—The Older Worker Benefit Protection Act (OWBPA) amended the Age Discrimination in Employment Act in part to regulate agreements providing for the release of age discrimination claims. OWBPA requirements are addressed in Chapter 3.

The American Jobs Creation Act—Depending on the terms of a particular separation agreement, the American Jobs Creation Act (AJCA), signed into law in 2004, may affect the agreement. AJCA issues are addressed in Chapter 3.

The Employee Retirement Income Security Act of 1974—The Employee Retirement Income Security Act of 1974 (ERISA) regulates, in part, employee welfare benefit plans. If an employer has a policy or practice of regularly providing severance pay to departing employees, the employer has a "welfare benefit plan" that is subject to ERISA regulation, including a requirement to provide employees with a summary plan description. A voluntary separation program (VSP), as discussed in Chapter 3, could also fall within ERISA regulation.[9]

A policy providing that employees will be paid a certain number of weeks of severance pay indexed to the number of years of employment would be deemed a welfare benefit plan subject to ERISA. If the employer provides severance only on an ad hoc basis (for example, to settle a discrimination claim asserted by a departing employee), that would not ordinarily be considered a welfare benefit plan.

Federal Protection of Whistle-blowers

Whistle-blowers are protected under the antiretaliation provisions of numerous federal statutes including the Sarbanes-Oxley Act.

Sarbanes-Oxley Act—The Sarbanes-Oxley Act (SOX) applies to public companies that have securities (stocks or bonds) registered with the Securities and Exchange Commission (SEC) and certain entities associated with the securities industry.

SOX made sweeping reforms as to corporate governance, accounting and auditing practices, corporate reporting, and legal enforcement. Additionally, whistle-blowers (who have been instrumental in detecting and prosecuting corporate misconduct) were afforded new protections against retaliation. With respect to termination of employment, SOX contains three important provisions.

First, SOX bars retaliation against employees of public companies who assist existing or anticipated proceedings related to alleged violations of SEC rules or federal securities laws.

A second SOX provision provides affected employers with a little more leeway, should they dare to exercise it. Affected employers may not discharge an employee who provides information about corporate conduct that the employee reasonably believes violates SEC rules or federal securities laws, provided that the information is given to (a) a federal regulatory or law enforcement agency; (b) any member or committee of Congress; or (c) a person who holds supervisory authority over the employee or has the authority to investigate, discover, or terminate misconduct. In other words, whistle-blowing to federal authorities or the internal chain of command is protected, but holding a press conference is not.

A third pertinent SOX provision applies only to certain employers in the securities industry and to a relatively small group of employees: securities analysts. Under this provision, a broker/dealer employer may not retaliate against a securities analyst involved with investment banking activities for an unfavorable research report that may adversely affect the current or prospective investment banking relationship of the broker/dealer with the public company that is the subject of the report.

The consequences of employer violations of SOX can be severe: reinstatement, back pay, interest, special damages, attorney fees, and other litigation costs—plus criminal liability.

State Statutes Regulating Termination Practices

When undertaking a termination of employment—whether a discharge or a layoff—employers must be careful to comply with state statutes and local ordinances, in addition to the federal laws discussed above.

States and municipalities typically legislate in seven general areas: (1) limitations on valid reasons for involuntarily terminating employment; (2) wage and hour laws regulating final paychecks; (3) employee benefits; (4) employee access to personnel records; (5) post-termination communications about the employee (e.g., reference checking, service letters, and blacklisting); (6) enforceability of noncompetition and nondisclosure agreements; and (7) laws similar to the WARN Act that require advance notice to employees, unions, and government agencies of mass layoffs and plant closures.

Figure 2-6 (on pages 30–31) is a state-by-state chart that illustrates which states have laws on 16 issues related to employment termination.

State Limitations on Valid Reasons for Involuntary Termination

Most states have laws similar to Title VII of the Civil Rights Act of 1964, the Age Discrimination in Employment Act (ADEA), the ADA, and the USERRA (discussed above). However, some states and localities go much further in creating classes of persons who are protected from termination. In addition to protecting against termination on the basis of race, color, national origin, sex, religion, age, disability, and military service, some states and localities have created protections for a variety of activities that are

Figure 2.6   States Having Various Statutes Affecting the Termination of Employment

Notes on Use: States may have added or repealed statutes since the preparation of this table. A check mark indicates merely that the particular state has some sort of statutory requirement on the general subject. In the absence of a specific statute, case law may contain similar requirements.

Key to Table Columns:

Statutes Limiting Grounds for Involuntary Terminations

  1. Leave to be a witness
  2. Leave to vote
  3. Whistle-blowing in private sector
  4. Marital status
  5. Sexual orientation
  6. Trans-gender identification
  7. Legal off-duty conduct
  8. Employee wages subject to garnishment

Wage/Hour Statutes

  9. Final paycheck: timing, delivery, amounts to be included]

Employee Benefits Statutes

10. State continuation of insurance benefits

Access to Personnel Records

11. Statutes regulating employee access to personnel records

Statutes Regulating Post-termination Communications

12. Anti-blacklisting
13. Service letters
14. Reference immunity

Statutes Regulating Noncompetition and Nondisclosure Agreements

15. Noncompetition and nondisclosure

WARN-type Statutes

16. States having WARN-type statutes

Type of Statute

State	1	2	3	4	5	6	7	8	9	10	11	12	13	14	15	16
AL			✓		✓			✓				✓			✓	
AK	✓	✓		✓	✓			✓	✓		✓			✓		
AZ		✓			✓				✓			✓		✓	✓	
AR		✓	✓						✓	✓	✓	✓		✓		
CA	✓	✓	✓	✓	✓	✓		✓	✓	✓	✓	✓	✓	✓	✓	
CO	✓	✓	✓	✓	✓		✓	✓	✓	✓	✓	✓		✓	✓	
CT	✓		✓	✓	✓			✓	✓	✓	✓	✓				
DE				✓	✓			✓	✓		✓		✓	✓		
DC				✓	✓		✓	✓	✓		✓					
FL	✓			✓						✓		✓		✓	✓	
GA	✓	✓						✓		✓				✓	✓	
HI	✓	✓	✓	✓	✓			✓	✓	✓		✓		✓	✓	✓
ID								✓	✓		✓	✓		✓		
IL	✓	✓	✓	✓	✓			✓	✓	✓	✓	✓		✓		
IN	✓		✓		✓				✓			✓	✓	✓	✓	
IA	✓	✓						✓	✓	✓	✓	✓		✓	✓	
KS		✓						✓	✓	✓		✓	✓	✓		
KY		✓		✓	✓		✓	✓	✓	✓	✓	✓		✓		
LA			✓					✓	✓	✓				✓	✓	
ME	✓		✓					✓	✓	✓	✓	✓	✓	✓		✓
MD	✓	✓	✓	✓	✓			✓	✓	✓				✓		✓
MA	✓				✓			✓	✓	✓	✓			✓	✓	✓
MI			✓	✓	✓				✓		✓			✓	✓	
MN		✓	✓	✓	✓		✓	✓	✓	✓		✓	✓	✓	✓	
MS		✓	✓					✓		✓		✓				
MO		✓						✓	✓	✓				✓	✓	
MT	✓		✓	✓	✓			✓	✓	✓		✓		✓	✓	✓
NE		✓	✓	✓				✓	✓	✓				✓		
NV	✓	✓			✓		✓	✓	✓	✓	✓	✓	✓	✓	✓	
NH			✓	✓	✓		✓	✓	✓	✓	✓					
NJ			✓	✓	✓			✓	✓	✓		✓				
NM		✓		✓	✓	✓		✓	✓			✓		✓		
NY	✓	✓	✓	✓			✓	✓	✓	✓		✓			✓	
NC			✓					✓	✓	✓	✓	✓		✓	✓	
ND	✓		✓	✓			✓	✓	✓	✓	✓	✓		✓	✓	
OH	✓	✓	✓					✓	✓	✓			✓	✓		
OK		✓	✓					✓	✓	✓	✓	✓	✓	✓	✓	
OR			✓	✓	✓	✓	✓	✓	✓	✓	✓	✓		✓	✓	
PA	✓				✓			✓	✓		✓			✓		
RI			✓		✓	✓		✓	✓	✓	✓	✓		✓		
SC	✓							✓	✓	✓				✓		✓
SD		✓	✓	✓				✓	✓	✓	✓			✓	✓	
TN		✓	✓					✓	✓	✓	✓			✓		✓
TX		✓	✓					✓	✓	✓	✓	✓	✓	✓	✓	
UT		✓						✓	✓	✓	✓	✓		✓		
VT	✓		✓		✓			✓	✓	✓						
VA	✓			✓				✓	✓		✓	✓		✓		
WA				✓	✓			✓	✓	✓	✓	✓	✓	✓	✓	
WV		✓						✓	✓	✓					✓	
WI	✓	✓		✓	✓	✓	✓	✓	✓	✓	✓	✓		✓	✓	✓
WY	✓	✓				✓	✓	✓	✓					✓		

deemed good as a matter of public policy or are not considered relevant to termination decisions.

Examples of activities that many states support through antitermination legislation are the performance of jury duty, giving testimony when subpoenaed to do so, and voting. Every state has enacted laws making it illegal, to one degree or another, to discharge an employee because he or she has been summoned to perform jury duty. In some states, temporary or relatively new employees are exempted from the protection; in other states, small employers are exempted. A minority of states protect employees from termination as a result of giving testimony. Of those, some differentiate between an employee who is called in a civil lawsuit and one who is the victim of a crime or the defendant in a criminal case; or between an employee who has been subpoenaed and an employee who is testifying voluntarily. Almost every state makes it illegal to use employment consequences to influence employee voting. Most states have statutes protecting employees from being fired in retaliation for exercising worker's compensation rights; in the absence of statutory protection, there is usually common law protection. Whistle-blowers are also seen as beneficial and deserving of protection against termination in many states. Nearly every state protects whistle-blowing public sector employees, and about half the states extend such protection to employees in the private sector.

States often create protected classes of persons in addition to those established under federal law. Various states outlaw termination decisions based on marital status, sexual orientation, transgender identification, political orientation, breastfeeding, legal off-duty conduct (e.g., smoking tobacco; consuming legal alcohol or food products; engaging in sports, games, or hobbies; watching television or movies; or engaging in political campaigning), free association, free expression, and wage garnishment.

The great majority of states prohibit termination of employment because the employee's wages are subject to garnishment. However, in many states, the protection is extended only if the garnishment is for spousal or child support; in a few states, the employer must tolerate only a certain number of garnishments before it can fire the employee.

Wage and Hour Laws

State wage and hour laws also come into play in the termination context. Here, the areas typically regulated are the timing of final paychecks, the means of delivering the final paycheck, required payments upon termination, and permissible deductions.

In some states, the final paycheck must be delivered immediately or within a specified number of days if the termination is involuntary, but it may be cut on the next regular payday in the case of voluntary termination. The laws sometimes direct that the paycheck be mailed to the employee or made available at the worksite, and sometimes give either the employer or the employee discretion to choose the means of delivery.

Usually, state laws require payment of all earned compensation (wages, salary, bonuses, and commissions) in the final paycheck. Disputes frequently arise as to whether a bonus or commission has been fully earned and, therefore, must be paid upon termination. Payment for accrued vacation is typically required; however, in some states employers do not have to pay for unused vacation. Two states specify that vacation pay is to be on a pro rata basis. Some require payment for unused holidays. Ordinarily, compensation is not required for accumulated sick leave (at least where such payment is not the regular practice or required by agreement); a few states require such payment. Five states mandate payment of severance benefits under various circumstances. Such statutes are sometimes referred to as "tin parachute" statutes.

States vary widely in their approach to permissible deductions from the final paycheck for such items as unreturned company property, employee advances, and training expenses.

Employee Benefits

Although unemployment insurance benefits are jointly administered with the federal government, states are heavily involved in establishing the qualifying and disqualifying conditions, the duration and amount of benefits, and the procedures for claiming and awarding them.

There is wide disparity among the states as to what kind of conduct should or should not prevent unemployed persons from receiving benefits. Because the legal framework can vary widely from one state to another, it is imperative for employers with multistate workforces to be aware of these differences when deciding whether or not to contest an employee's claim for unemployment benefits.

Another area in which states are active is the regulation of continuation of insurance coverage in situations in which COBRA does not apply because, for example, the employer has fewer than 20 employees. Many states extend COBRA-like benefits to employees of small businesses, subject to notice and election procedures that may be identical to COBRA's or quite different.

Finally, just as states have expanded the number of classes of persons protected against termination based on membership in the class, they are also expanding the circumstances under which employees may take family, medical, or other leaves of absence. Typically, where states expand the qualified reasons for taking a leave, they require reinstatement at the end of the leave or at least prohibit retaliation against the employee for exercising the right to take qualified leave.

Employee Access to Personnel Records

About 60 percent of states require employers to either copy or make available for inspection and copying an employee's or former employee's own personnel file. States differ as to the applicable time periods, the scope of records the employee must be permitted access to, and the means by which the state enforces the rule.

Post-termination Communications about Employees

Many states have laws against blacklisting, that is, preparing, using, or publishing a list of former employees deemed persona non grata and thereby hindering the efforts of those persons to obtain future employment or singling them out for ostracism.

Several states require employers to provide, at the request of a former employee, a service letter disclosing basic employment information about the individual, such as the nature, character, and duration of employment; the rate of compensation; and the reason for termination. The exact contents required, the amount of time allowed to comply, and whether the service letter must be given to the employee or to a person designated by the employee vary by state.

Similarly, recognizing the importance of a free flow of truthful job-related information, a substantial majority of states have passed reference immunity laws to encourage employers to provide employee references without fear of being sued for defamation, invasion of privacy, or tortious interference with business opportunities. The particulars of these statutes vary widely by state.

Noncompetition and Nondisclosure Agreements

Noncompetition and nondisclosure agreements are regulated, at a minimum, under the common law of the various states. However, a number of states have elected to regulate them by statute also. Some states have virtually outlawed employer/employee noncompetition agreements. Others have limited their enforceability to specific circumstances, such as where they are needed to protect trade secrets or where the employee was an executive or served as confidential staff to an executive.

Laws Similar to WARN

A number of states have enacted laws very much like WARN, requiring advance notice to employees, unions, and government agencies of mass layoffs and plant closures. However, these state statutes may differ from WARN in the definition of mass layoff and plant closure; the amount of notice that must be given; the persons to whom notice must be given; and the contents of the notice.

Chapter 3
Preparing for Terminations

I thatched my roof when the sun was shining, and now I am not afraid of the storm.

—George F. Stivers

The Beginning of the End

It's inevitable: Even before we hire a new employee, we know that sooner or later the employment relationship will end.

To minimize the potential for problems during termination, employers should plan carefully for both voluntary and involuntary job separations. This "beginning of the end" should occur on two levels. The first level of preparation involves the establishment of an infrastructure designed to shield the organization against lawsuits and other threats to the business. The second level involves the development of strategies and tactics for handling specific individual or group departures.

Creating the Framework for Terminations

Employment terminations take place in the context of the particular organization. The unique features of that context will either help or hinder a safe and smooth parting. To reduce the likelihood of negative outcomes, employers should establish a strong infrastructure consisting of

- protective policies and procedures;

- enforceable written agreements with employees about post-termination restrictions and dispute resolution; and

- adequate liability insurance to cover termination-related legal claims.

Termination Policies and Procedures

Start by spelling out your organization's approach to separations in written termination policies. Such policies should define various types of termination, discuss how these separations are handled, and give the employer flexibility to revise the policy or deviate from the policy as it deems necessary. As the samples in Part 2, Section A illustrate, some employers choose to address all types of termination in a single policy, while others draft separate policies for voluntary and involuntary job separations. The following topics are commonly addressed in termination policies:

- The amount of notice requested from resigning employees.

- The employer's right to place a resigning employee on paid leave during the employee's notice period.

- Circumstances under which an absence without notice will be deemed job abandonment.

- Compensation that will or will not be included in the final paycheck (e.g., earned pay, accrued vacation pay, unused sick leave, personal time off).

- Return of company property.

- Exit interviews/surveys.

- Eligibility for rehire or reinstatement.

- Handling of reference requests for the various types of termination.

The samples in Part 2, Section A also show that some termination policies contain a detailed description of the separation process and procedures, while others are deliberately general to give management flexibility in handling individual terminations. Whatever approach you adopt, take care to follow your written separation policies and procedures or be prepared to identify extenuating circumstances that justify a different process. When you want to deviate from your policies, document the reasons for such deviation. Of course, these reasons must be based on legitimate employer concerns, not on discriminatory or retaliatory motives.

Other Recommended Policies

You may also want to develop policies clarifying the nature of and expectations for the working relationship between your company and its employees. The following are three important issues to address:

1. **Employment-at-will.** If your organization wants to maintain the right to discharge at will, an employment-at-will policy, drafted or reviewed by an employment attorney, is a must. This policy should be prominently located and conspicuously formatted in your employee handbook, employment application, employment offer letters, and employment contracts of unspecified duration. It should state unambiguously the legal right of both employer and employee to end the relationship at any time, with or without just cause. A good at-will policy includes a disclaimer that nothing in the employee handbook or any statements or actions by management can be construed as creating an express or implied contract of employment. A signed acknowledgment of receipt of and consent to your employment-at-will policy will be helpful in the event of litigation. Obtain the acknowledgment from every employee, preferably during the employee's first days at your organization.

2. **Work rules.** It is difficult for a discharged employee to claim that he or she didn't know that a particular behavior was prohibited if your employee handbook includes a policy on employee conduct and work rules. This policy should give examples of specific infractions that may result in discipline or termination. Because it is impossible to identify in advance every possible type of employee misconduct that might merit discharge, your work rules policy should state that the

list of infractions is illustrative rather than inclusive and that the employer has the right to discipline or terminate an employee at will.

3. **Discipline.** Disciplinary policies and procedures let employees know the consequences of violating work rules. Some employers prefer progressive discipline policies, under which an employee is subjected to increasingly severe disciplinary action (typically, moving from verbal to written warnings, to suspension, and ultimately to termination) for repeated or additional policy violations. Caution: While it is usually a good idea to *impose* discipline progressively, overly specific progressive discipline policies can be used against your organization if an employee is fired without having gone through all phases of the stated process. Any discipline policy should specifically permit your company to terminate employees as it deems necessary without following any or all steps of a progressive discipline process.

Samples of employment-at-will, work rules, and discipline policies appear in Part 2, Section B.

In addition, your company may wish to include separate policies in the employee handbook on the following topics if they are not covered in your termination policies:

- Vacation and paid time off accrual and payment (Chapter 2).

- Severance pay and benefits, if applicable (this chapter).

- References (Chapter 5).

- Employee access to personnel file (Chapter 5).

- Return of company property (Chapter 4).

These topics are discussed in the chapters indicated. Sample policies are included in Part 2, Section B.

Written Agreements with Post-termination Restrictions

In most states, employees owe their employers a common law duty of loyalty. The nature and extent of this duty vary by state and, in certain states, by the employee's position. Generally, employees are restricted by law against competition and the use of confidential and proprietary information against a current employer. This duty of loyalty usually expires upon separation from employment. However, an employer can protect itself against unfair post-termination competitive practices and the disclosure of trade secrets if it requires signed agreements upon hire or during the course of an individual's employment.

Common written restrictions on an employee's activities after separation include (a) *noncompete* agreements, which prohibit former employees from competing with the employer for a specific amount of time in a specific area or with regard to specific products or services; (b) *nonsolicitation* agreements, which prohibit former employees from soliciting the employers' customers or encouraging other employees to go to work with the employee after termination; and (c) *nondisclosure* agreements, which prohibit the use or disclosure of confidential information.

The enforceability of noncompete and nonsolicitation agreements will usually depend on how reasonable the restrictions are in terms of the scope of the activities limited, the duration of the restriction, and the geographic area covered. Such agreements should be drafted as narrowly as possible while still protecting the company's legitimate business interests, such as preservation of trade secrets or goodwill. A noncompete lasting one year and covering one city is much more likely to be enforced than one that prohibits competition nationwide for 10 years.

Nondisclosure agreements are generally enforced according to their terms, provided that the protected information constitutes genuine trade secrets. Generally speaking, a trade secret is information that (a) has economic value or gives a competitive advantage; (b) is not generally known or legally obtainable; and (c) has been protected through reasonable steps. Figure 3-1 provides a checklist to help employers identify their trade secrets. If you determine that you have information worth protecting from disclosure, consider whether you have taken reasonable steps to protect its secrecy. These steps might include controlling physical access to the information; conspicuously stamping it "TRADE SECRET MATERIAL: DO NOT REMOVE OR DISCLOSE"; making sure that the information is disclosed only to those with a need to know; and requiring employees to sign nondisclosure agreements as a condition of access to the information.

Dispute Resolution Agreements

Over the past two decades, there has been an explosion of interest in alternative dispute resolution (ADR). The two most prevalent forms of ADR are *binding arbitration* (in

---

Figure 3.1   **Proprietary Information Checklist: What Trade Secrets Does Your Organization Need to Protect?**

Product Information
__ Product design
__ Formulas
__ Product performance
__ Plans for new products

Technical Information
__ Research result
__ Web site hits and click-throughs
__ Web site plans

Operations Information
__ Plant design
__ Methods of operation
__ Equipment
__ Materials costs
__ Suppliers

Customer Information
__ Customer lists
__ Customer purchases
__ Payment histories

Distributor/Dealer Information
__ Distributor/dealer lists
__ Discount structures
__ Distributor/dealer performance

Personnel Information
__ Employee lists
__ Telephone/home address lists

Financial Information
__ Financial plans
__ Financial operations
__ Profit margins
__ Banking relationships
__ Investors' names
__ Pricing lists/discounts

Other Information
__ Plans for acquisitions, divestitures, joint ventures
__ Licensing practices
__ Marketing plans
__ Market research
__ Advertising budgets
__ _____
__ _____

See: Sobel, Michael, "Keeping the Lid on Proprietary Information," SHRM HR Technology Exchange Forum Library (www.shrm.org/hrtx/library_published/nonIC/CMS_008547.asp)

which the parties agree to have their dispute resolved by a neutral third person or panel) and *mediation* (in which a neutral third party facilitates the parties in reaching a negotiated resolution). Arbitration or mediation agreements can be entered at hiring or after a dispute has arisen. After a dispute has arisen, employees would likely be reluctant to enter an agreement waiving the right to a trial by jury, but they are usually willing to undertake nonbinding mediation, especially if it doesn't cost them anything.

While ADR agreements can be very useful to employers in resolving termination disputes, they should not be entered without careful consideration of the advantages and disadvantages, and it is critical to consult an employment lawyer to ensure that the terms of the agreement will hold up under applicable federal and state law.

Arbitration has many advantages compared with traditional litigation. First, arbitration is conducted in private rather than in a public courthouse. Second, disputes are usually resolved faster in arbitration than in the courts, which are experiencing considerable backlogs. Third, employers are protected from the possibility of a "runaway jury"—a jury that is swayed by passion or prejudice and enters a huge damage award, including an exorbitant amount in punitive damages. Some would argue, however, that this benefit is offset by the tendency of arbitrators to "split the baby"; that is, to award the employee partial relief on a claim that has no actual merit. Fourth, depending on the discovery and motions procedures negotiated by the parties under a particular arbitration agreement, arbitration can be much less expensive than traditional litigation. Fifth, the parties will be able to select an arbitrator who is an expert on the legal issues involved. And finally, the grounds for appealing an arbitration award are extremely limited, which can be a very good thing—provided you're on the side that won.

An agreement that requires the parties to mediate before commencing either traditional litigation or arbitration can also be very beneficial, giving the parties the opportunity to try to reach a negotiated resolution with the assistance of a trained mediator, thereby avoiding the cost and disruption of litigation.

Internal appeal or grievance procedures have been used by some employers for quite some time, particularly in the public sector. Recently, some employers have used jury waiver agreements, which are agreements to resolve disputes through the court system, but with a judge rather than a jury deciding the case.

The enforceability of an ADR agreement depends greatly on the particular provisions in the agreement, the claims the employee asserts, whether the employment involves interstate commerce, and the federal and state laws that apply to the agreement.

Liability Insurance

An important component of your termination infrastructure is adequate insurance protection against employment-related liabilities. Liability insurance is supplementary to—not a substitute for—good termination policies, agreements, and practices. It insures the employer for employment risks that cannot be eliminated or reduced through effective internal HR measures.

Several types of insurance policies may cover assorted employment-related claims. Comprehensive general liability policies may provide coverage for employment-related claims resulting in bodily injury, personal injury, or property damage. Directors and officers insurance may cover a company director or officer who is named as a defendant in an employment lawsuit.

In contrast to those two types of insurance, employment practices liability insurance (EPLI) is designed to insure against losses sustained as a result of wrongful employment practices liability claims. Most EPLI policies cover wrongful termination, discrimination, breach of contract, and other employment-related tort and statutory claims. However, EPLI policies typically exclude a variety of employment claims, such as WARN, COBRA, and ERISA violations.

Employers should assess their employment liability insurance needs on the basis of their size, workforce composition, the states in which they do business, history of claims by current and former employees, and the deductibles or risk retention they are willing to carry.

Anticipating Employee-Initiated Departures

Surprise resignations and job abandonment create challenges to productivity, morale, and staffing. But if supervisors and human resource professionals are vigilant and proactive, they may be able to predict and prepare before the employee gives notice or goes absent without leave.

The first step in anticipating voluntary employee departures is gathering and analyzing turnover statistics and exit interview/survey data, with the goal of pinpointing turnover patterns. Typically, the HR department handles this task—sometimes using human resource information systems—and reports key findings to management. Useful information to track includes the following:

- Common reasons for resignation.

- Voluntary turnover ratio (the number of employees who leave the organization through resignation or job abandonment divided by the total number of employees in the organization during a particular time period).

- Number or percentage of employee-initiated departures in particular jobs and departments.

- Number or percentage of resigning employees by gender, age, race, national origin, and so on.

- Number or percentage of resigning employees by supervisor.

- The tenure of employees who resign or abandon jobs.

Understanding trends in these areas will enable supervisors to keep more careful watch on valued employees who fit common voluntary termination profiles.

Supervisors and HR professionals should be alert for signs of a possible resignation based on events occurring in an employee's life or marked changes in the employee's

---

Figure 3.2 **Resignation Triggers and Tip-Offs**

Events Triggering Resignations
- Suspension
- Demotion
- Spouse relocation
- Return to school full-time
- Serious injury or illness
- Expiration of family, medical, disability, or other leave
- Eligibility to receive company retirement benefits
- Eligibility to receive Social Security
- Attainment of a college degree
- Assignment of a new supervisor
- Marriage
- Pregnancy

Tip-offs to Upcoming Resignations
- Marked change in quality or quantity of work
- Increased negativity about job or company
- Low interest in future assignments and work activities
- Removal of personal items from work space
- Uncharacteristic organization or disorganization of files and projects
- Questions about COBRA and other termination benefits
- Questions about reference practices
- Questions about non-compete, non-disclosure, or other employment agreements
- Request for a copy of personnel file

---

behavior. Figure 3-2 lists early warning signs of potential resignations. If a supervisor believes that an employee may resign in the near future, he or she should discuss this possibility with HR or other managers to determine what to do when the employee gives notice or how to address the problem that is prompting the resignation. Chapter 4 addresses appropriate responses to resignations and apparent job abandonment.

Planning for Employee Discharges

Discharge is the most serious discipline an employer can impose on an employee. It is the "capital punishment" of employment terminations.

From the employer's perspective, one of the few positive aspects of the involuntary dismissal of a problem employee is that the company controls the termination decision, the timing, and the manner in which the employee is let go. The employer's power to discharge should be exercised judiciously, humanely, and only after a thorough pretermination review to ensure that discharge is the appropriate action in the situation.

Deliberation

A discharge decision should never be made in the heat of the moment. Hasty firings are almost always flawed by incomplete information, misinterpretation of employee behavior, failure to consider more appropriate corrective action, subjective and potentially unlawful personal bias against the employee, discriminatory or retaliatory motives, or disrespectful or other inappropriate treatment of the employee.

No employee should be dismissed unless he or she has been afforded a fair "trial" internally and found "guilty" of serious or repeated misconduct or unacceptable performance.

This trial should take the form of a formal pretermination investigation followed by a pretermination review.[10] The purpose of the investigation is to:

- fully and objectively evaluate the facts related to the employee's misconduct or performance deficiencies;

- review applicable policies and any written employment agreements with the employee that potentially establish employer obligations or employee rights;

- gather, prepare, and review disciplinary documentation; and

- assess other relevant evidence.

The purpose of the pretermination review is to go over it all again, make sure that nothing was missed, and then make an informed decision. Although the pretermination review should be an integral part of your dismissal process, it should be described in your termination policies in a very general fashion, if at all. Figure 3-3 provides a pretermination review checklist.

Figure 3.3   What to Review before Every Employee Dismissal

Policies
- Has the employee violated an employment agreement, company policy, or work rule? Is it written? When and how was it communicated to the employee?
- Has the employee received a copy of our employment-at-will policy? Do we have the employee's written acknowledgment of receipt of this policy?
- What do our discipline and termination policies, or any applicable employment or collective bargaining agreement, require or permit us to do?
- Do we have any severance policies that we need to follow?

Investigation Process
- Did the company conduct an investigation before making the decision to fire the employee?
- Who conducted the investigation? Was this person qualified to conduct the investigation? Was this person an unbiased party?
- Were all appropriate witnesses questioned? Were all relevant documents examined? Was other relevant evidence reviewed?
- Has the employee had the opportunity to present his or her side of the story related to alleged misconduct?
- If the employee is a member of a union, was he or she allowed, upon timely request, to have a union representative present during any investigatory interview that could result in discipline?
- Was sufficient evidence of the employee's misconduct discovered during the investigation? How persuasive is the evidence against the employee?

Documentation
- Do the employee's performance appraisals and disciplinary documentation support a discharge decision?
- Have we adequately documented the investigation of the employee's misconduct?
- Has the employee signed any agreements that restrict his or her post-termination activities?
- Should we ask the employee to sign a separation agreement when he or she is terminated? Why?

Evaluation of Proposed Dismissal
- Does the employee's conduct warrant dismissal? If so, why?
- Have other employees engaged in similar misconduct? If so, have they been discharged? If not, what is different about this employee's misconduct?
- Are there preferable disciplinary alternatives to discharge?
- Is the employee a member of a protected class? If so, has the employee made allegations of discrimination by the organization?
- Has the employee ever filed a complaint internally or with a government agency? Has the employee sued the company or a previous employer?

Otherwise, an employee could argue that he or she was wrongfully terminated if the pretermination review did not comply with standards set forth in the written policy.

Making Discharge Decisions

To fire or not to fire? Employers should ask that question only upon completion of the pretermination review, much as juries may begin deliberations only after the plaintiff and defendant have presented their cases. To ensure a fair and legally sound decision, contemplated dismissals should be analyzed according to (a) their appropriateness for the particular offense, (b) precedents set by past treatment of employees for similar behavior, and (c) aggravating or mitigating circumstances.

Let's assume that there is substantial, credible evidence that an employee has broken workplace rules, that company policy and any employment contracts or collective bargaining agreements allow termination for these violations, and that the violations and previous steps in the disciplinary process have been documented accurately and fully. The question at this point is whether and why termination is a suitable response to the specific infraction.

For example, a discharge based on sexual harassment seems reasonable if the employee has groped or sexually assaulted another employee but may be an unduly harsh response against an employee who has told sexual jokes that no one ever told him or her were offensive. The difference between these two situations is the extent of harm to other employees and the fact that the joker may not have realized that the jokes were offensive.

However, even if discharge is an appropriate response to the employee's infraction, your organization will be proceeding at its peril if a termination decision is made without considering organizational precedents. Have other employees engaged in similar misconduct or had similar performance issues? If so, were these employees fired, or were other (or no) disciplinary actions taken? Inconsistent treatment of employees who have committed the same workplace infractions can provide a basis for disparate treatment discrimination claims if the inconsistently treated employees differ in age, sex, race, national origin, religion, or another protected characteristic.

There are no hard-and-fast rules to apply to make the right decision about discharge. The employer must weigh all factors objectively, be consistent (unless there is a good reason not to be), and document the reasons for the decision, including the reasons for any inconsistency.

Alternatives to Discharge

In general, a discharge may be warranted if an employee engages in a single instance of serious misconduct (e.g., theft, violence, on-duty drug use); repeatedly violates important rules (e.g., safety standards, attendance) after being warned to change his or her behavior; or exhibits significant, ongoing performance deficiencies in spite of counseling or performance improvement plans. Even in these serious situations, however, your organization may want to consider alternatives to discharge if there are extenuating factors.

Instead of firing an employee, an organization may elect a lesser but still serious form of discipline, such as suspension or decision-making leave, in which the employee returns to the job after a paid or unpaid disciplinary absence. Other alternatives to discharge may involve changes in terms and conditions of employment, such as a transfer or demotion. Another alternative is for the employer to allow the employee to resign instead of being fired. Figure 3-4 describes these instead-of-termination strategies and

Figure 3.4   Discharge Alternatives

Form of Discipline	Description	Comments
Suspension	Paid or unpaid disciplinary leave	If the employee has previously been suspended for this infraction, this suspension should be more severe than the initial one (either in length or by docking pay, or both).
		If the individual is classified as a Fair Labor Standards Act (FLSA) exempt employee, his or her pay cannot be docked in less than full-day increments unless it is for violation of a safety rule of major significance
Decision-making Leave	A type of suspension (usually for a day, and usually with pay) in which the employee is given time to decide whether to (a) comply with all company policies, work rules, and expectations in the future, and face immediate termination for any future infraction; or (b) resign.	This leave provides the employee with a "last clear chance" opportunity to correct problem behaviors or resign before termination is imposed. Some employees may choose to resign and, thus, will not be able to file a wrongful termination lawsuit against the employer. If the person is ultimately discharged, the decision-making leave will provide strong evidence of the employer's fair treatment of the employee before termination.
		To avoid discrimination claims, employers should attempt to determine in advance what situations merit decision-making leave. To use this alternative to greatest effect, it should be offered to an employee only once. Otherwise, employees may view it as another type of suspension.
Transfer	Moving an employee to a different location, workshift, or job at the same level.	This action is appropriate if the employee's poor performance or misconduct is likely to be corrected or eliminated by the transfer. Otherwise, it is ill-advised to transfer an employee to another work setting where problem behavior may continue or worsen.
		Transfers are sometimes used instead of termination for harassment when the harasser's inappropriate conduct has been directed toward a single individual.
Demotion	A job reassignment to a lower level.	Demotion may be a viable alternative to termination for poor performance if the employee's performance at a lower level was acceptable. Keep in mind, though, that the typical employee will feel embarrassed by and resentful of a demotion, even if the employee knows that he or she would otherwise have been fired.
Resignation in Lieu of Termination	The employee is given the opportunity to resign instead of being discharged.	This option allows the employer and employee to part company on a less adversarial note than would occur if the employee were dismissed. If the employee resigns, he or she will not have a wrongful termination claim unless the employer's actions leading to the resignation can be viewed as a constructive discharge.
		For unemployment insurance purposes, a resignation in lieu of firing is generally deemed an involuntary termination, and the employer will need to show that the employee's actions are a disqualification for benefits.

highlights the pros and cons of each. None of these options to discharge should be made available to an employee until the legal and practical implications have been fully considered and potential negative consequences minimized to the extent possible.

Planning for Reductions in Force

Whether you choose to call it a reduction in force (RIF), a layoff, downsizing, or rightsizing will make little difference in the overall success of the process. The difference between disaster and success in involuntary group terminations is planning. A single termination exposes the employer to a single termination lawsuit. A RIF exposes the employer to multiple lawsuits and/or a class action lawsuit.

It's hard enough to dismiss an employee whose actions justify firing. When a group of employees must be let go because of financial or competitive pressures on the organization or as a consequence of a merger or acquisition, the pain intensifies and the challenges multiply. From the employer's perspective, the turmoil of a RIF can be even greater than that caused by a discharge based on performance or violation of policy, because most or all of these employees will lose their jobs through no fault of their own. It is difficult to select who will stay and who will go, and when; and how and when to communicate about and execute group departures—all the while trying to comply with the law. These tasks are especially difficult when the managers and HR professionals responsible for making or carrying out the decisions will themselves be terminated during the RIF.

Before implementing a workforce reduction, employers should consider other options that may enable them to avoid, postpone, or scale down a downsizing initiative. If a group termination becomes necessary, extensive preparation should be made.

RIF Avoidance Strategies

Various cost-cutting options that can be used to eliminate or delay workforce reductions are described in Figure 3-5. Some of these strategies—such as expense trimming, hiring freezes, temporary furloughs, natural attrition, retraining, and mandatory vacations— are seen by employees as fairly painless compared with a layoff, and they are relatively easy to implement. If an organization foresees the need for extensive cost-cutting for longer than a few months, other programs with more severe repercussions on the workforce—such as shortened workweeks, extended salary reductions, voluntary sabbatical leaves, and employee lending programs—can avert group layoffs.

To increase acceptance of and commitment to any of these strategies, it is important to inform employees of the specific business circumstances that necessitate the measures and of their possible duration, and to tell the workforce that a primary purpose of these activities is to avoid layoffs.

Voluntary Separation Programs

Even after implementing RIF avoidance activities, there may come a time when the organization has no choice but to reduce staff. At this desperate hour, employers have another alternative to mass layoffs: voluntary separation programs (VSPs).

VSPs have several potential advantages over involuntary workforce reductions. From the company's perspective, VSPs minimize the risk of termination lawsuits by departing

Figure 3.5	Reduction in Force Avoidance Strategies
Soliciting cost-reduction ideas from employees	Useful during a temporary business slowdown. Allows employees to contribute suggestions that may result in significant cost savings. Can improve employee morale during lean times if employees understand that the company is reducing costs to avoid layoffs.
Retraining	Gives flexibility to move employees from positions that would be affected by a RIF into other open positions that would be unaffected.
Hiring freeze plus natural attrition	Minimizes the human suffering but may result in important goals not being accomplished. Can be combined with retraining to reallocate current workforce to vacant yet critical positions.
Mandatory vacation	Requiring employees to take a certain number of vacation days within a specified time period. Reduces the amount of vacation pay owed if termination becomes necessary and spreads the available work among the current employees.
Reduced work week	Involves a temporary decrease in the number of hours in the workweek (e.g., from 40 to 34). Many workers would rather temporarily receive a smaller paycheck than be laid off. Some employees will also appreciate the opportunity to spend more time with their families.
Temporary facility shutdown	Closure of a work site for a designated period. Especially effective if used during holidays so that employees will have time off without using accrued vacation.
Salary reduction	Many employees would rather have a smaller paycheck temporarily than lose their job permanently or see their co-workers laid off. However, the longer this strategy is in effect, the greater the negative impact on employee morale. Can be combined with variable pay options to offset long-term financial losses to employees. Encourages attrition.
Voluntary sabbaticals	Allowing employees to take voluntary time off with no pay or reduced pay. Typically, employees receive the same level of benefits during the sabbatical period.
Employee lending	The employer allows employees to work for another company for a specific period. Typically, the borrowing company reimburses the lending company for the loaned employees' salaries and the lending company continues to pay employee benefits. A variation on this strategy is to give an employee the option to work for a nonprofit for a specific period for a portion of his or her normal pay and continued full benefits.

See: Vernon, Luke, "The Downsizing Dilemma: A Manager's Toolkit for Avoiding Layoffs," SHRM White Paper (March 2003); and Noe, Raymond A., John Hollenbeck, et al., *Human Resource Management,* 2nd ed. (Irwin, 1997), pp. 270–274.

employees. While VSPs may not totally eliminate the need for involuntary layoffs, they can help narrow the scope of a downsizing initiative. From the employees' perspective, the fewer involuntary terminations, the better. Some employees will eagerly volunteer to leave if the incentives to do so are more attractive than what they would receive in an involuntary termination.

Obviously, the value and type of incentives offered in a VSP are critical. Other important issues to address include the following:

- **Program eligibility.** Will all employees be eligible, or will the program be limited to certain facilities, departments, or job classifications where there is the greatest need to eliminate jobs? Limiting the pool of eligible employees will reduce the potential of having to reject many VSP applicants.

- **Veto criteria.** Most VSPs allow management to reject individual VSP applications on a case-by-case basis. To avoid potential discrimination claims, the company should accept or veto applications on the basis of predetermined factors, such as first-come, first-served; seniority; importance of the employee to business operations; or truly objective merit criteria.

■ **Time period to apply.** The time period in which eligible employees may decide to apply for a VSP is not legally mandated. However, as discussed later in this chapter, employees who are asked to sign a waiver of ADEA claims in connection with a group termination program must be given 45 days to consider the release and 7 days to revoke the release after signing. Consequently, the timing of the election period and the distribution of the release must be coordinated. Because neither ADEA nor other federal antidiscrimination laws allow releases of future claims, employers usually distribute releases for signature on the employees' final day of work.

Consider Adopting an ERISA-compliant Severance Plan

Another termination program your company might want to consider is a severance pay plan. Typically, such plans provide that, after a certain waiting period and upon involuntary separation, employees are eligible to earn severance pay benefits calculated according to length of employment and salary level, and conditioned on the employee signing a release of potential claims. If you adopt such a plan, as opposed to offering severance pay only on an ad hoc basis according to the perceived risk of each termination, you will need to comply with ERISA. ERISA-qualified plans have (a) a definition of eligibility for the severance benefit; (b) terms outlining the formula for determining the amount and duration of the severance benefit; (c) a description of when severance benefits will not be paid (exclusions); (d) a written procedure for claiming benefits; (e) a designated plan administrator; and (f) an appeal procedure for employees to contest a benefit denial. Because a severance pay plan is a benefit promised to employees in consideration for their labors, they have the right to sue to enforce the promise. However, employees must usually exhaust the internal administrative remedies before resorting to litigation.

There are several advantages to using an ERISA-compliant severance plan rather than the ad hoc method. First, when severance is paid on an ad hoc basis, employees have an incentive to exaggerate or invent employment-based complaints. Second, a severance plan rewards good employees as well as those who are leaving under disagreeable circumstances. Third, a severance plan can have a positive impact on unemployment insurance premiums.

Implementing a RIF

Sometimes a RIF cannot be avoided. The safe and successful implementation of a RIF requires attention to eight phases of the process. At every phase, the employer must consider both the success of the RIF (i.e., meeting business objectives) and the safety of the RIF (i.e., avoiding litigation). Sometimes these equally important goals conflict.

1. WARNing, WARNing—RIF about to Occur!—The first thing the employer should analyze is whether the Worker Adjustment and Retraining Notification Act (WARN) or any WARN-like state or local requirements will apply. The answer to this question may affect both the number of employees laid off and the timing of the RIF. This can be a complicated process, and you may need to consult an experienced employment attorney. Even if WARN compliance obligations are not triggered by the RIF, lawyers and consultants can be valuable partners to ensure that RIFs are conducted in compliance with the law and in furtherance of company objectives.

2. Developing a Working Concept—Next, the employer should analyze what is motivating the RIF and, in light of that, develop a preliminary concept of what the workforce looks like now and what it will look like after the RIF. The best defense in RIF-prompted litigation is a legitimate business reason. The RIF should be implemented in a way that addresses the root cause or causes. For example, a RIF might be handled in very different ways depending on whether the root cause is (a) abandonment of a line of business; (b) closure of a plant; (c) reduction of excess production capacity; or (d) reorganization of departments, functions, or layers of management. In this phase, the employer should start thinking about the selection criteria that will be applied. For example, would the criteria be based on seniority, maximizing cost reduction, merit, or some combination thereof? This is not the time to make a decision but simply to develop an overall strategy.

At this phase, the employer should also begin considering what, if any, severance pay or benefits will be offered to departing employees in exchange for signing a release of claims. If severance pay or benefits are to be offered, the employer should start the process of drafting suitable and enforceable agreements, leaving the particulars to be filled in at a later date. Management should consider whether the employees will be required to sign a release of claims as a condition of receiving severance pay or benefits. If the company has a serious chance of successfully reorganizing, severance-for-release is a good idea. If the RIF will only prolong the inevitable dissolution of the business, it may be better to apply those funds elsewhere.

In this phase, it is helpful to prepare organizational charts for the post-RIF company, to identify what existing and new positions will be needed and draft corresponding preliminary job descriptions, and to begin thinking about whether these positions can be filled from within or must be filled by outside applicants.

A degree of vision is required at this phase. At one level or another, management should answer the following questions:

- Which of our current employees will fit best into the new organization?

- Will we need to bring in new employees to satisfy our knowledge, skill, and abilities needs, or can we retrain?

3. Paper, Paper Everywhere—With this concept in mind, the third step is to begin collecting and reviewing documents pertaining to the possible candidates for separation: (a) individual employment and collective bargaining agreements; (b) written job descriptions; (c) performance evaluations and disciplinary histories; and (d) any existing ERISA severance plan. Having this information will prevent you from inadvertently violating contractual obligations and will help you decide what the selection criteria should be, who should make the selections, and what sort of severance package might be appropriate.

4. Choosing Your Selection Criteria—At this point, the employer will have a good idea of the number of layoffs and will be ready for the fourth step: making a decision on the selection criteria. The employer will also need to decide who will apply the criteria. For example, will it be a single person specifically designated for the task, a team of people, the existing management structure, or an outside consulting firm? The selection criteria should be documented and communicated, in writing, to the person or persons who will be applying them. The employer should also designate one or more people—referred to here as the *EEO watchdog*—who will be responsible for evaluating the selections made to determine whether there are any disparate impacts on protected classes. Again, this may be a single individual, a team, or outside consultants, but the EEO watchdog must be separate from the person or persons applying the selection criteria in the first place. In this phase, the employer should also make an initial decision about how much money will be budgeted to pay severance or provide benefits in consideration of employees signing a release of claims.

5. Selection: It's a Dirty Job, But Someone Has to Do It—The fifth step is to begin applying the selection criteria to the workforce. Care should be taken in applying the criteria and in selecting the persons who will apply them to avoid the possibility that discriminatory biases will infect the process. Although existing managers may be most familiar with candidates' strengths and weaknesses, the closer the relationship of the decision-maker to the candidate, the greater the risk of bias. At the conclusion of step five, the employer will have tentatively selected x individuals for layoff. If the employer plans to offer severance based on years of service or percentage of regular compensation, it can now apply its budgeted funds to the pool of persons selected to determine what formula for severance benefits will be used.

6. Unleashing the Watchdog—In the sixth phase, the EEO watchdog performs a situation-appropriate but deliberate and documented adverse impact analysis. This analysis should not be shared with the persons making the selections. (See Part 2, Section E.5.2 for a sample worksheet to use in this task.) What is situation-appropriate depends on a number of factors. If selection was based solely on seniority, the risk of disparate impact litigation is minor. Most antidiscrimination statutes deem seniority-based RIFs a "safe harbor." If a plant is being closed and all employees are being laid off and none reassigned, the risk of disparate impact litigation is also slight. But if the selection was based in part on perceived merit, the risk will be higher. If the number of persons being laid off is small, it may not be possible to perform a meaningful statistical analysis. Nevertheless, at least a commonsense analysis should be done from an EEO perspective.

As part of the watchdog's duties, he or she should meet with the persons making the selections and ask questions calculated to ascertain whether the selections were made in accordance with the prescribed criteria and whether any bias may have slipped into the process. If a picture of disparate impact emerges, the situation should be carefully analyzed to determine whether the selection criteria were correctly applied or whether the criteria themselves need to be adjusted. The mere fact that a statistical disparity exists doesn't necessarily mean the planned RIF violates the law. It does mean that the company must be able to explain why the disparity doesn't constitute discrimination.

7. "Huddle Up!"—In phase seven, the watchdog's findings should be discussed with the senior manager responsible for overall implementation of the RIF. At this point a decision can be made on whether to proceed with the selections already made, to require the selections to be made again with greater attention to the prescribed criteria, or to adjust the criteria and re-select. While the senior manager is evaluating the EEO implications presented by the watchdog, he or she can also review how the budget for severance pay and special benefits would be applied to the pool of persons selected. The budget may need to be adjusted upward or downward. Senior management should also consider whether the RIF, as conceived at this point, satisfies the objectives set forth in phase two. If not, the selection criteria may need to be adjusted for that reason as well.

At the conclusion of phase seven—including reapplication of all the previous steps as necessary—the employer will have a final list of persons who will be laid off and a timetable that complies with any applicable WARN or WARN-type laws.

8. Getting the Word Out—Phase eight consists of communicating the RIF decision to all stakeholders: the employees who will be laid off, those who will be retained, appropriate government agencies, and the media. We will deal with these in reverse order.

The company should consider the public relations aspects of its RIF and develop a plan for notifying the media. The media will report on the RIF anyway, so the company might as well share its side of the story up front. Holding a press conference or issuing a press release describing all the efforts undertaken by the company (a) to avoid and (b) to fairly and humanely implement a RIF will help write the stories by busy journalists who aren't looking for a way to discredit the company. Announcing a RIF can make a public company's stock price go up or down. By explaining to the media the benefits it hopes to derive from the RIF, the company increases the chances of a favorable impact on share prices.

Even if WARN or WARN-like laws do not apply, employers should notify affected government agencies and union representatives of an impending RIF at the same time they notify employees. Consider hand-delivering a letter to the mayor's office, city council, and the affected union representatives, and following up promptly with a phone call from a senior executive.

Don't forget about the survivors. Employees who are not selected for layoff worry about increased workloads, their ability to meet established objectives, the value of their employee stock ownership plans, and whether they could be next on the chopping block.

Most important, plan how you will communicate the bad news to the employees who will be let go. These people will remember forever how they were treated on their way out. Treating departing employees with tact, compassion, and honesty will reduce the likelihood of litigation. Will you send a memo or e-mail, or hold a meeting? Will all employees be notified at the same time, or just those who are being let go? Will the names of those selected be published to all employees, or will dissemination of that information be left to the grapevine? If a meeting is held, extreme care should be taken to maintain control so that it does not devolve into a debate over the selection process or a gripe session. Spend some time visualizing how the meeting will play out and what the company response will be if one or more employees become vocal, disruptive, or even threatening. Whose job will it be to maintain/regain control of the meeting? Remember, the main point of the meeting is to notify, not justify.

The crux of the RIF communication is like the first paragraph of a news story: who, what, when, where, why, and how. A large part of the planning for communicating the decision is being ready to tell the employees what steps the company took to ensure fairness in the process; what the company is willing to do in terms of a severance package, references, and service letters; and what steps the company has taken to simplify the process of filing for unemployment insurance benefits. Consider inviting a representative of the unemployment agency to give a presentation explaining what benefits are available and how people should go about applying for them. Even if you are not offering outplacement services or career counseling as part of a severance package, consider hosting a workshop on- or off-site for the departing employees. Employees who quickly attain unemployment insurance or reemployment have less of an incentive to sue. Be prepared to respond immediately and accurately to all questions related to COBRA and HIPAA. Especially where merit was a factor in the selection process, the employer should be thoroughly prepared with a truthful but tactful answer to the following questions:

- ■ "Why me and not him?"

- ■ "Who made this decision?"

- ■ "Are there other jobs in the company I can be reassigned to?"

- ■ "What if I were to offer to take a pay cut? Would you consider letting me keep my job?"

- ■ "Who, besides me, is being released; and why?"

These are perfectly natural questions from a person who is being laid off. If they are asked, it is important that management not perceive them as a criticism or an accusation of unfairness or unlawfulness. Management should be prepared to answer them. However, if the communication process is handled well, employees may not feel the need to ask the questions.

Developing the Separation Packet

Regardless of whether the separation is the discharge of a single employee or a RIF, employers should develop a separation *packet*—a collection of documents to be given to the employee upon termination. Depending on the nature of the separation, the packet might include the press release, applicable policies, RIF selection criteria, information about the timing of the process, a summary of severance benefits, a formal separation agreement, a description of unemployment insurance benefits, and COBRA and HIPAA notices. The packet should be appropriate to the context of the separation.

Consider a Separation Package

Regardless of whether the separation is the discharge of a single employee or a RIF, employers should consider whether to offer severance pay or benefits—a separation *package*. If the decision is made to offer severance, here are some things to consider:

- Will the company demand a release of claims in exchange? Offering severance pay without asking for a release is generally not recommended. It just gives the employee funds with which to hire an attorney. Countless employees have eagerly accepted severance benefits only to turn around and sue once the benefits ran out.

- How much money will be offered? Will it be a lump sum or paid out at the same rate as current compensation?

- What, if any, extension of insurance benefits can/will be offered without violating the group insurance plans?

- Will outplacement benefits or career counseling be offered?

- Will confidentiality of the terms be required?

- Will an employee forfeit consideration in the event of a breach of the agreement or on reemployment?

- How much legal overlay should be included? Will it be written in plain language or legalese?

Reasons to Use Separation Agreements

A separation agreement defines the rights and responsibilities of an employer and employee upon the termination of employment. Separation agreements provide the departing employee with something extra—over and above what the employee was otherwise entitled to—in exchange for the employee signing a broad release of claims against the employer. Separation agreements can provide an employer with cheap and effective insurance against claims asserted by separating employees. Additionally, the agreement helps separating employees cope with the challenges of termination of employment, thereby fostering positive relations between employer and employee as time goes on. Consequently, it is a good idea to use a separation agreement whenever an employment relationship is terminated, whether involuntarily or voluntarily, whether the position is management or entry-level, and regardless of whether the employee has asserted legal claims against the employer.

Separation agreements can be simple or complex, depending on the circumstances surrounding the separation. For example, if the separating employee is under 40 years old, resigned to take a better job, and has never voiced any complaints that could form the basis of a legal claim, the employer might use a very simple form.

In contrast, if the employee is 40 years or older, was laid off or fired, and has voiced complaints about discriminatory or other unfair treatment, a more complex form would be required for the employer to obtain a valid release of all claims. Because of the complexity of the form in this situation and the fact that the employment and tax laws applicable to such matters change over time, the employer may want to consult with legal counsel to ensure that it achieves all the goals of signing a separation agreement and does not violate the law in any way.

Three Basic Types of Separation Agreements—Thee Older Worker Benefit Protection Act (OWBPA) mandates that any agreement providing for the release of claims under the Age Discrimination in Employment Act (ADEA) must contain certain provisions to be legally enforceable. As a result of the OWBPA, there are three basic types of separation agreements for the following situations: (1) none of the employees being terminated are 40 years or older; (2) a single employee age 40 years or older is being terminated; and (3) more than one employee is being terminated and at least one terminating employee is 40 years or older. These forms are referred to in Part 2, Section G as Separation Agreement (non-OWBPA), OWBPA Release (single termination), and OWBPA Release (group termination), respectively.

If only one employee age 40 or over is being terminated, the release agreement should contain the following features to be deemed enforceable:

(a) The waiver is part of an agreement between the individual and the employer that is written in a manner calculated to be understood by the individual or by the average individual eligible to participate.

(b) The waiver specifically refers to rights or claims arising under the ADEA.

(c) The individual does not waive rights or claims that may arise after the date the waiver is executed.

(d) The individual waives rights or claims only in exchange for consideration in addition to anything of value to which the individual is already entitled.

(e) The individual is advised in writing to consult with an attorney before executing the agreement.

(f) The individual is given at least 21 days to consider the agreement.

(g) The agreement provides that for at least seven days following its execution, the individual may revoke the agreement, and the agreement shall not become effective or enforceable until the revocation period has expired.

If more than one employee is being terminated, the OWBPA increases the consideration period from 21 to 45 days and mandates the following additional requirements for the release of age discrimination claims to be legally enforceable. At the commencement of the 45-day period, the employer must inform the individuals in writing of

(a) any class, unit, or group of individuals covered by an exit incentive or other employment termination program;

(b) any eligibility factors for the program;

(c) any time limits applicable to the program;

(d) the job titles and ages of all individuals eligible or selected for the program; and

(e) the ages of all individuals in the same job classification or organizational unit who are not eligible or selected for the program.

Form G.4.1 in Part 2 provides a sample that can be used to satisfy these OWBPA disclosure requirements.

What to Cover in a Separation Agreement—Because business judgment plays such an important role in deciding what to include in a particular employee's separation agreement, there is no one "right" or "best" form. As a matter of business judgment, based on legal counsel if appropriate, an employer may choose a very simple form, a very complex form, or something in between.

Part 2, Section G offers several examples of separation agreements that reflect the legal framework and business judgment of employers in numerous actual situations.

A Word of Caution about Deferred Compensation—The American Jobs Creation Act (AJCA) made fundamental and significant changes to the federal tax rules applicable to deferred compensation. In some instances, separation agreement forms used before the enactment of the AJCA on October 22, 2004, are no longer suitable and should be revised to avoid violations of the new deferred compensation rules.

Most of the changes are contained in new section 409A of the Internal Revenue Code, which covers any plan or arrangement in which a "service provider" will have a "legally binding right" in one taxable year to receive "compensation" that will not be actually or constructively received until a later taxable year. The IRS has provided guidance in Notice 2005-1. If a deferred compensation arrangement fails to satisfy the new document and operational requirements, all amounts deferred for the year of the failure and all preceding years are included in the gross income of the individual, and a 20 percent penalty plus interest applies.

How do these changes in deferred compensation rules affect separation agreements? In the past, it has not been uncommon for employers to characterize the payment provided for in a separation agreement as "additional compensation." This was never recommended language for a separation agreement, because it suggests that the severance pay is given in exchange for the employee's past services rather than in exchange for the employee releasing potential claims. Such language is even more dangerous under the new deferred compensation rules. Similarly, separation agreements sometimes mention employees' post-separation consulting services to the company. A separation agreement that says a departing employee will be paid a certain amount for consulting services (regardless of whether the services are actually performed) but delays payment until a later date is at risk of violating the new deferred compensation rules if the payment date is in a later tax year than the tax year in which the employee/consultant's right to receive payment is vested.

Arrangements for post-employment consulting must be carefully structured in light of the new deferred compensation rules to ensure that employers do not inadvertently violate the AJCA in separation agreements with departing employees.

Determining Logistics for Involuntary Terminations

A critical part of the termination planning process is deciding how to deliver the bad news to employees who will be fired or laid off. In all but the most unusual situations (for example, a discharge involving a person who has demonstrated violent tendencies or made direct threats to company personnel), notice of involuntary termination should be given in a face-to-face meeting. Other methods of communicating termination decisions (e.g., by memo, letter, e-mail, or telephone) may be easier to implement and have less potential for uncomfortable confrontations; however, most employees (and juries, too) would view these methods as unduly impersonal. Additionally, employees who believe they were treated badly in termination are more likely to sue. For example, a survey of approximately 1,000 terminated workers in Ohio revealed that almost 15 percent of the workers who felt there was no dignity or respect in the way they were treated at termination sued their former employer, whereas less than 0.5 percent of the workers who felt they were treated with dignity and respect sued.[11]

Informing an employee in person that he or she is out of a job is a tough and touchy task. Handling these meetings in a way that is sensitive to the employee but protective of the company, the managers involved, and the workforce in general requires careful planning. Several logistical issues must be addressed in preparing for termination meetings, including who will participate in the termination, when and where it will take place, and what will be said and done. The next chapter will offer suggestions on how to prepare for and conduct such meetings.

Chapter 4
Conducting Terminations

All's well that ends well.

—William Shakespeare, *All's Well That Ends Well*

It's Never Easy to Say Goodbye

The communication of a termination decision—whether it is a discharge, a layoff, or a resignation—should take only a few minutes. But this brief encounter is likely to be one of the most stressful and challenging moments in the entire working relationship between employee and employer.

This chapter discusses how to sensitively and effectively notify employees of involuntary terminations, and how to proactively anticipate resignations and job abandonment. The chapter will also focus on exit meetings, providing guidance on how to maximize this final opportunity to obtain valuable, candid feedback from departing employees.

Setting the Stage for Involuntary Termination Meetings

Although the process toward a discharge or layoff begins long before the actual event, the scene that will be seared into the memories of departing employees and the persons charged with responsibility for conveying the news is the moment the employer communicates the termination decision. Several important decisions must be made to set the stage for a safe, sensitive, and smooth performance of the act of termination.

Opinions differ as to how best to handle various aspects of termination. Although there is no single "right" or "best" way to let an employee go, various procedures have foreseeable ramifications. Human resource professionals and managers should work closely together to orchestrate the "who, what, when, where, and how" of conveying involuntary termination decisions. Ordinarily, the information is conveyed first in a face-to-face meeting and then followed up by written documentation.

Who Should Attend?

Most human resource professionals and employment lawyers favor having two management representatives present at the termination. Typically, the two individuals who attend the meeting on the employer's behalf are the employee's immediate supervisor or manager and an HR department representative.

The main objective is to avoid a situation of one person's word against another's as to what occurred during the meeting. It is less likely that a former employee can mischaracterize what occurred if two employer representatives agree on what happened and was said. Usually, the supervisor or manager should communicate the termination decision, as he or she has worked directly with the employee and will be familiar with the facts and circumstances prompting the termination. The second person should function as a witness, a note-taker, and perhaps a backstop against serious mistakes being made by the primary communicator or a clarifier for the benefit of the employee as to what the process has been to date.

If the employee belongs to a union, the terms of the relevant collective bargaining agreement must be reviewed beforehand and followed during the termination process. Unless there is a written agreement to the contrary, the employee should not be allowed to bring a third party—such as a co-worker, family member, or attorney—to the termination meeting. If the employee wants his or her attorney to attend, the employer can explain, "Our business relationship is with you, not your attorney. You're free to retain an attorney and be represented in unemployment or other legal proceedings, but your attorney may not attend this meeting."

Similarly, if the employee sees the termination coming, he or she may ask permission to record the meeting. This is a difficult judgment call. How will it look to a jury if the employer brought a witness to the meeting but the employee was denied permission to bring a witness or record it? On the other hand, an employee who brings a tape recorder is probably looking for more than just a true record of the proceedings and may hope to elicit damaging admissions from the employer's representatives. You should anticipate the possibility of a request to record and have a response prepared. You should also be prepared if the employee says, "I don't care what you say. My attorney says I have a right to record the meeting, and I'm going to do it." If the employee plays that card, you have little choice but to proceed with the meeting, noting your objection "on the record." Seizing the tape recorder, calling security officers, or suspending the meeting and handling the termination entirely in writing are not attractive alternatives.

It is not unheard of for employees to surreptitiously record termination meetings or counseling sessions. This is legal in many states, although it doesn't make the employee look very good in front of a jury. Employers should always conduct themselves in termination meetings as though they are being recorded, because they just might be.

What Will Be Said?
Finding the right way to say goodbye to an employee is hard, and many managers beat around the bush or sugarcoat. But what employees want to know is the truth about the reasons for and consequences of being let go. And they want this information conveyed in a respectful and humane way.

To avoid saying the wrong things in the wrong way, managers need to plan what to say and rehearse saying it before the termination meeting. Essential topics to cover during the meeting include the following:

- That a decision has been made to terminate employment.

- The reason(s) for and key facts supporting the termination decision.

- Effective date of separation.

- Separation package and benefits.

■ Review of reference policy and procedures.

■ Review of applicable post-termination restrictions.

■ What happens immediately following the meeting (e.g., clean out office, return company property).

■ Other exit activities (e.g., exit interview, outplacement meeting).

■ Whom to contact about post-termination issues.

One of these subjects—the reason for termination—merits special attention. Although the employment-at-will doctrine is based on the principle that an employment relationship may be terminated for any reason, no reason, or a bad reason, an employee will want to hear the real reason—and that reason better be legal under federal, state, and local law. The reason should be founded on objective facts and behavior, not on the subjective whim of the supervisor. Otherwise, the employee is very likely to take the employer to court to get an explanation. According to a survey of approximately 1,000 terminated workers in Ohio, 20.3 percent of workers who were not told why they were being let go sued their former employer; while only 1.7 percent of workers who got an explanation for their termination sued.[12]

Further discussion of what to say and do in termination meetings appears later in this chapter.

When Will the Termination Occur?

Is there a best day or best time of day to conduct a termination meeting?

Many employers choose to terminate employees on Friday afternoon. The reasoning behind this timing is the belief that the employee will cool off over the weekend and won't be able to contact an attorney immediately. But the terminated employee may spend the weekend stewing with a spouse, friends, or attorney-acquaintances about the situation. By Monday morning, this employee may be boiling over.

Other employers choose the middle of the week, to enable the employee to take immediate constructive steps to deal with the job loss, including seeing a counselor or an outplacement advisor or looking for other work. Even if the employee decides to contact an attorney immediately, this may be a positive development for the employer. The terminated employee may learn that, although the termination seems totally unfair, he or she does not have a basis for suing the employer; that likely recovery is much less than the employee imagined (particularly after payment of the attorney's contingency fees and litigation costs); or even that one or more attorneys are not interested in the case because of the limited potential damages. A mid-week termination also allows the company to communicate appropriately with the terminated employee's co-workers before rumors run out of control and misinformation from the dismissed employee creates serious morale problems.

A second timing issue is the time of day when the termination decision is communicated. Many employers favor the end of the day, so that the employee can leave at the usual departure time without drawing undue attention or embarrassing questions from co-workers. End-of-day timing also makes sense if the employer has reason to believe the terminated employee will be disruptive or threatening.

On the other hand, some employers prefer to terminate an employee in the morning or early afternoon, so he or she has sufficient time to gather personal belongs and say good-bye to co-workers. This timing may be particularly appropriate if the employee is being laid off along with others for financial or business reasons and not for cause.

Because of the pros and cons of termination timing issues, employers should fully consider the ramifications of conducting the meeting on various days and times of day for each termination rather than scheduling a meeting for a particular day and time because "that's the way we always do it." Although the timing of the termination is unlikely to be deemed a sufficient basis for an employee to claim that he or she was discriminated against, it can lead to unexpected problems. Suppose, for example, the termination is done in the morning. If the employee is part of a carpool or took public transportation, you may have inadvertently placed the person in a difficult situation logistically.

Where Will the Termination Take Place?

The answer to this question should begin with a cardinal rule on where *not* to conduct a termination meeting. Under no circumstances should this meeting be held in a manager's or HR staff member's office. In this setting, one of the employer representatives will probably be sitting behind his or her desk and may be unable to leave the office if the employee blocks the door or makes physical threats.

The best place for the meeting is usually in a conference room or other neutral, private setting. Company representatives should always take the seats nearest the door, so they have a clear exit if needed. The room should also have a telephone, so the manager or HR representative can get immediate answers to any unexpected questions from the employee or can contact security personnel if necessary. To maintain the privacy of the meeting, any curtains or blinds facing work areas should be closed, unless the areas are empty.

How Will Security Issues Be Addressed?

While routine precautions should be taken in every termination, some security measures should be used only in extraordinary circumstances. Normal termination safeguards should include the following activities:

- Blocking computer system access as soon as the employee goes into the termination meeting.

- Having the employee return keys, identification badges, and other company property such as computers, cell phones, and company credit cards before leaving the premises.

- Changing pass codes to the building or secure areas.

- If applicable, removing the employee's name as signatory to bank accounts or post office boxes.

These and other steps to maintain security are included in the sample termination process checklists found in Part 2, Section D.

Ordinarily, there is no need to escort an employee out of the building. In fact, doing so may elicit a disruptive response from an individual who would otherwise have left without incident. Additionally, a departing employee who is seen by co-workers being escorted from the building will likely feel humiliated and may be inclined to seek legal redress for intentional infliction of emotional distress or invasion of privacy. Similarly, having someone watch while the employee packs personal belongings or packing the belongings for that person may be unnecessarily courting trouble.

The use of escorts and security personnel should generally be limited to situations in which there is reason to believe that the employee will become disruptive or pose a threat to people or property during and immediately after the termination meeting. In such cases, appropriate precautionary measures should be implemented in consultation with threat assessment and workplace violence experts.

What to Say and Do in Termination Meetings

Approach a termination meeting with four guidelines in mind. First, keep the meeting short. In most cases, it should take no longer than 10 to 20 minutes. Second, keep it sweet. In other words, be polite and compassionate in giving the difficult news and responding to the employee's reactions and questions. Third, make sure to cover all the topics on your termination outline, in the order and manner that you have practiced. Finally, stay "on message." Don't be drawn into a debate or a reconsideration of the termination decision. You are there to notify, not justify.

Opening Statements

When an employee is summoned to a termination meeting, he or she is probably anxious and may suspect the worst. The best thing to do is break the suspense with your first remarks. Inform the employee directly and briefly of the decision to terminate. Let the employee know whether the decision is effective immediately or at a later date.

Sample Opening Statements

For a discharge:

"[Employee name], please have a seat. I have some unpleasant news to deliver. Because of your [state the reason for the discharge, such as "failure to follow company work rules," "inability to improve your performance as necessary," "continued tardiness in spite of repeated warnings"], the company has decided to terminate your employment. This decision is final and is effective today."

For a layoff:

"[Employee name], as you know, the decision has been made to reduce the size of our workforce because of [give a general reason for the layoff, such as "the need to streamline our operations to become more competitive"]. We have reviewed all jobs to determine which ones are essential as we move forward. I am sorry to have to tell you that your position is being eliminated. Unfortunately, we do not have another position to offer you. Your last day will be on [give effective date of termination.]"

Responding to the Employee

After you've informed the employee of the termination decision, stop talking. This pause will give the employee an opportunity to absorb the news. Different people respond to a job loss in different, sometimes surprising, ways. Allow the employee to express feelings. Be ready to deal sensitively and appropriately with the following normal reactions:

- **Sadness.** Have tissues available in case the employee starts crying. Give the employee time to get control of his or her emotions before continuing. Ask the employee if he or she would like to have a few minutes to be alone. If so, leave the room for a short period, then come back and resume the discussion.

- **Shock.** If the employee exhibits no reaction to being let go, you should ask if he or she understands what you've said. If the person doesn't understand, repeat, paraphrase, and expand on your initial comments. If the employee still seems to be in a state of shock, ask, "Do you have any questions for me about what I've told you?" If not, you should inquire whether the employee would like to discuss the details of the termination later in the day.

- **Anxiety.** Many employees express immediate concern about their personal and financial status after the termination. Assure the employee that you are willing to listen and to answer or find answers to questions about post-termination compensation and benefits issues, and provide other support during the termination process.

- **Anger.** Anger is a normal response to being terminated. If the employee seems angry, paraphrase his or her comments without being defensive to show that you are listening. Acknowledge that it is normal to be upset in this situation.

If the employee's behavior becomes extreme at any time during the meeting, respond promptly and appropriately. For example, if an employee becomes hysterical, it may be best to stop the meeting and give the person some time alone before continuing. If the employee becomes verbally abusive or physically threatening, stay calm and state firmly in a normal voice that you will not tolerate aggressive behavior. End the meeting and take immediate steps to protect yourself and other company representatives present in the meeting and to defuse potential violence by the employee. Contact internal security and outside professionals as necessary to protect employees and the organization.

Your actions in the meeting and reactions to the employee will have as much impact on him or her as your words.

Providing Details

When the employee seems ready for more information, explain key aspects of the termination, including final pay, accrued vacation, and employer-paid benefits on separation, as well as the terms of any severance package. Review the company's reference policy and any post-termination nondisclosure, noncompete, or nonsolicitation restrictions the person agreed to in writing during the course of employment. If any of these topics will be covered instead, or in more detail, in a separate exit meeting, say so. It helps to refer to a checklist during this phase of the meeting to ensure that all necessary issues are discussed. Part 2, Section D includes sample termination process checklists.

During this phase of the meeting, give the employee a packet containing written materials for him or her to review (e.g., termination letter, COBRA notice, retirement benefits information, reference policy, outplacement program description) and documents for his or her consideration and signature (e.g., separation agreement, reference authorization, COBRA election form), unless this information will be given to the employee by another company representative later.

Be prepared to answer the employee's questions about the termination. These may range from very general questions such as "Why me?" to very specific questions such as "Will I be eligible for unemployment benefits?" It is important not to react defensively or engage in a debate when asked the former types of questions and to provide accurate answers to the latter types. If you don't know the answer to a question, make a phone call during the meeting to someone who can answer it, or tell the employee when you will provide the answer. It is also helpful to tell the employee whom he or she can contact after the meeting with further questions and to provide a termination contact list for this purpose.

Once the employee has finished asking questions, describe what will happen immediately after the meeting. Identify the person who will collect company property in the employee's possession, and cover the logistics of when and how the employee can collect personal belongings and leave the premises. If an exit interview will take place, explain the purpose and timing, and say who will conduct it.

Closing Remarks

Your last words in the termination meeting may leave a lasting impression on the employee. Help the employee maintain his or her dignity with supportive and humane final comments. To avoid saying something offhand that the employee may perceive as callous or may seek to use in litigation against the company, plan and memorize a closing remark.

Sample Closing Remarks

For a discharge:
"[Employee, name], I am sorry to have to deliver this difficult news. I wish you the best in the future. Please call me if I can be of assistance."

For a layoff:
"[Employee name], I appreciate the contributions you have made in the department. I am sorry we no longer have a role for you. This was a very difficult decision for the organization to make. We will provide as much support as we can during this transition. Please let me know if I can be of assistance to you in the future."

After the Meeting

When the termination meeting is over, the managers involved should take time to de-stress, debrief, and document.

Although the pain of involuntary termination meetings will be much greater for the employees, those who have delivered the news may have feelings of loss, sadness, or "survivor's guilt." These reactions are particularly common during RIFs. Those who handle terminations should recognize these emotions and find positive ways to handle them. One activity that may help is a termination debriefing with others who are involved in the process to discuss feelings about and perspectives on the termination. This session also can provide the opportunity to review what went well and what could be handled more effectively in the future.

Separation records should be completed while memories are fresh. Part 2, Section E.2 includes sample forms to document separation. It is also prudent to prepare a memo summarizing what was said and done in the meeting. This memo should note any intentions to sue, accusations, threatening statements or actions, and any unusual behavior by the employee, as well as admissions by the employee that could be used to defend against later legal claims.

Figure 4-1 provides a summary of the foregoing guidelines on handling termination notification meetings.

Handling Legally Risky Terminations

Whenever an employer initiates an involuntary termination, the door is opened to the possibility of a wrongful termination lawsuit. That door opens even wider—with possible charges of discrimination—when the terminated employee is a member of a class that is protected by federal, state, or local laws. The door opens even wider still—with potential retaliation allegations—if the employee has filed an internal or external complaint of harassment, discrimination, or violation of other laws before being fired.

Employers should not allow the fear of increased legal exposure to prevent them from dismissing individuals whose performance or misconduct warrants it. But they should

---

Figure 4.1   Conducting a Termination Meeting

- Prepare the room where the meeting will be held. Make sure to have all pertinent written information and separation packet materials at hand. Have tissues and water available for the employee if needed.
- Get right to the point of the meeting. Don't exchange pleasantries or make conversation.
- Be clear that the termination decision is final.
- Avoid debating the merits of this decision. Don't say, "It wasn't my decision."
- Allow the employee to express feelings about the termination. Listen carefully and empathetically.
- Don't discuss your own feelings about the termination. Don't say, "I know how you feel." You don't.
- Provide specific answers to the employee's questions. If you don't know the answer to a question, call someone who does or tell the employee when and how the question will be answered.
- Mention any resources (such as employee assistance counselors or outplacement services) that are available to the employee.
- Keep your cool. Remain calm even if the employee becomes emotional. Don't argue with the employee.
- Before ending the meeting, ask if the employee has any other questions.
- When concluding the meeting, stand. This will be a nonverbal signal to the employee that the meeting is over.

be very careful before, during, and after the termination not to say or do anything that might create the appearance of unlawful discrimination or retaliation.

Consistency and specificity are two keys to closing and barring the door to termination discrimination or retaliation claims. Company managers, supervisors, and human resource staff should make conscious and concerted efforts to treat employees who are members of a protected class, or who have filed complaints, fairly and similarly to other employees, and should clearly and fully explain the reasons and circumstances leading to termination. Figure 4-2 provides pointers on minimizing potential legal exposure in risky situations.

Dealing with Job Abandonment

Employers have obvious challenges in communicating with employees about involuntary termination decisions. And, as we discuss later in this chapter, employers must react appropriately after employees give notice of resignation or they will run the risk of parting on bad terms. In the case of job abandonment, however, no pertinent communication occurs before an employee decides to jump ship. The employer's challenge in potential job abandonment situations is to investigate the circumstances and attempt to communicate with an employee who is absent, without prematurely "pulling the plug."

In most cases, an AWOL (absent without leave) employee has surrendered his or her job. Sometimes, though, an apparent job abandonment is not what it seems. Perhaps the missing employee has experienced a health emergency, has been the victim of a crime, or is stranded somewhere without access to a phone. The employee may have left a message about the absence with someone in the office other than his or her supervisor, and that person forgot to relay the message.

Supervisors should look into "no call, no show" situations within hours after an employee has failed to report to work, beginning with a call to the employee's home. If

---

Figure 4.2	**Reducing Your Risks in Legally Risky Terminations**

■ Don't start building a file against an employee just because he or she has made a complaint—even if unwarranted—of discrimination or other illegal employer practices.

■ Be sure to follow all requirements established in your organization's discipline and termination policies. Refer to and show the employee these policies during the termination notification meeting, and explain how they apply to the employee.

■ During the termination meeting, fully explain the reasons for the termination. Without getting drawn into a debate, cite specific examples and dates of performance deficiencies or misconduct.

■ Make a general statement (if it is true) that other employees have been discharged in the past for the same performance problems or policy violations, but don't provide specifics about these terminations.

■ If the employee threatens to see an attorney or sue, don't be defensive. Acknowledge the person's right to seek legal advice. In such situations, your organization should contact its employment counsel immediately.

■ When providing references for a former employee, never make comments about the person's age, race, national origin, religion, or other protected characteristics. Do not disclose the fact that the person has made internal complaints or complaints to a government agency, or has sued your organization.

no one answers or provides information about the employee's whereabouts, leave a message inquiring whether the employee is okay. The supervisor can also check with co-workers to find out whether they have heard from the employee or know why he or she is not at work. A second call home should be made the next day to let the employee know that the organization will assume that he or she has quit the job without notice if the employee doesn't report to work or call back within the period stipulated in the organization's job abandonment policy.

If the employer discovers or knows facts that suggest an absence without leave is related to a medical or psychiatric problem, terminating the employee for job abandonment may run afoul of the Family and Medical Leave Act, the Americans with Disabilities Act, or similar state laws.

If there is no indication of extenuating circumstances for an employee's failure to report, the organization may proceed with finalizing a termination for job abandonment. Status change documentation, with the date and reason for the termination, should be placed in the employee's file. The organization should also attempt to notify the employee that he or she is no longer employed. Part 2, Section F.3 contains sample termination letters for job abandonment situations.

Responding to Resignations

The scene is a familiar one: An employee walks into the supervisor's office, closes the door, sits down, and breaks the news, "I've decided to resign. My last day will be two weeks from today." Once the employee gives notice, the employer has important questions to ask, decisions to make, and steps to take to ensure a smooth parting of the ways.

First, Probe for Information

When an employee gives notice, a supervisor should not act offended or take it personally. The resignation may have nothing to do with the supervisor or the company. If it does, the resigning employee's negative feelings may be an indication of more widespread discontent in the organization or may be related to the person's interactions with other employees. Or the employee may be dissatisfied with assigned duties, pay, benefits, or work schedule. Supervisors should take the time to probe for information. Specific topics to cover and questions to ask include these:

- **Reasons for resignation.** *Why are you leaving?*

- **New job.** *Do you have another job? With whom? What will you be doing for them? When do you start this job?*

- **Status of current work.** *What assignments are you working on? What still needs to be done to complete these projects? How much of this work do you think you will be able to complete before your last day?*

- **Who knows?** *Have you told other managers or employees that you'll be leaving the organization? Do any customers or clients know of your plans yet?*

The answers to these questions will enable the supervisor and the HR department to create an exit plan that is appropriate in the particular situation.

Then, Get on the Right Track

The period between a resignation and the employee's last day typically proceeds according to the employee's stated departure plans and the organization's usual exit process. Sometimes, though, the company will want to fast-track or sidetrack the employee's exit from the organization. At other times, an employee might want to back-track from a resignation given in the heat of the moment. In general, employers should tread carefully before taking detours from the normal resignation path.

How much notice is too much? Two weeks is the typical notice period *requested* by most employers. An organization may choose to request longer notice from executive or professional employees. Employers should not establish resignation policies that *require* a certain notice period, as that requirement may suggest that your employment arrangement is not really at-will.

In certain situations, it may be in the organization's best interest to ask an employee to leave the day he or she gives notice. This may be warranted, for example, if a salesperson is leaving to work for a competitor, if the company is concerned about the security of confidential or proprietary information, if the employee is likely to be disruptive or unproductive after giving notice, or if the employer and employee are in the midst of addressing discrimination or harassment claims. In such cases, the employer should pay the employee for the notice period in lieu of having the person actually show up for work. Failure to pay may make the resigning employee eligible for unemployment benefits or a claim of wrongful discharge. Moreover, a practice of giving employees the boot the day they resign without paying them for their notice period sends a strong message to other employees not to give advance notice when they resign.

Should a company ever try to convince an employee not to quit? Perhaps. But only in special circumstances such as these: (a) The resigning employee is a high-performing "star"; (b) the position will be very hard or costly to fill; (c) the employee is working on a critical project that will be difficult to complete on time if he or she leaves; (d) the company is operating under a hiring freeze; or (e) changes are already under way to resolve the problem that prompted the resignation (i.e., moving an ineffective manager into a nonsupervisory position).

In these situations, a mere plea not to leave is unlikely to make an employee who has resigned change his or her mind. Instead, the supervisor should engage in a thoughtful and specific conversation about what the supervisor or organization could do to retain this valued worker. While more money may be a key to keeping a "keeper," it's possible that different duties, a new title, career development opportunities, or a more flexible schedule may be more important to the person. Once the organization understands the factors that might make the employee reconsider, it can decide whether to make a counteroffer that would address the person's immediate and long-term career needs.

Before attempting to get the employee to reconsider, the company should assess the likely consequences. If the employee agrees to stay, will he or she go looking for another job soon? The answer to this question is probably "yes" if the employee resigned because of dissatisfaction with a supervisor, company policies, or the organizational culture. And how will other workers respond to attempts to get the employee to stay? Will such offers make other employees resentful of the individuals who receive and accept them? Will it stimulate others to put themselves on the market, in hopes of getting similar treatment?

What if the employee has a change of heart? Sometimes the situation is reversed, and the employee wants to un-resign. How should an employer respond? If a replacement has been hired for the resigning employee, it would be unfair to the new hire and legally risky for the organization to retract the offer and allow the original employee to continue in the position. In other cases, the company should evaluate whether it is consistent with the organization's termination philosophy and permissible and consistent with company policy to allow an employee to rescind a resignation. If there are no restrictions in this area, and the company has not already taken steps or incurred expenses to hire a replacement, the employer should evaluate whether there is a good reason (such as the reasons listed above for attempting to get the employee to stay) to allow an employee to continue working for the company despite having been sufficiently dissatisfied to resign in the first place.

Regardless of an organization's view on resignation retractions, it should ask a resigning employee to give written notice. When an employee tenders resignation verbally, the employer should immediately ask the employee to prepare a letter or complete a resignation form. If the employee fails or refuses to do so, the company should prepare a written confirmation of receipt of resignation. Sample resignation forms and a confirmation of receipt appear in Part 2, Section F.1. If the employee later claims to have been wrongfully discharged, these records provide evidence that the employee's departure was voluntary.

Finally, Pave the Way to the Exit

Several activities should take place during the employee's notice period to ensure a seamless transition of the employee's work to others and to end the employment relationship as professionally and positively as possible.

After the employee has tendered a resignation, he or she will probably want an opportunity to notify certain individuals before a general announcement is made. Other staff members should be informed of the employee's resignation as soon as possible thereafter, either in a group meeting or through an e-mail or memo. These announcements give the remaining employees the opportunity to say goodbye and discuss work transition issues with the departing employee. A sample departure announcement, suitable for any type of termination, appears in Part 2, Section F.6. Customers, clients, and vendors with whom the employee has worked should also be notified, either by telephone or in writing. In many instances, it is appropriate for the departing employee to contact these parties, although obviously this would not be the case if an account executive has taken a job with a competitor or the employee has expressed great dissatisfaction with the employer.

In addition to promptly spreading news of a resignation, the supervisor should develop plans with the departing employee for the completion of key assignments and ongoing tasks. It is a good idea to have the employee prepare a list of pending assignments and the status of each. The supervisor may also want to review the departing employee's job description with him or her, to determine if it should be revised before seeking a replacement.

A formal exit meeting should be conducted with the departing employee to ensure that necessary administrative tasks are taken care of by the individual's last day. The next section provides guidance for effective exit meetings.

It's important to remember that an employee's notice period can be a very emotional time, not only for the individual who is leaving the organization but also for the employees who remain. Doing something nice for the departing employee—such as giving a gift, recognizing the employee's service and contributions in a staff meeting, or holding a goodbye lunch or party—can make a big difference in how everyone feels about the organization after the employee is gone. The types of farewell gestures that may be appropriate depend on the organization's culture and traditions, and should take into account the person's position and length of service.

Making the Most of Exit Meetings

A formal exit meeting should be the final rite of passage for all separating employees. The purpose of this meeting is to tie up loose ends administratively, address employee questions, and gain insights on the separating employee's experience with and opinions about the organization.

The timing of the exit meeting depends on the type of separation. In most cases, discharged employees should attend an exit meeting immediately after the termination notification meeting. Exit meetings with resigning or laid off workers should be scheduled for the individual's last or next-to-last day. Obviously, such meetings can't be scheduled in the case of job abandonment. In these separations, the employer will need to handle termination issues by telephone or through written communications.

Cover the Administrative Bases

Common administrative activities handled in termination meetings include

- collection of company property, such as identification badges and keys;

- delivery of the final paycheck;

- discussion of COBRA and other post-termination benefits;

- review of the company's reference policy and completion of a reference authorization form; and

- review of any applicable policies or written agreement relating to noncompete, nonsolicitation, or nondisclosure covenants.

It is helpful to use an exit checklist to make sure that all necessary administrative actions have been taken before the employee's departure. Several sample checklists appear in Part 2, Section D.

Obtain Feedback from Departing Employees

One very important aspect of the separation process is the exit interview. Usually, it is conducted during the exit meeting, although some employers prefer to conduct a telephone interview a few weeks after the employee's last day or have the employee complete and return an exit survey. Some employers outsource the exit interview to a third party. There are pros and cons to each approach. Face-to-face exit interviews provide the opportunity for a structured but interactive dialogue. During these interviews, separating employees have the chance to vent about perceived problems and offer suggestions for improving the work environment, and interviewers can ask probing questions and observe the employee's demeanor and reactions. On the other hand, some employees will respond more candidly to a written exit survey—particularly if the surveys are tabulated anonymously—or if they are interviewed by phone sometime later. Outsourcing exit interviews offers the advantages of a personal, probing interview by a trained and objective interviewer with whom employees are more likely to be candid, but they will be more costly than internally conducted exit interviews.

Assuming that exit feedback is obtained during an interview rather than from a written exit survey, there are several issues to consider, including these:

- **Which employees to interview.** Most organizations do exit interviews only in connection with resignations. Although it is a far less common practice, some employers conduct exit interviews for involuntary terminations as well. Of course, discharged or laid off employees may be hostile, but it is better to hear about employee complaints such as discrimination and harassment in the exit interview than to learn about them later from a plaintiff's attorney, the Equal Employment Opportunity Commission, or another government agency. In fact, if an involuntarily terminated employee is given the opportunity to discuss working conditions during an exit interview and fails to raise complaints, that failure could later be used as evidence in the employer's defense that alleged discriminatory or harassing behavior never occurred or, if it did, that the employer had no knowledge of it.

- **Who should conduct the exit interview?** Departing employees are more likely to open up in exit interviews if they are speaking to someone they perceive as neutral. That person should not be in the employee's chain of command. Consequently, exit interviews frequently fall into the HR department's bailiwick. Interviewers not only should be impartial, but also should be trained in active, empathetic listening and effective interviewing techniques.

- **What topics to discuss.** There is considerable variation from company to company in the scope and focus of exit interviews. This is understandable, as exit interview questions should emphasize areas of primary interest and concern for the particular business. Common subjects covered are reasons for leaving, working conditions, compensation and benefits, training, and supervision. There are often general questions about what the employee liked most and least about working for the company. Some exit interviews include inquiries about the individual's new job and whether he or she would recommend your organization to others. Some sample exit interview questionnaires are included in Part 2, Section I.2. Sample exit surveys, to be completed by the employee, can be found in Part 2, Section I.3.

- **Confidentiality.** Departing employees are more likely to be honest and cooperative during exit interviews if they know that their comments will be kept confidential or anonymous. Understandably, they may be hesitant about giving negative feedback if they fear this information will get back to their supervisor or others who might retaliate against them, particularly if the exit interview takes place before the last day. Interviewers should explain from the outset who will have access to exit interview notes and how the employee's feedback will be used. As a general rule, exit information should be kept confidential and shared with management only on an anonymous basis. An important exception to this rule is situations in which a departing employee makes assertions of discrimination, harassment, or other illegal conduct by the employer. In such cases, the individual's comments will need to be investigated, and he or she should be so informed.

If handled professionally and sensitively, the exit interview can create good will and help the employee leave with positive feelings about the company. Figure 4-3 provides guidelines interviewers should follow to achieve these goals.

Put Findings to Good Use

All too often, exit interview documentation is filed away without being carefully analyzed and used. That is unfortunate, because exit interviews can provide benefits to employers that go beyond the positive conclusion of employment relationships. In some cases, comments made by departing employees (including allegations of discrimination, harassment, or violations of other laws) should prompt an immediate investigation and possible corrective measures. More typically, the information gathered in these interviews or surveys can help pinpoint the causes of job dissatisfaction and turnover.

But don't jump to organizationwide conclusions just because one or two employees make negative comments about employment conditions such as compensation, training, or management. As recommended in Chapter 3, the information garnered during exit interviews should be compiled and analyzed on an aggregate basis to identify common concerns and suggestions, as well as termination patterns and trends. A report that summarizes key exit statistics, commonalities, and trends should be distributed to management at least annually. This information can be a valuable tool in developing recruiting, retention, management development, and litigation avoidance strategies and programs.

Figure 4.3   How to Conduct Exemplary Exit Interviews

- Start by thanking the departing employee for his or her time and explaining the purpose of the interview and how the employee's feedback will be shared and used. Stress the importance of full and honest answers.
- Act friendly and interested in what the person has to say. Don't convey the impression that the exit interview is just a perfunctory administrative task.
- Spend most of the interview listening carefully.
- Expect and allow the separating employee to let off steam during the interview.
- Don't react defensively to negative comments and criticisms. Avoid the temptation to defend the company or management.
- Take notes of important points, but don't take so many notes that you are unable to maintain eye contact or respond sincerely and appropriately to the departing employee's comments.
- End the interview by expressing appreciation. As appropriate, thank the employee for his or her service, contributions to the company, and candor in the exit interview.

Chapter 5
Dealing with Post-termination Challenges

The game isn't over till it's over.

—Yogi Berra

Gone, But Not Forgotten

Lingering ties may bind the employer to a former employee in the days, weeks, months, and even years following termination. Although the employee is gone, there may be reasons he or she cannot or should not be forgotten. First, the employer might need to take immediate and ongoing steps to protect itself from possible harm by the former employee. Second, the organization will need to engage in post-termination conversations internally and may also have occasion to respond to inquiries and requests by the former employee or third parties. Third, the company must decide what to do with the personnel files of terminated employees. This chapter identifies problems that frequently arise in these three areas and suggests strategies to handle them.

Covering Your Assets: Post-termination Security Measures

Your company has three kinds of assets: human, tangible, and intangible. Human assets can be enticed to leave and are vulnerable to violence. Tangible assets are subject to theft or destruction. Intangible assets, such as trade secrets, can be misappropriated for use by competitors. Appropriate steps should be taken to prevent harm to these valuable assets by former employees who want to get even for perceived unfair treatment or hope to get ahead in their new jobs at your company's expense.

Ensure Workplace Safety

"It would never happen here"—that's what many employers believe about workplace violence. Unfortunately, violence is alive and kicking in U.S. workplaces. According to the Occupational Safety and Health Administration (OSHA), about 2 million U.S. workers are victims of some form of workplace violence each year.[13] Additionally, a 2004 SHRM workplace violence survey revealed that 10 percent of violent incidents in the respondents' organizations were committed by former employees toward their supervisors and another 7 percent were committed by former employees toward other employees.[14]

Employer passivity regarding this issue before, during, or after involuntary terminations can lead to disastrous consequences: dead or injured managers, HR staff, employees, or other innocent bystanders; destruction of or damage to company property and facilities; a fearful and traumatized workforce; or legal liability to workplace violence victims and perpetrators. To minimize the chances that any of these nightmares will ever become reality at your company, your organization should establish adequate premises security measures to prevent intrusions by uninvited, unwelcome parties, including former employees, and be prepared to respond to threats from potentially violent persons. These activities should be part of a broad-based strategy to prevent and respond to workplace violence, not just by former employees but also by other possible parties, including employees, customers, relatives or acquaintances of employees, or other third parties. Figure 5-1 lists some key dimensions of workplace violence prevention.

If a discharged or laid off employee makes threats or attempts violent acts directed toward the organization or its workforce, the organization should seek immediate

---

Figure 5.1   **Dimensions of Workplace Violence Prevention**

Premises Security Measures
- Building access
- Physical barriers
- Locks
- Lighting
- Intrusion detection systems
- Video surveillance

Security Personnel
- Company-employed security guards
- Private security company
- Termination escorts

Professional Advisors
- Employee assistance program (EAP) provider
- Threat assessment/workplace violence experts
- Attorneys

Crisis Management Plan
- Violence and weapons policies
- Response procedures for actual incidents, threats, suspected problems
- Crisis management team
- Relationship with local law enforcement agency
- Crisis communication
- Crisis logistics
- Public relations during or after crisis

Violence-aware Human Resource Practices
- Pre-employment screening
- Background checking
- Drug testing
- "Discipline without punishment"
- Dignity and respect in termination
- Security precautions during terminations
- Violence awareness training

assistance from qualified professionals. The following actions may be necessary in these situations:

- Convening the company's crisis management team to monitor and manage the situation.

- Warning individuals who are targets of threats by the former employee.

- Keeping HR staff and managers and supervisors who were in the former employee's chain of command informed of the situation.

- Advising company security personnel and persons posted at reception areas and entrances to alert security personnel if the potentially violent employee attempts to enter the premises or work areas.

- Adding security guards.

- Seeking advice on how to handle the situation from workplace violence experts, counseling professionals, and attorneys.

- Contacting the local law enforcement agency.

Many of the measures taken to protect employees from workplace violence will also protect employers from loss of tangible assets by denying the former employee the opportunity to create harm.

Protect Intangible Assets

Just as organizations should be vigilant in safeguarding their human and physical assets from potential harm from former employees, they should also be careful about maintaining the integrity of valuable proprietary information and goodwill. The misappropriation of trade secrets can have serious financial or competitive repercussions, or even put a company out of business. Even if the employee does nothing more than badmouth the former employer, harm can be done to the company's reputation, ability to retain valued employees, and ability to recruit new employees.

Many businesses have had firsthand experience with the problem of misappropriation of trade secrets. A survey conducted by the American Society for Industrial Security of 138 *Fortune 1,000* companies revealed that from July 2001 through June 2002, 40 percent had lost proprietary information, including research and development information, customer lists, and financial data.[15] Despite this alarming statistic, according to a 2004 SHRM poll of human resource professionals, 30 percent of the respondents said their organizations had not taken any measures to protect trade secrets.[16]

Former employees may have had access to confidential information during their employment, and they may have a motive to disclose this information if they go to work for a competitor or harbor hard feelings when they leave. Unless proper steps are taken, employees also may have the opportunity to misappropriate and misuse trade secrets.

For the most part, protecting trade secrets is a matter of planning and infrastructure, as discussed in Chapter 3, and actions taken during the termination process, as discussed in Chapter 4. However, your company can take additional steps to protect trade secrets after termination.

In the event that a former employee is poised to misappropriate or disclose trade secrets—or is already doing so—the company must take prompt, situation-appropriate action, such as the following:

- Have a manager, attorney, or private investigator telephone the former employee to ask pertinent, and possibly pointed, questions and to remind the employee that the company expects the employee to honor contractual and statutory obligations not to misappropriate or disclose trade secrets. A face-to-face meeting can be even more effective, if it can be arranged. The key here is the element of surprise. Don't leave a voice message. In selecting the person to perform this task, recognize that your company may want him or her to testify in court later.

- Send a letter to the employee demanding that the employee immediately cease and refrain from activities prohibited by a noncompete agreement, nondisclosure agreement, or trade secrets statute, and alert the employee to the potential consequences for failure to do so. Unless the letter is signed by an attorney, it may not be taken seriously by the offending employee.

- Send a letter to the party to whom the former employee has disclosed, or may disclose, trade secrets, stating the former employee's contractual obligations not to disclose confidential information and the potential liability for interfering with contractual relations or violating applicable trade secret statutes.

- Sue for an injunction to prohibit misappropriation or misuse of trade secrets, or to prohibit the employee from engaging in competitive employment.

- Sue the former employee and/or his or her new employer for damages for the misappropriation or misuse of trade secrets.

Words of Wisdom: Communicating about and with Former Employees

Employers should be prepared for a number of post-termination communication challenges, including inquiries from other employees, government agencies, prospective employers, and the former employees themselves. It is important that managers and human resource professionals speak sensitively and safely to avoid negative consequences from post-termination communications about and with former employees.

What to Tell Other Employees about Terminations

The first post-termination communication challenge is breaking the news to other employees. This announcement should be made as soon as possible, preferably on the same day the employee is officially let go. Usually, the terminated employee's immediate supervisor will tell the work group or department about the termination.

Before notifying employees of the termination, the supervisor should prepare a clear, brief, and general explanation of why the employee is no longer working at the company. The supervisor should anticipate likely questions and prepare responses. To minimize exposure to a defamation lawsuit, tell the truth, but limit the information to the facts the employees need to know to do their jobs. Avoid telling white lies, even if the point of doing so is to protect the employee. In some situations, you may want to discuss your planned explanation with an employment attorney beforehand. Although e-mail or a companywide memo lacks the personal touch, you may want to make the announcement this way because of the extreme importance of the words used. In fact, your organization might establish a policy of using e-mail or a memo for all termination announcements.

Keep in mind that the main purpose of the announcement is to convey the simple fact that the employee will no longer be working for you. The secondary purpose is to explain why the employee is gone. Under no circumstances should the announcement be an apology for the termination. The supervisor might make one of the following statements, or a variation thereof:

> *"[Employee name] is no longer with the company because [give very general reason for the discharge such as "it wasn't a good fit."]"*

> OR

> *"[Employee name] left the company today to pursue other opportunities."*

> OR

> *"Today was [employee name's] last day. As a matter of employee privacy, I can't discuss the specific reasons she is no longer with the company."*

These statements should be made with tact and concern. You should then give the employees the opportunity to ask questions, although you may not be at liberty to answer them. If warranted, provide assurances that the terminated employee was treated fairly and respectfully. After employee concerns have been addressed, discuss how the terminated employee's work will be completed and how incoming calls for this individual should be handled.

If a verbal announcement is made, a follow-up memo or e-mail communication, similar in content to the announcement used for employee resignations, should inform the entire workforce of the employee's departure. A sample departure announcement can be found in Part 2, Section F.6.

Communicating with Former Employees

From time to time, managers or human resource professionals will communicate with a former employee about business matters. Perhaps the separated employee has a question about the final paycheck, health continuation benefits, the rollover or distribution of retirement account funds, or a possible employment verification or reference check. Or the employer may need to ask the employee something about the work the employee was doing at the time of the termination, such as where a certain spreadsheet is filed. Whatever the reason, if the employee left the organization on good terms, these contacts can provide a pleasant opportunity to catch up. On the other hand, if the employee was fired, laid off, or quit without notice, the idea of communicating with him or her may trigger anxiety, annoyance, or avoidance.

Regardless of the circumstances of a former employee's departure, company representatives should respond promptly and courteously to post-termination inquiries. Not only is this the respectful way to treat a former employee, it is the smart way. Separated workers who are treated insensitively may be more likely to badmouth or pursue legal action against their former employer. Employers should document the date and content of all such communications.

Responding to Unemployment Insurance Claims

It is not uncommon for employers who are otherwise very careful about adopting HR best practices to fall asleep at the wheel when it comes to responding to claims for unemployment insurance (UI) benefits. They may routinely contest UI claims without giving serious thought to the merits or risks of doing so. Or they provide inaccurate or incomplete information and then have to change their story when a hearing is conducted.

What happens when you contest a former employee's UI claim? Well, first, he or she gets angry. (So much for all you've done up to that point to create a smooth departure.) Second, the employee starts thinking about getting a lawyer. If the employee does contact one, that attorney may attempt to determine whether the employee has potential claims for wrongful discharge, discrimination, harassment, wage/hour violations, defamation, and so on. Suddenly, the employer has gone from trying to save a few bucks on UI premiums to the possibility of a full-blown lawsuit. The employee, with or without the assistance of the attorney, may subpoena records and witnesses to testify at the UI benefits hearing. This is an opportunity for the employee or attorney to obtain "free discovery" about other claims much earlier than would otherwise be the case. It is also an opportunity for the company to be ambushed, having to answer damaging questions without having been thoroughly prepared for them by its own attorney.

If the employee is successful in the UI hearing, he or she may go on to file other claims. One of those claims may be a discrimination claim. The employee might also tack on a claim for unlawful retaliation, asserting that the company contested the UI claim in bad faith as a means of retaliating against the employee for exercising statutory civil rights. When the discrimination case eventually goes to trial, the employer may offer much more, or different, evidence than it did when it made its halfhearted attempt to contest UI benefits. At that point, you can almost hear the former employee's attorney: "Ask yourselves, ladies and gentlemen of the jury: Were they lying then, or are they lying now? Because this is not the same story they told two years ago in the UI hearing."

The proper way to respond to UI claims is as follows: First, collect all the information needed to respond to the claim in sufficient time to undertake a thoughtful review and make an informed decision before the deadline to respond. Second, determine whether the employee's claim has merit. If it does, tell the agency that. If it doesn't, consider carefully, in light of the above scenario, whether this is a situation in which it makes more sense to "lie low and keep your powder dry." You may want to consult legal counsel in making this determination. Ultimately, you may decide not to respond to the request for information (in which case the employee will probably be granted benefits by default) or to respond with the requested information and inform the agency that you do not contest the right to benefits. "Won't that be admitting we're wrong?" employers often ask.

No. Unemployment insurance statutes typically provide that the granting or denial of benefits cannot be used as evidence in another case. Third, if you decide to contest benefits, do it right. Muster your documents and witnesses, prepare your questions, prepare your witnesses, and go in and win. Think twice about trying to do this without the assistance of legal counsel. But if you do, here are some guidelines to follow:

- Be thoroughly prepared with witnesses and exhibits, having complied with all rules for providing copies to the former employee or hearing officer ahead of time or at the hearing.

- Appear in person. Your witnesses will be more credible in person, you'll be a better questioner, and you'll have better rapport with the hearing officer.

- Treat the hearing officer with deference and respect. Refer to him or her as "Your Honor" unless instructed to do otherwise.

- Treat the employee with respect, but don't be a patsy.

- Be cool, calm, and collected. Avoid the temptation to act the way attorneys do on television programs.

Handling Reference Requests

Although you may never hear directly from a former employee after his or her last day, sooner or later you will probably receive reference inquiries about this individual. This prospect often sends employers ducking for legal cover behind a "name, rank, and serial number" or "no comment" reference policy. This approach is often prompted by advice from attorneys who are overly concerned with liability and without regard to the business consequences.

It is true that an employer who knowingly or recklessly provides false, disparaging reference information may be liable for defamation. So, too, an employer who gives a misleading positive reference about a former employee who demonstrated dangerous tendencies may be sued for misrepresentation if the individual is hired on the basis of the reference and subsequently causes harm. However, it may be overkill to implement highly restrictive policies and practices for responding to reference requests. These practices have the ironic and counterproductive consequences of hurting good former employees (by making it difficult for them to provide proof of capable performance and exemplary work behavior to prospective employers) and making it easy for problematic former employees to hide their past workplace misdeeds and move into other unsuspecting organizations, where they can continue to perform poorly or cause harm.

Employers can avoid these consequences and still protect themselves against legal claims by adopting reference policies and procedures that permit the safe disclosure of useful and substantive information about job performance, duties, qualifications, work behavior, and reasons for leaving.

As discussed in Chapter 2, many states require employers to provide service letters describing various aspects of a former employee's service at the request of the employee or a prospective employer. A substantial majority of states have enacted reference immunity statutes. These laws protect employers who provide good faith references to prospective employers from liability for defamation or other torts.

Even in states that do not have a reference immunity statute, the potential legal risks of providing references to prospective employers can be greatly reduced when the information provided is (a) given with the employee's prior written consent (for federal agency employees, written consent is required by the federal Privacy Act of 1974; (b) true; (c) job-related; (d) based on documented facts; and (e) provided in response to a specific question rather than volunteered. To ensure that these conditions are met, your organization should develop and distribute a written reference policy and consistently implement realistic and effective procedures for handling reference requests.

Your reference policy should cover who may provide references, the types of information that may be disclosed, and conditions for releasing reference information. A sample reference policy appears in Part 2, Section B.5. Prior written consent of the reference subject is the primary condition. This authorization can be obtained at the exit meeting or at a later date, upon request by the former employee. The authorization form may include a waiver provision stating that the employee releases the company, its agents, and prospective employers from any liability arising from the company's furnishing of reference information. (See Part 2, Section C.3 for sample authorizations.) If the employee is unwilling to sign the consent form, the only information that should be shared about him or her in reference checks is dates of employment, title, and verification of earnings, or information required by an applicable service letter statute.

Reference requests should not be dealt with on an ad hoc basis. Instead, your organization should establish sound and workable procedures. It is important to decide who in the organization will be permitted to provide references. A standard practice is to centralize and limit reference-giving responsibility and authority in the HR department. According to a 2004 SHRM reference and background checking survey report, 85 percent of employers gave HR staff primary responsibility for providing references, and only 9 percent designated the former employee's supervisor.[17] Although there are several advantages to allowing only HR staff to respond to reference requests (including expertise, awareness of liability issues, greater consistency in response, and access to personnel files), employers should recognize that reference-checkers (including HR professionals) routinely attempt to bypass HR departments in favor of contacting former supervisors directly and that supervisors frequently provide references "under the table" for good former employees.

Rather than having references sought and given under the table, your organization could decide to allow both HR representatives and supervisors to provide references—as long these individuals are trained to handle reference inquiries effectively. Figure 5-2 provides tips on responding to reference requests.

Regardless of your policies on who gives references and what type of information may be disclosed, it is a good practice to document reference requests and the responses. A sample that can be used for this purpose appears in Part 2, Section E.6. These reference records should be kept in former employees' personnel files.

Figure 5.2   **How to Respond to Reference Requests**

■ Communicate only with parties that have a legitimate need for a reference about a former employee. Ask the party requesting a reference whether he or she represents a prospective employer of the individual. A former employee may have a friend or a professional investigator call to find out what you are saying about him or her in reference checks.

■ Ask the party requesting a reference if he or she has the former employee's permission to contact you.

■ When in doubt about the identity and motives of the person making a telephone inquiry, call the prospective employer to verify the inquirer's position, or require that the reference checker submit the request in writing on the company's letterhead. If you ask for a phone number and call back, you can ascertain whether you are speaking to a real or phony reference checker.

■ Provide only truthful, job-related information when providing references. Don't provide overly positive, misleading information to reference checkers.

■ Use specific examples and facts to provide informative, concrete answers to reference checkers' questions. Ideally, factual information given in references should be based on documentation.

■ Don't volunteer information that is not requested.

■ Provide the same type of reference information about former employees at all levels, to the extent the employee has consented to disclosures.

■ Consult an attorney if a reference request pertains to a former employee who exhibited dangerous tendencies or has complained of violations of his or her workplace rights.

Adapted from Bliss, Wendy, *Legal, Effective References: How to Give and Get Them* (SHRM, 2001), pp. 50–51.

On the Records: Managing the "Ex-Files"

A former employee's personnel file may continue to expand even after he or she is gone. How do you manage the files of these former employees? In the words of singer Kenny Rogers, "You got to know when to hold 'em, know when to fold 'em." The three major issues are (1) allowing access to records by former employees, (2) records retention, and (3) records destruction.

Avoid "Random Access" to Records by Ex-employees

A current or former employee's right to access his or her own personnel file is a matter of company policy and, in about 60 percent of the states, a matter of state statute. Currently, no comprehensive federal law requires employee access to personnel records in the private sector. Neither the federal Privacy Act nor the Freedom of Information Act covers private sector personnel files. The Occupational Safety and Health Act requires employers to permit employees to inspect their personal medical records in connection with possible exposure to hazardous workplace substances. The Fair Credit Reporting Act, under some circumstances, requires employees to be given access to background checks considered to be "consumer reports."

The fact that 60 percent of the states have enacted access statutes reflects the twin realities that employees have a legitimate interest in accessing at least some parts of their personnel files and that many employers have refused such access. Typically, one of the first things an involuntarily terminated employee does is ask for a copy of his or her personnel file. Frequently, this request is made at the suggestion of an attorney. What should your company do, in the absence of governing federal or state law, in response to such a request? Ideally, you will respond according to your pre-existing policy on the subject. A sample policy appears in Part 2, Section B.6.

But what *should* your policy be? In discharge and discipline situations, employers are frequently apprehensive about giving employees access, fearing that the information will somehow be used against the company. However, denying a current or former employee access to—at a minimum—his or her application for employment, performance evaluations, and records of changes in employment status will make a jury think the company has something to hide or, worse, is trying to aggravate the employee. If some employees are granted access but others aren't, you open yourself to charges of unlawful discrimination or retaliation. If a lawsuit is initiated, the employee will be able to obtain the records through discovery anyway, so employers who are inclined to deny access should consider whether their reasons are good ones.

However, it is reasonable for employers to protect from disclosure certain types of confidential information, such as references other persons have given about the employee and, usually, details of internal investigations, such as a sexual harassment investigation.

If access is permitted, it should be done in a consistent and orderly fashion. You may want to require that the employee submit the request in writing. It is wise to create a record showing that the employee requested and was given access to specific records on a specific date. You should consider whether your policy will be to permit the employee access to the actual file or to a copy (the recommended course). Finally, you should consider establishing a flexible timetable for responding to such requests.

Records Retention: Let's Hang on to What We've Got

The issue of records retention can be a real challenge. Different federal laws contain different retention requirements, and states may impose their own requirements where federal law does not apply because of, for example, the small size of the business. States may impose additional requirements even where the federal laws do apply. Some retention requirements apply only to government contractors, while others apply to employers in general. Different laws can require retention of the same types of documents but for different periods of time. When different periods apply to the same records, employers should retain the records for the longest period specified. Where a charge or lawsuit is filed, all relevant records should be kept until final disposition.

For summaries of record retention requirements under federal employment laws, see "Federal Records Retention Requirements for Employers" by Wallace Bonaparte and Cornelia Gamlem (www.shrm.org/hrresources/whitepapers_published/CMS_000270.asp) or "Record Retention Requirements Summary Guide" (www.mnwfc.org/winona/record_retention_requirements1.htm).

Records Destruction: How to Fold, Spindle, and Mutilate Them

The flip side of records retention is document destruction. Storing paper records for years on end can be an expensive proposition. Moreover, as long as the record exists, there is a risk that it will be accessed by the wrong person for improper reasons.

Although microfilming and electronic scanning technology help reduce the amount of space needed to store records, these methods can be costly, and they do not address the problem of inappropriate disclosure. Thus, at some point, your company will want to destroy old personnel files that are no longer legally required to be maintained.

Document destruction should be carried out according to an established written policy providing for periodic destruction of old records. A human component is critical to the destruction regimen because, for example, some records cannot be destroyed until final action has been taken regarding a charge or lawsuit. And one employee's file may be relevant to another employee's lawsuit, so it wouldn't be safe to retain only the charging employee's records. In some jurisdictions, if an employer destroys documents before they cease to be relevant to a pending charge or lawsuit, the employer can be sued for "spoliation of evidence." Legal advice is sometimes required in making document destruction decisions.

Once you decide to destroy old documents, do you simply throw them into the dumpster behind the building? Absolutely not. Common sense dictates that sensitive personnel information, some of which could be used in identity theft, must be shredded, burned, or pulverized—whether it is recorded on paper or disk, magnetic tapes, CD-ROMs, or discarded computer hard drives. As of June 1, 2005, the Fair and Accurate Credit Transactions Act (FACTA) requires such reasonable measures of destruction of consumer information derived from a consumer report. Under FACTA, violators are subject to civil liability and stiff per-day fines levied by the federal and state governments.

PART 2

SAMPLES

List of Samples

Sample	Comments
A. Termination Policies and Procedures	
A.1. Employment Separation	
A.1.1. Employment Termination Policy and Procedures	A very detailed statement of policies and procedures applicable to all types of separation from employment.
A.1.2. Policy: Separation from Employment	A detailed policy form addressing all types of separation from employment. Note especially the provisions on rehire.
A.1.3. Employment Termination Policy	A very short policy statement with minimal verbiage and an at-will disclaimer.
A.1.4. Terminating Employment Policy	A moderately detailed policy form that defines various types of separation from employment, containing a prominent at-will disclaimer. Also addresses return of property upon separation.
A.2. Voluntary Termination	
A.2.1. Resignation from Employment Policy	A policy statement on resignation that describes the exit interview process and provides information about final paycheck and health continuation benefits.
A.2.2. Resignation Policy	A very short policy statement on resignation requesting that the employee give two weeks' notice and indicating that an exit interview will be scheduled.
A.2.3. Resignation Policy and Procedures	A more detailed statement of policies and procedures applicable to resignation, including a discussion of final paycheck and benefits.
A.3. Involuntary Termination—Individual Discharge	
A.3.1. Involuntary Termination from Employment Policy and Procedures	A statement of policy and procedures devoted exclusively to involuntary terminations.
A.3.2. Procedure for Discharging Employees for Cause	A statement of procedures for involuntary terminations. This document would be "eyes only" for supervisors.
A.4. Involuntary Termination—Reduction in Force	
A.4.1. Layoff/Recall Rules	A detailed statement of policies and procedures governing layoffs and recalls.
A.4.2. Reduction in Force "Bumping" Process Flowchart	A flowchart is an effective way to communicate procedures governing layoffs and recalls.
A.5. Exit Interview	
A.5.1. Exit Interview Process	This form defines two general categories of termination and establishes separate documentation and exit interview procedures for each category. The form begins with an introduction describing the purpose and goals of the exit interview.
A.5.2. Terminations and Exit Interviews—Policy and Procedures	A to-the-point statement of policies and procedures for exit interviews.
A.6. Reinstatement	
A.6.1. Reinstatement Rules	This form provides a moderately detailed statement of procedures applicable to reinstatement following a layoff. Note that changes would be required if the form were used in the context of reinstatement following FMLA or USERRA leave.
B. Other Policies Related to Termination	
B.1. Employment-at-Will	
B.1.1. Employment-at-Will Policy and Disclaimer	A must-have form for every employer who wants to maintain the right to discharge at-will. The written acknowledgement form is valuable evidence in the event of litigation.
B.1.2. Employment-at-Will Disclaimer	Another sample of this must-have form. Employers should consider modifying the forms to make them suitable for use other than as part of an employee handbook; for example, as a stand-alone form or a paragraph in the employee's offer letter.
B.2. Employee Discipline	
B.2.1. Employee Conduct and Work Rules	A list of specific infractions that may result in termination prevents an employee from saying that he or she didn't realize a particular behavior was prohibited. This form reserves the right to terminate employment even in situations not specifically listed.
B.2.2. Disciplinary Procedures	This is a classic progressive discipline policy. Although imposing discipline progressively has its benefits, adopting a policy stating that the company will do so can sometimes be used against the employer. This form is drafted to limit the likelihood of that happening.

Sample	Comments
B.3. Vacation/Paid Time Off Accrual and Payment	
B.3.1. Paid Time Off (PTO) Policy	A detailed PTO policy containing provisions for forfeiture in the event of involuntary termination or failure to use PTO within a calendar year. Such forfeiture provisions may not be legal under the laws of some states.
B.4. Severance Pay and Benefits Policy	
B.4.1. Severance Benefits-Non-Disciplinary Discharge	A simple policy discussing benefits of salary and health insurance extension and severance pay. Note: This would constitute a welfare benefit plan subject to the provisions of ERISA.
B.5. Reference Policies and Procedures	
B.5.1. Policy on Providing Employment References	A comprehensive policy on providing employment references. Reprinted with permission from *Legal, Effective References: How to Give and Get Them*.
B.6. Employee Access to Personnel File.	
B.6.1. Policy: Access to Employee's Personnel File	Employee access to his or her own personnel file may be mandated by state law or merely permitted by the employer. This policy places some parameters on what is considered reasonable access.
B.7. Return of Company Property	
B.7.1 Policy: Return of Company Property	Disputes over whether an employee has returned all company property are a recurring problem. This form will help to systematize the process, giving both employer and employee proof of compliance. Unreturned property sometimes leads to employers withholding final paychecks, a practice that may be illegal or regulated under some state laws.
C. Employee Acknowledgment and Authorization Forms	
C.1. Payroll Deductions	
C.1.1. Consent to Payroll Deductions	A form like this one is useful to explain what employees can expect in terms of payroll deductions, and it provides the consent necessary under some state laws to make deductions for items such as unreturned company property.
C.2. Employment Termination	
C.2.1. Employee's Termination Certificate	A form such as this can be helpful in reminding an employee of continuing duties of nondisclosure, noncompetition, and return of company property. An employee who is considering violating a noncompete agreement may reconsider upon realizing that he is going to be asked upon termination to certify that he intends to abide by it. If an employee refuses to sign after having agreed to do so when hired, it is a heads-up that the employee may be up to something.
C.2.2. Separating Employee's Certification to Employer	A second form illustrating other topics for which employers might find it useful to have departing employees provide a certification.
C.3. References	
C.3.1. Employee Consent to Disclose Personal Information and Release of Liability	A short but useful form combining a job reference policy statement, consent to disclose personnel information, and a release of liability in consideration for the employer agreeing to provide more than "name, rank, and serial number" in response to reference requests. Reprinted with permission from *Legal, Effective References: How to Give and Get Them*.
C.3.2. Instructions for Providing References with Reference Summary and Authorization	A form such as this, used in conjunction with the exit interview process, can be very useful to update information about the employee's performance since his or her last regular evaluation. This form also functions as a reference consent form.
C.4. Release of Employee Contact Information	
C.4.1. Departing Employee's Mailing Address	A basic form addressing issues of how the employee can be contacted, to whom the employer may provide such contact information, and e-mail auto-reply.
C.5. Election of Exit Incentives	
C.5.1. Early Exit Incentive Program Election Form	A form describing a hypothetical early exit incentive program, with election form.
C.6. Receipt of Termination Materials	
C.6.1. Receipt of Early Exit Incentive Program Materials Acknowledgement Form	An OWBPA-compliant form acknowledging receipt of documents and information in connection with a hypothetical early exit incentive program applicable to a group of employees.

Sample	Comments
D. Checklists	
D.1. **Termination Process**	
D.1.1. Separation Process Checklist	A checklist to ensure that all the details of separation have been taken care of by (a) the employee's supervisor, (b) the payroll department, and (c) HR.
D.1.2. Associate Termination Checklist	An alternative separation checklist.
D.1.3. Voluntary Separation Process Timeline	A checklist organized according to four phases of the voluntary termination process.
D.1.4. Involuntary Separation Process Timeline	A checklist organized according to three phases of the involuntary termination process.
E. Termination Process Worksheets and Records	
E.1. **Record of Employee Counseling and Discipline**	
E.1.1. Employee Counseling Form	A form with checkboxes that is helpful in standardizing the description of performance problems on a companywide basis. The form also provides checkboxes for the employee to agree/disagree with the supervisor's assessment and to promise/refuse to comply with supervisor expectations.
E.1.2. Employee Counseling Form	An alternative form that prescribes documentation and recordkeeping procedures for verbal warnings that are different from procedures for more serious discipline.
E.1.3. Record of Employee Discipline	A form requesting identification of persons who witnessed the employee's infraction (useful in the event of litigation).
E.1.4. Documented Warning	An alternative form that notes the existence of an appeal process.
E.2. **Record of Separation**	
E.2.1. Employee Separation Form	A record memorializing the conditions of separation.
E.2.2. Employee Separation Report	A record memorializing the conditions of separation along with information about final paycheck, return of property, and COBRA processing.
E.2.3. Employee Separation Record	A record memorializing the conditions of separation, including leave of absence. Also addresses eligibility for rehire, final paycheck, and return of property. Form is designed to be signed by employee.
E.3. **Final Paycheck Calculation**	
E.3.1. HR/Accounting Final Pay Checklist	A simple form for calculating the final paycheck.
E.4. **Termination Benefits**	
E.4.1. Benefits upon Termination Worksheet	A form to keep track of COBRA entitlements and record payment of final paycheck.
E.4.2. COBRA Payment Form	A form to monitor employee payments for COBRA insurance and cancellations by employee.
E.5. **Reduction in Force**	
E.5.1. Position Reduction and Severance Process Timeline	A form to organize the numerous tasks to complete a RIF.
E.5.2. RIF Adverse Impact Worksheet	A worksheet to help prevent adverse impact discrimination when implementing a RIF.
E.6. **Employee References**	
E.6.1. Record of Employee Reference Form	A form used to document when an employer has provided a reference about a current or former employee. Reprinted with permission from *Legal, Effective References: How to Give and Get Them*.
F. Termination Notices and Letters	
F.1. **Employee Resignation**	
F.1.1. Employee Resignation Form and Company Confirmation of Resignation Form	A form signed by employee and employer to document voluntary resignations, which are frequently given only orally.
F.1.2. Voluntary Resignation Notice	An alternative form signed by employee and employer to document voluntary resignations.
F.2. **Employment Separation**	
F.2.1. Confirmation of Employment Separation	A form signed by employee and employer to document involuntary as well as voluntary separations.
F.3. **Job Abandonment**	
F.3.1. Job Abandonment Letter	Contemporaneous proof that an employee is deemed to have abandoned the job, thereby terminating employment.
F.3.2. Job Abandonment Letter (for incarceration)	Another form to document job abandonment; in this instance, because the employee is incarcerated.

Sample	Comments
F.4. Discharge	
F.4.1. Termination Letter (leave of absence)	Documenting termination because of inability to return to work following medical leave.
F.4.2. Termination Letter (leave of absence)	Documenting termination because of failure to return from worker's compensation leave within one year, and noting that employee is eligible for rehire.
F.4.3. Termination Letter (proof of U.S. employability)	Notice of termination because of employee's inability to provide proof of U.S. employability as required by the Immigration Reform and Control Act.
F.4.4. Termination Warning Letter (incorrect Social Security number)	Notice of termination because of failure to provide accurate Social Security number.
F.5. Layoff	
F.5.1. Layoff Memorandum	A notice that the employee is being laid off because of lack of work; describes severance pay that is available upon signing a release of claims. The notice can be used by the employee to demonstrate to unemployment insurance authorities and potential employers that termination was not based on poor performance.
F.6. Employee Departure	
F.6.1. Employee Departure Announcement	A form that can be used by employers to notify other employees, in a consistent and nondefamatory manner, of an employee's separation from employment.
F.7. Service Letter	
F.7.1. Service Letter	Some states require employers to provide service letters reflecting basic facts about a former employee's employment. Note that the required content of service letters varies by state. Such letters can be useful to employees when applying for unemployment insurance, future employment, and loans. Of course, employers are free to provide such letters even when they are not mandated by law.
G. Separation Agreements and Releases	
G.1. Separation Agreement (non-OWBPA)	
G.1.1. Employee Separation Agreement (non-OWBPA release form)	A simple, one-page separation agreement with a release of claims that is suitable for situations in which the departing employee is under 40 years old. The form is notable as an example of a modern trend to avoid legalese and use plain English.
G.1.2. Separation Agreement (non-OWBPA release form)	Another simple separation agreement with a release suitable for non-OWBPA situations.
G.2. OWBPA Release (single termination)	
G.2.1. Confidential Separation and Release Agreement (OWBPA release form for single terminations)	This separation agreement has a release suitable for use in situations where only one employee is being terminated and he or she is 40 years or older (i.e., OWPBA situations). The form has many of the bells and whistles favored by employment lawyers who are attempting to provide employers with maximum protection under the law.
G.2.2. Employee Separation Agreement (OWBPA release form for single terminations)	This separation agreement also has a release suitable for use in situations in which only one employee is being terminated and he or she is 40 years or older. However, this agreement attempts to use plain language instead of legalese. A departing employee may feel more comfortable signing a plain English form without retaining an attorney.
G.2.3. Separation and Release Agreement (OWBPA release form for single terminations)	Another form of separation agreement containing an OWBPA-compliant release suitable for single employee terminations. This form also has many bells and whistles, and follows the traditional style. Reprinted with permission from *Ending the Employment Relationship Without Ending Up in Court*.
G.2.4. Separation Agreement and Release (OWBPA release form for single terminations)	Another example of a separation agreement containing an OWBPA-compliant release suitable for single employee terminations.
G.2.5. Resignation Agreement (OWBPA release form for single terminations)	A short and simple form for OWBPA terminations of a single employee.
G.3. OWBPA Release (group termination)	
G.3.1. Confidential Separation and Release Agreement (OWBPA release form for group terminations)	This separation agreement has a release suitable for use in situations in which a group of employees is being terminated and a release of age discrimination claims is sought. The form has many of the bells and whistles favored by employment lawyers who are attempting to provide employers with maximum protection under the law. OWBPA group layoffs require employees to be given certain information about other employees eligible for the early exit incentive program (29 U.S.C. §626(f)(1)(H)). This form contains that disclosure in the separation agreement at paragraph 4(e)-(h).

Sample	Comments
G.3.2. General Release Agreement and Waiver of Claims (OWBPA release form for group terminations)	A simpler form containing an OWBPA-compliant release of claims suitable for a group termination. OWBPA group layoffs require employees to be given certain information about other employees who are eligible for the early exit incentive program. This form should be used in conjunction with a separate disclosure form such as Form G.4.2 in order to disclose the information required by 29 U.S.C. §626(f)(1)(H).
G.3.3. Separation Agreement (OWBPA release form for group terminations)	Another short form containing a release suitable for OWBPA group termination situations. This form should be used in conjunction with a separate disclosure form such as Form G.4.1 or G.4.2 in order to disclose the information required by 29 U.S.C. §626(f)(1)(H) when the waiver is requested from a group or class of employees.

G.4. OWBPA Group Disclosure

Sample	Comments
G.4.1. OWBPA Group Disclosure Memorandum (with exhibit)	OWBPA disclosure in memo form plus spreadsheet.
G.4.2. Early Exit Incentive Program Disclosure	OWBPA disclosure in memo form.

H. Employee Separation Packet Materials

H.1. Benefit Package Summary

Sample	Comments
H.1.1. Termination Benefits Information	A basic notification of COBRA continuation rights.
H.1.2. Voluntary Resignation Incentive Benefit Package Letter	Employers who need to reduce their workforce may consider offering employees incentives to resign, such as those described in this letter. Note how the employer makes it clear immediately that "this is not a layoff notice."

H.2. Unemployment Benefits

Sample	Comments
H.2.1. Unemployment Benefits Information (Arizona)	When implementing a RIF, employers should attempt to make the situation as painless as possible for departing employees. Providing detailed information about available unemployment benefits, such as this letter does, is a good example of how employers can ease the impact on employees simply by acting as a conduit for information.

H.3. Severance Pay FAQs

Sample	Comments
H.3.1. Severance Package Questions and Answers	Question-and-answer (Q&A) sheets are an excellent way to disseminate important and helpful RIF information to employees in an easy-to-understand and easy-to-access format.

H.4. Severance Pay Examples

Sample	Comments
H.4.1. Severance Pay Examples	In this document, RIF information is conveyed in a tabular format that makes it easy for employees to compare the consequences of voluntary resignation, involuntary RIF, and being retained through the regular retirement date. Again, an excellent way to convey information that is of concern to employees.

H.5. Reduction in Force FAQs

Sample	Comments
H.5.1. Reduction in Force (Bumping) Frequently Asked Questions	Bumping rights, if available, can be difficult but critical for employees to understand in evaluating early exit incentive options. Here, an employer explains affected employees' bumping rights in detail in easily understood Q&A format.

H.6. Retirement Benefits Summary

Sample	Comments
H.6.1. Retirement Benefits	This is a comprehensive description of retirement benefits provided by a large employer. Particular topics are highlighted with clear boldface type, and the Q&A format is used to address some points. Employees are given the name and number of a person to call for further information.

I. Exit Interview Tools

I.1. Exit Interview Schedule

Sample	Comments
I.1.1. Termination and Exit Interview Schedule	Establishing a termination and exit interview schedule systematizes the termination process and reduces tension by letting employees know what will happen when they leave.

I.2. Exit Interview Questionnaire (for exit interviews conducted by company representatives)

Sample	Comments
I.2.1. Exit Interview Template	This is an example of a template to be used by a trained HR representative to conduct an exit interview. Using a template results in systematization of the interview on a companywide basis, permitting meaningful comparisons among interviewees.
I.2.2. Exit Interview	Another good example of an exit interview template.

Sample	Comments
I.3. Exit Survey (completed by employee)	
I.3.1. Exit Survey	This survey combines multiple-choice and short-answer formats. Multiple-choice responses make it easy to conduct comparative analyses. The short answer format allows employees to express themselves more freely, to explain their responses contextually, and to offer suggestions.
I.3.2. Exit Interview Questionnaire	This survey focuses mainly on multiple-choice questions, while still affording the employee an opportunity to comment on whatever he or she considers important.
I.3.3. Exit Interview Questionnaire	This survey integrates the multiple-choice format and the short-answer format on a topic-by-topic basis.
I.4. Supervisor Exit Questionnaire	
I.4.1. Employee Separation—Supervisor Questionnaire	A supervisor's record of the conditions of separation, and requiring a performance evaluation with rehire recommendation.
J. COBRA Notices	
J.1. General Notice of Continuation Coverage Rights	
J.1.1. Model General Notice of COBRA Continuation Coverage Rights (for use by single-employer group health plan)	This form comes from the U.S. Department of Labor (DOL) web site (www.dol.gov/ebsa/compliance_assistance.html). A Spanish version is also available.
J.2. Occurrence of Qualifying Event	
J.2.1. Employer's Notice to Plan Administrator of Occurrence of COBRA Qualifying Event	To be sent to the plan administrator when the employer becomes aware of a COBRA qualifying event.
J.2.2. Qualified Beneficiary's Notice to Plan Administrator of Occurrence of COBRA Qualifying Event	This form permits a qualified beneficiary to notify the plan administrator of a COBRA qualifying event, such as divorce from the covered employee or loss of dependent child status under group health plan rules.
J.3. Election Notice	
J.3.1. Model COBRA Continuation Coverage Election Notice (for use by single-employer group health plan)	This form comes from the U.S. Department of Labor web site (www.dol.gov/ebsa/compliance_assistance.html). A Spanish version is also available.
J.4. Unavailability of COBRA Coverage	
J.4.1. Plan Administrator's Notice to Applicant of Unavailability of COBRA Continuation Coverage	This form is used to notify an applicant for COBRA coverage that coverage is unavailable and to explain why; for example, the employment of the covered employee was terminated for "gross misconduct."
J.5. Early Termination of COBRA Coverage	
J.5.1. Plan Administrator's Notice to COBRA Beneficiary of Early Termination of COBRA Continuation Coverage	COBRA coverage can be terminated early for failure to pay required premiums or for other reasons. This form is used to give a covered beneficiary notice of termination of the coverage and the reason for it.
K. HIPAA Certificate	
K.1. Certificate of Group Health Plan Coverage	
K.1.1. Certificate of Group Health Plan Coverage	This form comes from the U.S. Department of Labor web site (www.dol.gov/ebsa/compliance_assistance.html).
L. WARN Notices	
L.1. To Affected Employees	
L.1.1. WARN Act Notice to Affected Employees	The WARN Act requires different notices by employers to different types of persons. This form is compliant with the requirements for notice to affected employees.
L.2. To Employee Representative	
L.2.1 WARN Act Notice to Representative of Affected Employees	As stated above, the WARN Act requires different notices by employers to different persons. This form is compliant with the requirements for notice to representatives of affected employees (unions).
L.3. To Government	
L.3.1. WARN Act Notice to Government (standard form)	Again, the WARN Act requires that two types of government officials be provided with notice. This form is fully compliant with the requirements for this notice.
L.3.2. WARN Act Notice to Government (short form)	As just stated, the WARN Act requires that two types of government officials be provided with notice. Providing just the limited information on this short form is expressly authorized by WARN. However, *the omitted information must be readily available on-site*. If the employer has the information, it is probably better to use the standard form rather than the short form.

SECTION A

Termination Policies and Procedures

The foundation of the paper piece of the termination puzzle is an organization's written policies and procedures. This section includes sample policies and procedures that cover both voluntary and involuntary separations.

Resignations are specifically addressed in some of these samples. This is an area in which some employers have not developed specific procedures but perhaps should. Other samples in this section address disciplinary or performance-based discharges, reductions in force (RIFs), retirement, and rehiring issues.

The section also contains policies and procedures for exit interviews. Specific tools for exit interviews and exit surveys are presented in Section I.

Sample A.1.1   Employment Termination Policy and Procedures

Subject: Terminations of Employment

Supersedes: Supersedes Policy Dated [Date], Origination Date [Date]

Effective: [Date]

Page(s):   [# Pages]

Approved by: [Human Resources Leadership Team (HRLT)]

1.0 Philosophy/Purpose

While [Company Name] hopes that its employment relationships with all employees are long-term, it is recognized that not all employees are suited for employment with [Company Name]. This policy is designed to state [Company Name]'s policy for employees who voluntarily terminate their employment relationship with [Company Name] or have their employment relationship involuntarily terminated by [Company Name].

2.0 Scope

This policy applies to all employees at all business units and corporate offices of [Company Name].

The policy and procedures enumerated below shall apply unless such policy or procedures are otherwise specified in a contract to which [Company Name], or a covered business unit, is a signatory. In such cases, the terms of the contract shall govern for employees covered by that contract, and such terms will take precedence over this policy.

3.0 Responsibility

The interpretation, administration and monitoring for compliance of this policy shall be the responsibility of the Chief Operating Officer or his/her designees, and [Company Name] Human Resources.

4.0 Policy

It is the policy of [Company Name] to establish and maintain at-will employment relationships with all non-represented employees. At-will employment means that either the employer or the employee may terminate the employment relationship at any time, with or without notice and with or without cause. This policy addresses the protocol for [Company Name]'s termination of employment relationships. This policy does not address terminations due to reductions in work force. *See Reductions in Work Force Policy, Resignations Policy*, and *System-Wide Involuntary Terminations HR Policy.*

Although [Company Name] may terminate employees at any time, with or without cause and with or without notice, [Company Name] may terminate employees for specific reasons such as, but not limited to, unsatisfactory work performance, violation of work rules or company policies or procedures, and/or disciplinary problems.

Prior to finalizing any termination decision, a review of the facts and approval are required by Human Resources.

5.0 Practice/Procedure

5.1 Separation Process

5.1.1 Voluntary

Employees who voluntarily terminate their employment are requested to provide [Company Name] with a minimum two (2) week written notice. Management may accept the notice and allow the employee to continue working. In certain instances, such as where the employee has access to sensitive or confidential information, the manager or supervisor may relieve the employee of his/her duties and pay the employee for the time remaining within the two (2) week notice period. An employee who is demonstrating performance or behavioral difficulties after submitting his/her notice of resignation may be released immediately without pay. Prior to the employee's last day of work the manager and employee will review the exit checklist for any final return of [Company Name] property as well as for the employee to receive a terminated benefits summary information sheet.

5.1.2 Involuntary

All involuntary terminations must first be reviewed by Human Resources. Based on the circumstances of a situation, an employee may be suspended without pay from the workplace while his/her employment is being reviewed for termination. If an employee is alleged to have been involved in an act of violence, theft, or threat/intimidation, [Company Name] Security is required to be notified.

Notification of a decision to terminate an employee from [Company Name] will be communicated in a meeting between the employee and her/his supervisor or manager and (when possible) another member of [Company Name] leadership. In some circumstances an employee may be notified either by telephone or in writing (certified letter). Decisions to provide notification via telephone or in writing must be reviewed in advance with Human Resources. Meetings where employees are terminated in person may require the presence of any of the following parties: Human Resources, Employee Assistance Program (EAP), Security or other members of management as appropriate.

If the termination occurs at a meeting between the employee and management, the manager or supervisor is required to collect all [Company Name] property and to complete the questionnaire checklist. If the termination occurs via telephone or certified letter, the manager or supervisor is required to inform the employee that he/she must return all [Company Name] property. The manager or supervisor is required to return the employee's identification badge and keys to Security.

Employees who are involuntarily terminated may reference and as appropriate utilize the [Company Name] Alternative Dispute Appeals (ADA) process that is used by their operating unit to appeal the termination decision.

Once an employee has voluntarily given notice of his/her termination or has been involuntarily terminated, the following steps will be taken:

Process for managers/supervisors to follow for both Voluntary and Involuntary Terminations:

5.1.3 Preparation of Electronic Personnel Transaction Form (EPTF)

A) Complete an e-PTF and send directly to Employee Services, with a copy to local Human Resources.

B) Notify Security and Information Technology (IT) via email requesting employee building (badge) access and computer access to be terminated. For employees having access to specialized systems, contact the appropriate departments to terminate access.

5.1.4 Benefit Summary Sheet

The supervisor or manager of a terminating employee will provide the employee with a benefit summary sheet on his/her last day of employment. If the supervisor or manager is unable to provide this in person, she/he may mail it to the employee's last known address.

If an employee has additional questions concerning his/her termination of employment or benefits thereof, she/he may contact the local Human Resources department for further information.

5.2 Payment of Paid Time Off (PTO)

Employees who are PTO eligible and who have one (1) year or more of service are eligible for a payout of any existing PTO bank. The PTO bank will be paid out in either the employees' last check or a separate check following their termination.

5.3 Termination of Benefits

Medical, vision, dental, term life, and accidental death and dismemberment insurance coverage will terminate at the end of the month in which employment is terminated. Short- and long-term disability coverage, unless the employee is currently disabled and collecting either of those benefits, will terminate on the last day of active employment. *See specific benefit plans or contact local Human Resources for more detailed information.*

5.4 Continuation of Benefits

5.4.1 Medical, Vision, Dental Insurances and Health Care Flexible Spending Accounts

Within fourteen (14) days of separation, a terminating employee will receive, by certified mail, information regarding continuation of benefits options pursuant to COBRA. *See also Continuation of Benefits Policy.* Contact Employee Services for more details.

5.4.2 Term Life (Employee and Dependent) and AD&D Insurances

Term life and accidental death and dismemberment insurances can be converted to individual policies if application for conversion is made within thirty-one (31) days of termination and other criteria are met. Contact Employee Services for more details.

5.4.3 Long-Term Disability Insurance

Long-term disability insurance can be converted to individual policies if application for conversion is made within thirty-one (31) days of termination and other criteria are met. Contact Employee Services for more details.

5.4.4 Voluntary Benefits

Employees who elect to participate in the system's voluntary benefit program have thirty (30) days from the date of termination to convert their voluntary benefits (auto/home, group legal or pet insurance) by calling [Phone Number].

5.5 Pension

If the employee is vested in any [Company Name] retirement program, retirement benefit status will be determined and reported within three (3) months following the close of the plan year. These amounts will be calculated by Human Resources or [Company Name]'s actuary and any questions regarding the calculation or discrepancies should be directed to the business unit Human Resources department. Contact Employee Services at [Phone Number] for more details.

5.6 Return of [Company Name] Property

On the terminating employee's last day of work, it is the responsibility of the employee's supervisor/manager to retrieve all [Company Name] property, including but not limited to I.D. badges, company-owned apparel, credit and debit cards, parking access cards, building, office and locker keys, and equipment. Any property not returned must be immediately reported to the Security Department by the employee's supervisor/manager.

See also: *Continuation of Benefits (COBRA) Policy*
Employment Statement Policy
System-Wide Involuntary Terminations HR Policy
Reduction in Work Force Policy
Resignation Policy
Specific benefit policies and plans

Sample A.1.2 Policy: Separation from Employment

Separation from employment occurs for various reasons, including resignation, the end of a seasonal or temporary assignment, reduction in force, job abandonment, or termination for unsatisfactory job performance. This policy provides guidance as to how the various types of separation are handled by Company.

Resignation

Resignation is voluntary termination of employment by the employee.

Company requests that resigning employees provide not less than two weeks' notice of resignation, and that employees provide a written resignation in addition to any verbal resignation. Employees may use Company's resignation form, or draft their own letter of resignation.

Resigning employees who fail to provide two weeks' notice or to submit a written resignation will not be eligible for re-hire. Additionally, Company may inform persons requesting references that the employee failed to comply with this policy upon resignation.

Company reserves the right to place resigning employees on paid leave for the duration of their two-week notice period.

Job Abandonment

An employee who, for two consecutive workdays, fails to report to work when scheduled and fails to notify his or her immediate supervisor (or, if the supervisor cannot be reached, the HR department) of the reason for absence prior to the second scheduled workday will be deemed to have abandoned his or her job as of the first missed workday. Employees who abandon employment will not be eligible for re-hire. Additionally, Company may inform persons requesting references that the employee abandoned his or her job.

Involuntary Termination

Employment is a voluntary relationship. Unfortunately, relationships do not always meet both parties' expectations or needs. In such situations, either the employer or the employee may elect to end the employment relationship. This is what is meant by employment at-will. Unless employees have a formal written employment contract with Company, their employment with Company is at-will.

Company reserves the right to terminate the employment of any at-will employee at any time, for any legal reason, and without any advance notice. Employees have the same right, although resigning employees are subject to the resignation procedures stated above.

Employees who are involuntarily terminated will be presumptively deemed ineligible for re-hire. However, if the separation from employment was due to reasons other than violation of Company policy, Company may make an exception in light of the particular circumstances.

Involuntary termination for reasons other than layoff may impact an employee's right to receive unemployment insurance benefits. Additionally, Company may inform persons requesting references that Company chose to terminate the employee's employment with Company.

Layoff or Reduction in Force

Unfortunately, changes in business conditions sometimes necessitate that employers lay off employees. This is sometimes referred to as a reduction in force. Layoffs may be triggered by changes in the market for the employer's goods or services, lack of venture capital funding, organizational changes, or other changes in economic circumstances. When and if layoffs are necessitated here, Company will comply with all applicable laws concerning non-discrimination, notification, etc.

Generally, separation from employment due to a layoff will not make an employee ineligible for unemployment insurance benefits.

Release from Employment

Some Company employees are hired to work for a specific season (e.g., a growing season, shopping season, or tourist season). Some Company employees are hired to work for the duration of a specific project (e.g., development of new computer software). When a seasonal or project employee's employment comes to an end, Company refers to that as a "release from employment."

Separation from employment due to release from employment may impact an employee's right to receive unemployment insurance benefits. Employees who are released from employment should be careful to notify applicable unemployment insurance agencies of the precise terms of their employment and release from employment.

Scheduled Termination at End of Leave of Absence

Leaves of absence may be either: (a) required by law under certain circumstances, or (b) granted by Company on a case-by-case basis. Subject to applicable laws (for example, Family and Medical Leave laws and Armed Services Leave laws) an employee on leave will be expected to return to work by a specific date, and, if the employee fails to do so, employment will be deemed abandoned, as described above. Employees taking leaves of absence should work closely with Company to ensure that both parties' expectations are met.

Sample A.1.3 Employment Termination Policy

Effective Date: _____

Revision Date: _____

There can be many reasons why employment may terminate. The following are two of the most common reasons for termination of employment:

- Resignation—voluntary employment termination initiated by an employee.
- Discharge—involuntary employment termination initiated by the organization.

We will usually schedule an exit interview if an employee resigns. At the exit interview, we can go over such topics as benefits, benefits conversion rights, repayment of any outstanding debt to Company, or return of Company-owned property. Employees may also make suggestions or complaints and ask questions regarding their employment at the exit interview.

Since employment with Company is voluntary and at will, an employee may terminate his/her employment at any time, with or without cause or advance notice. Likewise, Company may terminate an employee's employment at any time, with or without cause or advance notice.

Sample A.1.4 Terminating Employment Policy

Employment with Company is not for any specified duration and constitutes at-will employment. Either the employee or Company can terminate the employment relationship at any time, with or without notice and with or without cause. The employment-at-will relationship remains in effect regardless of any statements made in policies and practices or any other written or oral communications. An agreement for other than at-will employment may be entered into solely by the President of Company, and must be in writing.

Employment separation with the Company is normally conducted through one of the following actions:

- Resignation: voluntary termination by the employee;
- Dismissal: involuntary termination by the Company for any reason at any time with or without cause; or
- Layoff: termination due to reduction of the work force or elimination of a position or a reduction in labor requirements.

Terminations are to be treated in a professional manner. Terminating employees are entitled to receive earned pay, including accrued vacation pay. Unused sick or personal time will be forfeited upon termination.

Resignation

To ensure smooth operations, Company asks that employees desiring to voluntarily terminate employment provide advance notice when possible.

In the event an employee resigns to join a competitor, if there is any other conflict of interest, or the employee refuses to disclose the identity of the future employer, the Company may require the employee to leave the Company immediately rather than work during the notice period. Such action is not to be construed as a reflection upon the employee's integrity but rather sound business practice. When immediate voluntary termination occurs for the above reasons, the employee will receive pay "in lieu of notice," the maximum being two weeks of pay based upon a 40-hour workweek at the employee's straight-time rate or salary.

Dismissal

An employee may be dismissed at any time, for any reason, with or without cause, at the sole and absolute discretion of Company management. In the case of dismissal, the Company may, at its sole discretion, give some notice of its intent to dismiss an employee, but the Company is not required to give any such notice.

Layoff

When a reduction in force is necessary, or one or more positions are eliminated, the Company will, at its sole discretion, identify the employees to be laid off. The Company may give two weeks' notice to the laid off employee, but it reserves the right to substitute two weeks' severance pay in lieu of notice. Such pay will be based upon a 40-hour workweek at the employee's straight-time rate or comparable salary equivalent.

Return of Company Property

On the final day of employment, the Company must receive all keys and Company property from the employee. An appropriate representative may conduct an exit interview with the employee.

Sample A.2.1 | Resignation from Employment Policy

Resignation

Resignation is voluntary termination of employment initiated by the employee.

Company requests that resigning employees provide a written resignation letter in addition to any verbal resignation. Employees may use Company's resignation form, or draft their own letter of resignation.

In order to assist Company in filling the resigning employee's position, Company requests that employees provide not less than two weeks' notice of resignation. For reasons of security and maintaining effectiveness of other employees, Company reserves the right to place resigning employees on paid leave for the duration of their two-week notice period.

Exit Interview

Resigning employees may be asked to complete an exit questionnaire or participate in an exit interview by a Human Resources representative. The information obtained is invaluable to Company in its ongoing efforts to create a productive and pleasant work atmosphere, attractive compensation and benefit packages, and long-term employees with high morale. Please be candid in responding to exit interview questions.

Resigning employees will also be asked to complete forms authorizing Company to respond to reference requests.

Final Paycheck and Benefits

Resigning employees will receive their final paycheck on the next regular payday following resignation. The final paycheck will include all earned compensation through the last day worked, including pay for accrued but unused personal time off (PTO). Accumulated but unused sick leave is not compensated upon separation from employment. Any questions about final paychecks should be directed to Human Resources and, where appropriate, the employee's supervisor, as soon as possible—preferably before the final day of employment.

Separating employees will also receive written notice from Human Resources as to the status of any employee benefit plans the employee participated in, including any rights to continue health insurance coverage under COBRA (the Consolidated Omnibus Budget Reconciliation Act).

Sample A.2.2 | Resignation Policy

Effective Date: _____

Revision Date: _____

Resignation means that an employee voluntarily terminates his/her employment with Company. Company requests a resignation in writing at least 2 weeks before the date the employee will leave. Although advance notice is not required, this does help the remaining staff in reassigning work as well as providing time to replace the position and train if necessary.

Before an employee leaves, an exit interview will be scheduled. The exit interview helps Company to understand why the employee is resigning. Any changes to benefits can also be handled at this time.

Sample A.2.3 **Resignation Policy and Procedures**

1. Employees are encouraged to provide two weeks' notice of resignation in order to facilitate a smooth transition out of the company and filling the departing employee's position. Employees who fail to provide two weeks' notice may be deemed ineligible for rehire.

2. In addition to any verbal resignation, Company requires that all resignations must be documented by the departing employee in writing, either using Company's "Employee Resignation Form" or a letter drafted by the employee. The written resignation should be delivered either to the employee's supervisor or to Human Resources. Supervisors receiving verbal or written notice of resignation must inform Human Resources immediately. Employees who fail to provide a written record of resignation may be deemed ineligible for rehire.

3. Company will provide resigning employees with a written Confirmation of Resignation that may be used by employees as proof of the circumstances of the termination of employment.

4. An employee may not rescind his or her notice of resignation. Continued employment after the scheduled final day of employment will be at the discretion of Company, and may require application for rehire.

5. Employees contemplating resignation due to dissatisfaction with working conditions are strongly encouraged to discuss their concerns with either Human Resources or one of their supervisors. Company will attempt to resolve any concerns raised.

6. In some resignation situations, Company may elect to place the departing employee on leave without pay for the duration of the notice period. Such a decision should not be perceived as reflecting badly on the employee because it may be based on a number of reasons not known to the departing employee or other employees.

7. Resigning employees in good standing and whose most recent performance evaluation reflects an overall performance rating of "exceeds expectations" will be eligible for rehire for six months from the last day of employment, with benefits tied to seniority reinstated in full. Former employees will be considered for open positions along with all other candidates, and must go through the same application procedures as other applicants.

8. Regardless of the reason for termination of employment, Company provides notice to all employees on a monthly basis of the names of employees who have left the Company. Company also provides notice on a monthly basis of all new hires. Those persons having a need to know (such as certain persons in Human Resources, management, Information Technology, and Security) may be provided with detailed information about the circumstances surrounding a particular employee's separation from employment.

9. Resigning employees will be scheduled for an exit meeting to ensure that all company property is returned, to fill out forms regarding reference requests and final paycheck, to discuss benefits matters, and to provide employees with an opportunity to discuss any questions or concerns they may have regarding their employment or termination of their employment.

10. Final paychecks will be mailed to the resigning employee on the next regular payday following the final day of employment. Accrued but unused vacation time is paid. Accumulated but unused sick leave is not paid.

Sample A.3.1   Involuntary Termination from Employment Policy and Procedures

In order to promote consistent, nondiscriminatory, and effective procedures for the separation from employment, Company has established the following policy and procedures.

1. A termination of an employee's employment initiated by Company is considered an involuntary separation from employment. Such a termination may be the result of a layoff or in response to an employee's violation of Company policy or work performance below Company's expectations.

2. All involuntary terminations of employment must be approved by the employee's manager and coordinated with Human Resources. If a manager is presented with a situation of serious employee misconduct, the manager may immediately suspend the employee with pay pending discussion with Human Resources and other managers as to an appropriate response to the situation.

3. Company attempts to order its affairs in such a way as to avoid laying off employees. However, sometimes changing business conditions necessitate layoffs. An employee who is laid off is eligible for rehire.

4. Similarly, Company hopes, through sound hiring and training practices, to attain a workforce that performs up to Company expectations and adheres to all Company policies. And, when deficiencies are identified, Company prefers to attempt to correct them through counseling. However, some situations may be so severe as to require immediate termination of employment. Even where counseling is deemed an appropriate response to an undesirable situation, the persistent failure of an employee to satisfy required standards after repeated attempts at counseling may warrant the involuntary termination of the employee's employment. An employee whose employment is involuntarily terminated for reasons other than layoff is not eligible for rehire.

5. All warnings, counseling, other disciplinary actions, and terminations are required to be documented using Company's forms available from Human Resources.

6. No employee whose employment has been terminated involuntarily is entitled to severance pay. However, depending on the particular circumstances of any particular situation, Company may elect to offer severance pay to a departing employee upon the employee signing a separation agreement including a standard release of claims.

7. Regardless of the reason for termination of employment, Company provides notice to all employees on a monthly basis of the names of employees who have left the Company. Company also provides notice on a monthly basis of all new hires. Those persons having a need to know (such as certain persons in Human Resources, management, Information Technology, and Security) may be provided with detailed information about the circumstances surrounding a particular employee's separation from employment.

8. Employees whose employment has been terminated involuntarily will be scheduled for an exit meeting to ensure that all company property is returned, to fill out forms regarding reference requests, to discuss benefits matters, and to provide employees with an opportunity to discuss any questions or concerns they may have regarding their employment or termination of their employment.

9. Final paychecks will be given to involuntarily terminated employees on the employee's final day of employment. Accrued but unused vacation time is paid. Accumulated but unused sick leave is not paid.

Sample A.3.2   Procedure for Discharging Employees for Cause

1. An employee cannot be terminated without the consent of the General Manager and the General Manager being present. If the General Manager is unavailable, contact your Area Manager, the Director of Operations, or the Director of Human Resources.

2. Documentation for counseling performance issues and performance warnings is a mandatory procedure using the Company's Employee Warning Notice form.

3. You must have a witness present for all verbal or written warnings and terminations. All must be documented and put in the employee's file.

4. When terminating an employee, be direct and candid about the reasons for terminations. Discuss any odd or unusual termination with Human Resources before terminating an employee.

5. Explain that the termination was a company decision.

6. Know what you're going to say. Have the facts available. Do not waiver or seem equivocal. Do not allow the dialogue to ramble off subject.

7. Evaluate in advance if you are to seek a written release or resignation from the employee. If the employee decides to resign on his or her own accord, have the employee sign a resignation notice. Human Resources will provide this form.

8. All reference checks of former employees should be forwarded to the Director of Human Resources.

9. Strive to make the process of discipline and documentation fair and consistent.

Sample A.4.1 Layoff/Recall Rules

A. Procedures of Notification:

Whenever it becomes necessary, through lack of work or funds, or any other cause, to reduce the number of employees in any given class, the head of the department concerned shall notify the Personnel Director of the number of employees to be laid off from each class within the department. The Personnel Director shall thereafter transmit to the department head whose employees will be affected by the layoff a listing of the names of the employees who shall be laid off within the department in accordance with the provisions of these Rules. Employees in job sharing positions shall be excluded from the layoff process. However, if the position that two job-sharers occupy is eliminated from a department's budget, the incumbent job-sharers shall have seniority rights based on the seniority rating score (SRS) specified in this Rule.

B. Order of Layoff:

The order of layoff will be based upon the SRS of employees in the affected class. The employee in the affected class who has the lowest SRS shall be laid off first. If additional layoffs are necessary, they shall be made in like manner. Provisional employees of the same class within the Company service shall be laid off ahead of certified employees.

1. Except as otherwise provided in this Rule, an employee whose layoff is anticipated, as hereinabove provided, shall:

a. Assume a position (i.e., "bump back") in the next lower class in which the employee has certified Company service, provided that:

1. The employee's SRS in the lower class is higher than that of the lowest employee in that class; and **2.** The employee meets the physical requirements of the class and can perform the required duties;

Or, if possible:

b. Be transferred to a vacant position in a related equivalent or lower classification without examination, provided that such lower classification is equal to or higher than the next lower class in which the employee has certified service and provided further that the employee meets the requirements for performance in that class as determined by the Personnel Director and the appointing authority.

c. An employee who refuses a transfer or reduction, as described in Paragraph B.1.b. above, shall be considered to have forfeited further protection of this Rule and shall be considered to have resigned.

d. An employee who is reduced to a class at a pay range lower than that from which he was promoted, because the employee is physically unable to perform the duties of the higher class, shall be deemed to have had his "bumping rights" satisfied.

e. The provisions of this Rule in no way affect an employee's rights under the provisions of The Probation Rule.

2. The employee with the lowest SRS in the lower class shall have rights as in Rule 16.b.1 above, or be laid off.

3. In all cases, if in the judgment of the Personnel Director and with the approval of the Company President, retention of employees with special skills is required, or if those employees remaining would not have the demonstrated ability and qualifications to perform the required services, layoffs may take place out of the order of SRS.

4. When two or more employees in the same class have an identical SRS, the one with the least amount of certified time in Company employment shall be laid off first. If further determination is necessary, the appointing authority shall make the determination.

C. Determination of Seniority Rating Score:

Seniority shall be computed by adding one point for each full month of service within the classification from which layoffs are under consideration, and 1/30th of a point for each additional calendar day of service in the class. Points may only be added for service in regular full-time positions of the classified service. In addition, the following shall apply:

1. Time service in a part-time, hourly, or temporary position, including all federally-funded positions of a temporary nature, shall not receive seniority points under the provisions of this Rule; provided, however, that a regular Company employee who is placed in a temporary position in connection with an approved leave of absence and whose employee benefits have not been terminated shall have points credited for such period of service and job share employees will have a combination of their regular employment and the pro-rated credits earned in job share, if there has not been a break in service.

2. Creditable time in a class shall date from the earliest certified appointment date to a position in that class, except that time served prior to resignation, retirement, or dismissal will not be credited for seniority in conjunction with this Rule. Time of any officially-approved leave of absence shall be allowed as creditable time in determining the SRS of an employee.

3. Length of creditable time served in a higher class shall be allowed as creditable time in computing SRS in a lower class in which the employee actually served, provided service in the higher class occurred subsequent to service in the lower class.

D.   Recall List:

Recall lists shall be maintained for each class of position in which layoffs have occurred. Such lists shall consist of names of persons laid off from a position in the class and who were granted recall privileges in accordance with the provisions of this Rule. The names of the employees with the highest SRS in the class shall be placed highest on the recall list. When the scores of two or more laid-off employees are equal, they shall all be certified to the appointing authority for selection.

E.   Recall Eligibility:

Any employee who has been certified and appointed and has been laid off, or reduced in lieu of layoff, will have his name placed on the recall list of the classification from which the employee has been laid off or reduced. A laid-off employee, at his request within one year of layoff, may be placed on reinstatement lists of any lower classification in which the employee has served.

1. Any department with a position vacancy in a class with a recall list will give absolute selection preference to the individual with the highest SRS on the recall list for that particular class, who possesses the required knowledge, skills and abilities for the position vacancy. If the highest-scored employee on the list is not selected because of a failure to possess the required knowledge, skills, and abilities for the position, such employee shall retain his position on the recall list.

2. When an employee whose name is on the recall list is reemployed as described above, that employee shall be restored with the SRS held prior to layoff in the class to which he is reemployed, and seniority points shall begin to accrue on the date of reemployment.

3. The name of any employee which is placed on a recall list pursuant to Rule l6.e may be maintained on such list for a period not to exceed three years from the date that the employee was laid off.

4. If an employee on a recall list is offered a position in that class and refuses it, the employee's name shall be removed from the recall list for that class.

Sample A.4.2 Reduction in Force "Bumping" Process Flowchart

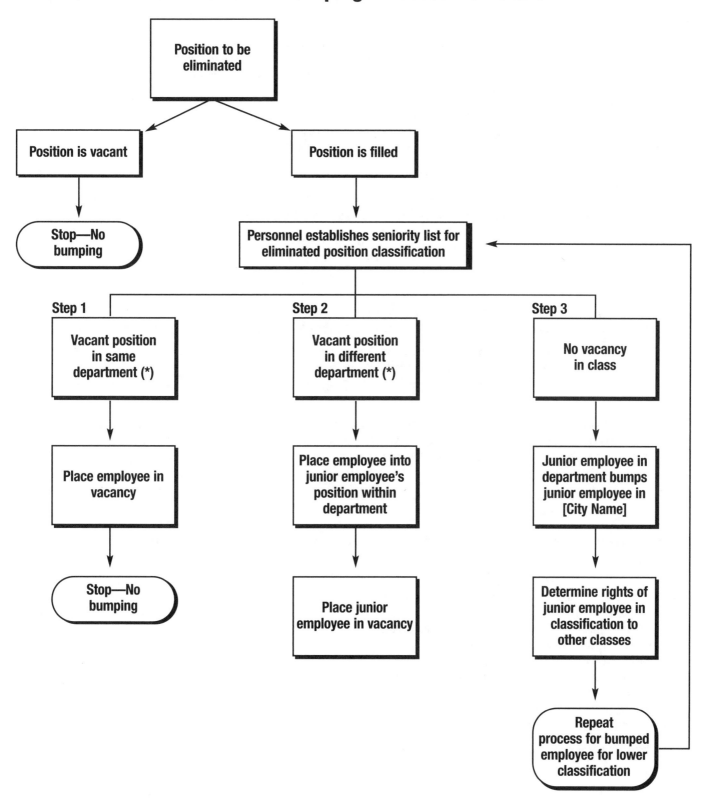

(*) Transfer to lateral vacancy in another class may occur

Sample A.5.1 Exit Interview Process

Introduction

To assist [Company] and its leaders in recruitment and retention efforts, an exit interview process has been established for employees, both full-time and part-time [position name] and [position name], who are terminating their employment with Company. Every full-time and part-time employee leaving Company is to be extended the courtesy of a final interview. This process is designed to elicit information from employees about their experience at Company and their reasons for leaving. The purpose of the exit interview is to:

- Obtain reliable data on problem areas, enabling management to initiate corrective measures and reduce turnover.
- Inform the employee of terms and conditions of employment affected by the separation (e.g., benefits, last paycheck, supplies or equipment to return, etc.).
- Foster good public relations with an employee who separates either voluntarily or involuntarily.

Procedure

To the extent possible, Human Resources will conduct a personal interview with all employees who are leaving the employ of Company. Occasionally, the employee's immediate division head, manager, or supervisor may also want to conduct an exit interview. However, the employee should still meet with Human Resources to discuss benefit and payroll information.

If an employee is unable to meet personally with the Human Resources representative for an exit interview, an interview may be conducted by phone.

Resignation and Retirement

Voluntary employment separation from employment is initiated by the employee's submission of a letter of resignation to his/her supervisor. This letter should be forwarded to Human Resources for the employee's personnel file. Company requires written notification at least two (2) weeks prior to last workday.

The supervisor should notify Human Resources when notice is given to allow adequate time to schedule an exit interview meeting with the departing employee. The interview should take place prior to the employee's last day of work for voluntary separations.

Dismissal

Human Resources should also visit with an employee in the case of an involuntary employment separation to cover benefits, payroll, and other issues as needed. In the event of a release or dismissal, the supervisor should contact Human Resources so a meeting time can be coordinated with the employee. Typically, only items from the "Employee Separation Report" (see below) will be discussed for an involuntary separation.

Forms

Employee Separation Report

The following information will be reviewed with the employee during the exit interview and noted on the "Employee Separation Report" form:

- Reason for termination
- Separation date
- Status of insurance and medical coverage, and COBRA insurance continuation rights, if applicable
- Final pay calculation
- Status of other payroll deductions and Flexible Spending Plan, if applicable
- Payment for earned/unused vacation, if applicable
- Retirement Plan issues, if applicable
- Items to be returned—Keys, equipment, library books, calling or credit cards, ID card
- Outstanding bills to pay (phone) or credits to use
- Address to which correspondence is to be sent (W-2 form)
- Other information relevant to job or individual

The complete Employee Separation Report will be filed in the employee's personnel file once all items have been discussed and processed.

Exit Survey Form

The following information will be discussed during the exit interview and noted on the "Exit Interview" form:

- Reason for leaving
- Evaluation of supervision/administration
- Evaluation of working conditions and work environment
- Evaluation of pay and benefits
- Thoughts and comments on working conditions and the work environment
- Suggestions for improvement at Company

The employee will be informed that the information gathered on this form will be shared with the President and his/her immediate supervisor or manager unless he/she requests it remain confidential. If he/she requests confidentiality, the results will only be tabulated and reported with the summary report (see below).

This form will be kept separate from the employee's personnel file and be filed with other completed exit surveys for periodic or annual summary.

Summary Report

Data from the exit interview will be collected, analyzed, and reported to Company leaders to help them make improvements to Company management practices and policies, improvements in working conditions, and to reduce turnover. The summarized report will be an anonymous compilation of responses from the exit interviews and will be reported on an annual basis. Depending on the number of separations each year, this data could be reported on a more frequent basis if necessary or requested to analyze areas where improvement is needed to address retention issues.

Sample A.5.2 Terminations and Exit Interviews—Policy and Procedures

I. Policy

Upon termination of employment, employees will have an exit interview with the Human Resources Administrator. The exit interview is mandatory. Its intent is to: foster good relations with the departing employee by discussing his/her service to Company; discuss the reasons for the termination; discover the employee's attitudes toward the job, the supervisor, and Company; and listen to any suggestions for policies or procedures that might make an improvement in Company work environment.

II. Procedures

The supervisor, as soon as a termination date is known, should do the following:

A. Fill out Termination Report.

B. Retain a file copy and send the original to the Human Resources Administrator with backup material (letter of resignation, written reprimands, etc.). The Human Resources Administrator will set the time for the interview.

C. The Human Resources Administrator will do the necessary paper/computer work to process the final check.

D. The employee will interview with the Human Resources Administrator on the final day. All company property must be turned in prior to the interview. At the completion of the interview the final pay will be received.

E. In the case of a discharge, the interview may be with the discharged employee's immediate supervisor and the Human Resources Administrator.

F. During the interview, forms and/or information for COBRA extended health coverage and for the Profit Sharing/401(k) Plan will be given to the employee. These may be filled out during the interview or completed and mailed back.

G. The Termination Report and Exit Interview Questionnaire will be routed to the General Manager and Executive Assistant. At this time, recommendations will be made for follow-up of problem areas or for recognition of good supervision and work environment.

H. The Human Resources Administrator will coordinate any follow-up activity to be taken upon direction of the General Manager.

Policy Approved: _____   Date _____
                                General Manager

Sample A.6.1   Reinstatement Rules

A. Reinstatement Lists:

Reinstatement lists shall be maintained for each classification. Such lists shall consist of the names of persons who previously had occupied positions in the class and have been granted reinstatement privileges in accordance with the provisions of these Rules.

B. Application for Reinstatement:

Written application for placement on reinstatement lists must be made within two years of the date of resignation. Application shall be filed with the Personnel Director.

C. Eligibility (for Reinstatement):

1. Any employee who has been certified and appointed to a regular, full-time position with the Company and who resigns from such position may apply for reinstatement within two years after date of resignation.

2. Any employee who qualifies for reinstatement may also, if he requests in writing, have his name placed on the reinstatement list of lower classifications in which he has completed the probationary period.

3. Any employee who resigned from Company service and applies for reinstatement pursuant to Paragraph C.1 above will have his or her name maintained on this list for a period not to exceed two years from the date that the name is posted to this list.

4. Any employee who requests reinstatement within 90 days following the date of resignation may have his or her name placed on the reinstatement list if he or she satisfies the other provisions of this Rule, and if the Personnel Director determines that in the event that the resigned employee has in the intervening period withdrawn or applied for withdrawl of the amounts standing to his credit as his contributions into the Company Retirement System, the employee has returned or agreed to return said funds to his or her retirement account pursuant to the provisions of the Company's Retirement System Rules. Failure of the employee to return such funds in full shall constitute grounds for immediate discharge of such employee at the expiration of six months following return to Company employment.

D. Disqualifications:

Any employee who resigns while under charges brought against him or her by the appointing authority shall not be eligible for reinstatement. Any employee who resigns shall not be eligible for reinstatement if his or her overall performance rating at the time of resignation was not satisfactory.

SECTION B

Other Policies Related to Termination

This section contains a variety of policies relevant to the termination of employment, including policies on discipline, payment for accrued vacation, return of company property, severance pay, employee references, and access to the employee's personnel file. Two forms of employment-at-will disclaimers are also provided.

Sample B.1.1   Employment-at-Will Policy and Disclaimer

Authors' Note: Place your employment-at-will policy and disclaimer in a conspicuous location in your employee handbook, such as the first page of the handbook.

(Important Note to Employees: Read this policy and disclaimer carefully before you sign the "Acknowledgment of Receipt of Employee Handbook and Employment-at-Will Policy" below.)

The policies and procedures in this handbook are designed to serve as guidelines for management action. They are not intended to create any contract or binding agreement between the employer and any employee. All policies and procedures outlined in this handbook are subject to change or modification at the employer's discretion any time that particular circumstances warrant.

This handbook is provided for information purposes only. No provision or portion of the handbook constitutes an implied or expressed contract, guarantee, or assurance of employment or any right to an employment-related benefit or procedure. Employer reserves the right to change, modify, eliminate, or deviate from any policy or procedure in this handbook at any time and to hire, transfer, promote, discipline, terminate, and otherwise manage its employees as it deems appropriate.

Under no circumstances will this handbook or any statement contained herein constitute or create a contract or duration of employment. All employment is entirely "At-will," which means staff members may voluntarily terminate the employment relationship at any time for any reason and the company retains the same right. An agreement for other than "At-will" employment will be entered into solely by the President, and only in writing.

If you have any questions concerning these guidelines, please see the President.

· ·

**Acknowledgment of
Receipt of Employee Handbook and
Employment-at-Will Policy**

I hereby acknowledge that I have received a copy of the Employee Handbook of Company, dated _____, consisting of _____ pages. I further acknowledge that I am employed by Company on an at-will basis, and that either Company or I may terminate my employment at any time, with or without notice, and with or without cause.

_____
Date

_____
Print Name

_____
Signature

Sample B.1.2   Employment-at-Will Disclaimer

This handbook has been prepared to help you become familiar with your new company and to make your integration into our organization a smooth one. It is not a contract or an agreement of employment for a definite period of time; rather, it is a summary of company policies, work rules, and the benefits you enjoy as an employee. From time to time, conditions or circumstances may cause the company to change, amend, or delete some of the policies and benefits contained in this handbook. When such changes are made, the company will notify you of the new or revised policy and its effective date.

All employees are employed at will. This means that either the employee or the company is free to terminate the employment relationship at any time and at either party's discretion. No supervisor or other company representative has the authority to alter this relationship, and you should never interpret such person's remarks as a guarantee of continued employment. The company's policy on separations is set forth more fully later in the handbook.

Reprinted with permission. *Ending the Employment Relationship without Ending Up in Court,* p.43, Francis T. Coleman, Esq.: Alexandria, VA: Society for Human Resource Management, 2001.

Sample B.2.1   Employee Conduct and Work Rules

Effective Date: _____

Revision Date: _____

We expect employees to follow certain work rules and conduct themselves in ways that protect the interests and safety of all employees and Company.

While it is impossible to list every action that is considered unacceptable conduct, the following lists some examples. Employees who break work rules such as these may be subject to disciplinary action, up to and including termination of employment:

- Theft or inappropriate removal or possession of property
- Falsification of timekeeping records
- Working under the influence of alcohol or illegal drugs
- Possession, distribution, sale, transfer, or use of alcohol or illegal drugs in the workplace, while on duty, or while operating employer-owned vehicles or equipment
- Fighting or threatening violence in the workplace
- Disruptive activity in the workplace
- Negligence or improper conduct leading to damage of employer-owned or customer-owned property
- Insubordination or other disrespectful conduct
- Violation of safety or health rules
- Smoking in prohibited areas
- Sexual or other unlawful or unwelcome harassment
- Possession of dangerous or unauthorized materials, such as explosives or firearms, in the workplace
- Excessive absenteeism or any absence without notice
- Unauthorized use of telephones, mail system, or other employer-owned equipment
- Unauthorized disclosure of business "secrets" or confidential information
- Violation of personnel policies
- Unsatisfactory performance or conduct

Since employment with Company is voluntary and at will, employees may terminate their employment at any time, with or without cause or advance notice. Likewise, Company may terminate an employee's employment at any time, with or without cause or advance notice.

Sample B.2.2 Disciplinary Procedures

The Company reserves the right to impose discipline upon employees, up to and including termination of employment, for poor performance or for any infraction of work rules or conduct that is detrimental to the interests of the Company.

If the conduct is not such that immediate termination of employment is deemed warranted, then the Company generally will use a progressive discipline procedure as follows:

1. The employee will be given a verbal warning by his or her supervisor. When giving a verbal warning, the supervisor should advise the employee that he or she is being given an "official verbal warning." The supervisor should promptly document the verbal warning using the Company's "Record of Employee Discipline" form, provide a copy of this form to the employee and file the original form in the employee's personnel file.

2. If there is a second violation, the employee will be given a written warning by his or her supervisor. A written performance improvement plan may also be imposed. The supervisor will document the written warning on the Company's "Record of Employee Discipline" form, and have the employee sign the form to acknowledge receipt. The refusal of the employee to sign the form is deemed insubordination, and is grounds for immediate termination of employment. After the employee has signed the written warning form, a copy should be made for the employee, and the original should be filed in the employee's personnel file.

3. If there is a third violation, the employee will be subject to suspension. A written performance improvement plan may also be imposed upon conclusion of the suspension. As with a written warning, the supervisor will complete the Company's "Record of Employee Discipline" form shown below, and have the employee sign it to acknowledge receipt. The refusal of the employee to sign the form is deemed insubordination, and is grounds for immediate termination of employment. After the employee has signed the form, a copy should be made for the employee, and the original should be filed in the employee's personnel file.

4. A fourth violation will result in termination of employment.

The Company reserves the right to terminate employment at any of the above steps or without imposing discipline progressively.

Record of Employee Discipline

Employee _____

Date and Time of Infraction _____

Nature of Infraction _____

_____

_____

_____

_____

Witnesses To Infraction _____

_____

_____

Discipline Imposed   ❑ Verbal Warning
                       ❑ Written Warning
                       ❑ Suspension   Dates _____
                       ❑ Termination

Performance Improvement Plan _____

_____

_____

_____

_____

_____

Signature of Supervisor _____

Signature of Employee Acknowledging Receipt _____

(Refusal of Employee to sign to acknowledge receipt is deemed insubordination, and is grounds for immediate termination of employment.)

Sample B.3.1 Paid Time Off (PTO) Policy

Authors' Note: The following policy includes a provision on payment of accrued, but unused, time off upon termination.

Effective Date: _____   Revision Date: _____

Definition:

Company provides Paid Time Off (PTO) to all regular full- and part-time employees for paid time away from work that can be used for vacation, personal time, or time off to care for dependents. Employees are encouraged to schedule sufficient time off for relaxation to promote good physical and mental health. PTO must be scheduled in advance and have supervisory approval, except in case of emergency. All time away from work should be deducted from the employee's PTO bank in hourly increments with the exception of fixed company holidays and time off in accordance with company policy for jury duty, military duty or bereavement, and parental leave for school visits.

Eligibility:

All full- and part-time employees are eligible to earn PTO. Part-time employees earn it at a rate equal to 1/2 of full-time employees for months when a minimum of 80 hours up to 119 hours is worked (if 120 hours or more are worked, PTO will accrue at the full-time employee rate).

PTO is earned on a weekly basis and credited to the employee's PTO bank the first day of the week following the week that PTO was earned.

In the first calendar year of employment for new hires and rehires, PTO eligibility is determined by the month in which employment begins. New and rehired employees begin accruing PTO the first day of employment and may use PTO after successfully completing a 90-day introductory period. Any PTO that will be accrued in the calendar year can be taken after that date.

PTO is not earned for months when unpaid leave is taken. PTO is not earned by temporary or contract employees or those whose job descriptions specifically exclude this benefit. PTO is earned on the following schedule:

Years of Service	Non-Exempt Positions
0 – 5 years	80 hrs/yr or 6.66 hours/mo or 1.54 hours/pay period
6 – 10 years	96 hrs/yr or 8 hours/mo or 1.85 hours/pay period
10+ years	120 hrs/yr or 10 hrs/mo or 2.31 hrs/pay period

Years of Service	Exempt Positions
0 – 5 years	96 hrs/yr or 8 hours/mo or 1.85 hrs/pay period
6 – 10 years	136 hrs/yr or 11.33 hrs/mo or 2.62 hrs/pay period
10+ years	176 hrs/yr or 14.66 hrs/mo or 3.38 hrs/pay period

Administration:

PTO should be scheduled as early as possible in advance, according to department policy, and have supervisory approval. PTO can be scheduled if it is already accrued or will be earned in the calendar year. Use of PTO that is not scheduled and approved 24 hours before the scheduled start time and use of PTO in excess of the amount that will be accrued in the calendar year will be considered an unscheduled PTO (UPTO) incidence. PTO taken in excess of the amount that will be earned during the calendar year will be without pay and may be subject to disciplinary action, up to and including termination.

Exempt employees who use time off in addition to the maximum amount to be accrued for the calendar year should take full days only. Pay will be reduced for any full days away from work in excess of accrued PTO and a UPTO incidence will be incurred and the employee may be subject to disciplinary action, up to and including termination.

Any employee who incurs four (4) absences during the 90-day introductory period is subject to disciplinary action, up to and including termination.

Extended Leave:

Absences for family leave should use PTO available for the calendar year and the remainder will be unpaid. At the employee's option, one (1) week of PTO may be reserved for later use.

Payment of Unused Time Off:

Employees who are terminated voluntarily without two-week notice and employees who are terminated involuntarily for any reason are not entitled to payment for accrued, unused PTO.

Employees who resign or retire with two-week notice will be paid for all unused, accrued PTO. Pay will be automatically reduced for any unearned PTO that has been taken. PTO cannot be paid out while employed. It is expected that a terminating employee will work the entire designated period by his/her notice, at the convenience of the company without utilizing PTO.

Absence Reporting:

Exempt absences of an hour or more per day are to be deducted from the employee's PTO bank. Exempt absences will be reported weekly on the Exempt Absence Report and submitted to the department supervisor by Tuesday of the following week, whether or not PTO has been used.

Rehire:

If an employee is rehired after voluntary resignation, prior service will be added to current service to determine the PTO accrual rate in the years following the year of rehire, unless the time away from the company exceeds the length of prior service.

Carry Over:

A maximum of 16 PTO hours can be carried over to the next calendar year. Any PTO in excess of 16 hours will be lost if it is unused in the calendar year unless extenuating business circumstances have prevented the employee from taking scheduled PTO. In these cases, PTO may be carried over and taken in the first half of the next year with approval of the department head.

Sample B.4.1 Severance Benefits—Non-Disciplinary Discharge

In the case of a non-disciplinary dismissal by the Company for reasons over which the employee has no direct control (dissolution of job classification, reorganization change, reduction of force, etc.), benefits shall be earned and paid in accordance with those for an employee serving proper voluntary termination notice on the Company. In addition, these employees will be entitled to severance pay and extension of health insurance benefits as follows, provided the employee has completed his/her training period:

1 week extension of salary and health insurance for each year of service completed to a maximum of 26 weeks. For employees with less than 1 year of service and past their training period, the company will pay 1 week of severance and no continuation of medical benefits.

(Example: If an employee has 11-1/2 years of service, he/she will receive 11 weeks' severance and continuation of medical coverage.)

For part-time employees, 1/2 of a week's severance pay will be paid for each year worked to a maximum of 13 weeks. A minimum of 1 week will be paid for any part-time employee who has completed his/her training period.

Sample B.5.1 **Policy on Providing Employment References**

Scope

This is a mandatory policy governing any release of information about current or former employees. Violation of this policy will be considered cause for discipline up to and including termination.

Persons Who May Provide References

References may be provided only by the human resourses department or management representatives in the chain of command above the person regarding whom a reference is being requested.

To Whom May References Be Provided

References may be provided only to bona fide prospective employers of current or former employees. Precautions should be taken to ensure that reference requests are legitimate, such as a) requiring the prospective employer to send a letter on company letterhead requesting the reference; b) obtaining the business card of the person requesting the reference; or c) telephoning the person back to verify that he or she is indeed employed by the company.

What Information May Be Provided

Only job-related information may be provided to persons requesting information on current or former employees. Under no circumstances should information be provided regarding the employee's race, religion, national origin, health, childrearing, sexual preference, veteran status, workers' compensation history, union involvement, complaints about alleged discrimination, political views, or private affairs.

Employee Consent/Release Form

It is the policy of the company not to disclose any information about employees unless and until the company has received an originally signed Employee Consent/Release Form (ECR Form) signed by the employee for whom the reference is requested. A copy of the required form—available from the human resources department—is reproduced below. The ECR Form must be delivered to the human resources department *before* any information is released.

Record of References Provided

It is the policy of the company that whenever an employment reference is given, the person giving the reference must complete a Record of Employee Reference Form (RER Form) so the company will have documentation of what information was—and was not—provided to the person requesting the reference. A copy of the required form—available from the human resources department—is reproduced below. The RER Form must be delivered to the human resources department within twenty-four hours of any information being released.

Confidentiality

Except as provided by this policy, all employee information is considered confidential.

Policy Guidance

You are encouraged to contact human resources with any questions about this policy.

Reprinted with permission. *Legal, Effective References: How to Give and Get Them*, pp. 37-38, Wendy Bliss: Alexandria, VA: Society for Human Resource Management, 2001.

Sample B.6.1 Policy: Access to Employee's Personnel File

Company employees who:

a) are currently employed by Company;

b) have been laid off by Company with reinstatement rights; or

c) are on Company-approved leave of absence

may obtain access to the official personnel file Company maintains on the employee upon reasonable notice. Upon written request from such employees, the Human Resources Department generally will attempt to make available for inspection and copying an employee's own personnel file within 72 business hours.

The above categories of employees may review their files in the presence of an HR representative, and identify to the HR representative those items the employee desires to have copied. Alternatively, Company reserves the right to copy the entire file and provide the employee with a complete copy without the employee inspecting the file in the presence of an HR representative.

Notwithstanding the foregoing, Company employees entitled to have access to their own employee personnel file may not have access to or inspect reference letters, other reference documentation, or records of internal investigations.

Former employees of Company will be allowed access to, and inspection of, the employee's own personnel file only to the extent required by applicable federal or state law.

Sample B.7.1 Policy: Return of Company Property

On an employee's final day of employment, the employee must arrange to return to the employee's supervisor any and all items of property that Company has issued to employee for purposes of performing the employee's job. This includes without limitation laptop computers and peripherals, personal digital assistant devices, cell phones, equipment, Company-provided uniforms, technical manuals, training materials, business cards (the employee may retain a photocopy of the business card), keys, access cards, and identification badge.

The employee should complete the following form and provide it to his or her supervisor, along with all items of property being returned, prior to the employee departing Company premises.

The employee's supervisor should verify that all listed items have been returned, sign the acknowledgement of receipt, and provide a copy of the signed form to the employee.

....

I, _____ [employee signature], certify that on this date, _____ [insert date], I have returned all items of property that Company has issued to me for purposes of performing my job, consisting of the following items:

1.	11.
2.	12.
3.	13.
4.	14.
5.	15.
6.	16.
7.	17.
8.	18.
9.	19.
10.	20.

I, _____ [supervisor signature], certify that on this date, _____ [insert date],
_____ [insert employee name] has returned to me all items of property listed above.

SECTION C

Employee Acknowledgment and Authorization Forms

This section includes a variety of forms in which an employee either acknowledges receipt of some sort of termination information or authorizes the employer to take certain actions, such as making payroll deductions, providing references, or releasing information to other employees.

Also contained in this section are two samples of a type of form that is not widely used but perhaps should be: the termination certificate. In this form, the departing employee is asked to certify that he or she has complied with company policies and agreements and intends to continue doing so. Termination certificates are particularly useful when protection of proprietary information or protection against unfair competition is important.

Sample C.1.1 Consent to Payroll Deductions

(All employees must sign the following consent to payroll deductions as a condition of employment.)

Notice: Employee's execution of this form constitutes consent to make deductions from employee's wages, commissions, salary, and other forms of monetary compensation. Read this form carefully.

I, the undersigned employee, hereby authorize Company to deduct from any sums due to me, including wages, commissions, salary, and other forms of monetary compensation, the following deductions (to the extent allowed by law):

1. All state, federal, and local taxes required to be withheld by Company;

2. Garnishments;

3. All premiums for group insurance;

4. Payroll advances, overpayments, or loans;

5. Expense advances that have not been timely accounted for;

6. Charges for Company products that I have purchased from Company;

7. The fair market value of any Company property lost or destroyed through my gross negligence;

8. Any funds belonging to Company I have been entrusted by Company to collect or administer on behalf of Company that I have failed to turn over to Company as required;

9. The fair market value of all tools and equipment issued to me that I fail to return in good condition and working order (including laptop computer, personal digital assistant device).

I understand that no deduction may be made for any period that would cause my compensation for such period to be less than the minimum wages required by applicable law. Any deductions not taken for such a period may be carried forward to successive pay periods.

Employee Name _____
(Print)

Employee Signature _____   Date _____

Social Security # _____

Sample C.2.1 Employee's Termination Certificate

This is to certify that my employment with Company is terminated effective _____.

I further certify I do not have in my possession, nor have I failed to return, any Confidential Information as defined in my employment agreement dated _____ with Company (the "Employment Agreement"), including, without limitation:

a) Lists of Property Owners;

b) "Open" Files;

c) "Closed" Files;

d) "Canceled" Files;

e) Telemarketing Leads;

f) Advertising Leads; and

g) All personal and financial information pertaining to clients and potential clients.

I hereby acknowledge the proprietary and confidential nature of such information, and certify that I will keep all such information strictly confidential. I certify, in accordance with the terms of the Employment Agreement, that I will not at any time, either directly or indirectly, divulge, disclose, communicate, or use Confidential Information I obtained or was otherwise exposed to while employed by Company.

This is also to certify that, in accordance with the terms of the Employment Agreement, for a period of twelve (12) months following the termination of my employment on _____ [insert date], I will not, either directly or indirectly, compete (including, without limitation, contacting the customers and potential customers of Company, and soliciting the employees of Company to leave the employment of Company) with Company in the Territory, as defined in the Employment Agreement.

_____   _____

Date   [Print Employee Name]

                                                                                _____

                                                                                [Employee Signature]

Sample C.2.2 Separating Employee's Certification to Employer

The undersigned employee certifies as follows:

Return of company equipment:

_____ Keys/ Security Card   _____ Lap Top

_____ Calling Card   _____ Pager

_____ Cell Phone   _____ Other _____

I have returned all [Company] ("Company") equipment, including any equipment that I purchased for business use and was reimbursed for with Company funds, to the Department Manager or Human Resources. _____ (initial here).

Benefits:

I understand that I will be mailed information on COBRA which will allow me to extend my health insurance benefits beyond my termination date. I realize I must send back the "Health Continuation Election Form" to the Company within 60 days from the date of the letter to continue the insurance. _____ (initial here).

I am aware that my insurance ends on the date of my termination unless I elect to continue coverage through COBRA. I am aware that I am personally liable for charges incurred by the use of my prescription/medical cards after the date of my termination from the Company. _____ (initial here).

I am aware that I may convert my standard life insurance policy to a personal policy if I have five years of employment service. I realize I must fill out and send in the application for this conversion within 31 days from the date of my termination. _____ (initial here).

I have reported all industrial injuries to you and I am not now disabled or in need of treatment because of a job connected injury. _____ (initial here).

I will not disclose to any person or company outside [Company] any confidential information as agreed to in my signed confidentiality agreement. _____ (initial here).

Receipt of Final Paycheck: (Please initial the applicable statement):

I have received my final paycheck including accrued vacation _____ (initial here).

I will pick up my final paycheck in person _____ (initial here).

I would like to receive my final paycheck by mail _____ (initial here).

Your Current Mailing Address:

_____

_____

_____

_____

_____   _____   _____
Employee's Signature   Date   Witnessed by (Signature & Title)

Sample C.3.1 Employee Consent to Disclose Personnel Information and Release of Liability

Without prior written authorization from former employees, the company will provide only the following information in response to reference requests:

1. Hire date and termination date

2. Job titles

3. Earnings

If you desire the company to provide additional information—for example, evaluation of job performance or reason for termination—then you must authorize the company to do so and you must release the company from liability for doing so as provided below.

Employee Consent to Disclose Personnel Information and Release of Liability

I, the undersigned employee, hereby authorize the company to provide written and verbal information about my employment by the company in response to any request for such information by a person representing himself or herself to be checking references in connection with my possible future employment.

In consideration of the company agreeing to provide such additional information, I hereby release the company and its officers, directors, agents, and employees from any and all claims I may have arising out of the furnishing of such information.

In further consideration of the company agreeing to provide such additional information, I hereby release any person representing himself or herself as checking references in connection with my possible future employment from any and all claims I may have arising out of the furnishing of such information.

Employee

_____   _____

(Signature)   Date

_____

(Print Employee Name)

Reprinted with permission. *Legal, Effective References: How to Give and Get Them*, p. 40, Wendy Bliss: Alexandria, VA: Society for Human Resource Management, 2001.

Sample C.3.2 Instructions for Providing References with Reference Summary and Authorization

Upon termination of employment, the employee's supervisor must complete an Employee Exit and Performance Review form for the departing employee. This form consists of three parts: part A, basic information on the employee (position held and dates worked); part B, a rating of the employee on job related characteristics; and part C, comments by the supervisor and rehire status. The employee must initial which part(s) of the review he/she authorizes Company to release to a potential employer or to use as a basis for a job reference. Part A will be released to individuals seeking a reference regardless if the employee initialed for permission. The employee must initial parts B and C before the information will be released, unless Company is provided with further written permission by the former employee. Both the supervisor and employee will sign the form which becomes part of the employee's personnel file.

Only the immediate supervisor and Human Resources are authorized to provide professional references for a past or present employee. Coworkers are not authorized to provide references for other coworkers on behalf of Company.

The following descriptions should be used as a guide when completing Employee Exit and Performance Review form. The characteristics are indicative of what a supervisor would expect for each factor. Employees should be rated on whether they meet the expectation.

Each category should be *evaluated* using the following scale:

- Unsatisfactory (does not meet expectations)
- Needs Improvement (partially or occasionally meets expectations)
- Satisfactory (regularly meets expectations)
- Good (occasionally exceeds expectations)
- Excellent (consistently exceeds expectations)

Quality of Work:

- Follows guidelines for neatness and thoroughness.
- Works accurately.
- Completes work consistently.
- Completes assignments, processes, maintenance, etc., thoroughly.
- Works independently when necessary.

Quantity of Work:

- Produces an acceptable volume of work.
- Completes assignments in time allocated or less.
- Produces acceptable quantity of work (e.g., numbers of tasks, reports, problem solving, etc.).
- Works at a steady pace regardless of environmental pressures.
- Attains conclusive, measurable results.

Knowledge of Job:

- Fully uses job-relevant technical skills.
- Maintains and updates knowledge of equipment and machinery.
- Keeps informed of current technical skills relevant to the job.
- Applies technical, professional knowledge to the job requirement.
- Uses past experience to solve problems.
- Uses necessary company and industry information to perform work.

Reliability and Punctuality:

- Is reliable and responsible in attendance.
- Works flexible hours to meet deadlines.
- Informs supervisor in advance of necessary leave.
- Is prompt in arriving to work and returning from breaks.
- Does not exhibit patterns of absence on Mondays, Fridays, or after holidays.
- Historically has good attendance.

Impact on Coworkers:

- Maintains a positive approach to the job.
- Accepts and follows policies.
- Demonstrates a constructive response to criticism.
- Works with others as a team.
- Displays a positive attitude.

Safety:

- Works safely (consider any accidents, injuries, or near incidents).
- Uses safety equipment provided.
- Reports defects in tools or equipment promptly to supervisor.
- Attends safety meetings as scheduled.

Interpersonal Relationships:

- Responds to suggestions or criticism appropriately—not defensive.
- Keeps supervisor and others advised of problems, ideas, or decisions when needed.
- Provides information, help, or coverage to others when needed.
- Is respectful of coworkers and customers.

Acceptance of Responsibility:

- Performs work as assigned.
- Takes responsibilities for errors.
- Takes personal ownership of job responsibilities.
- Works with minimal supervision.

Initiative:

- Generates workable ideas, concepts, and techniques.
- Is willing to attempt new approaches.
- Attempts to simplify and/or improve procedures, techniques, and processes.
- Is a self-starter.
- Performs preventive maintenance to keep tools in working order.
- Works with minimal supervision.

Appearance of Work Area:

- Maintains a neat work area.
- Keeps company vehicle clean and in good order.
- Respects customer's premises by leaving it at least as clean as before the work was performed (e.g., cleaning up extra wires and drill dust, not tracking in mud).

Reference Summary and Authorization

As part of the exit interview, it is important to provide an overview of the employee's performance. This review becomes the basis for any job reference we will provide for future employment opportunities.

Part A

This information will be released at the request of a potential employer.

Employee's Name: _____

Position: _____

Dates employed: from _____ to _____

Part B

PLEASE RATE THE EMPLOYEE ON THE FOLLOWING CHARACTERISTICS:

	EXCELLENT	GOOD	SATISFACTORY	NEEDS IMPROVEMENT	UNSATISFACTORY
Quality of Work	❑	❑	❑	❑	❑
Quantity of Work	❑	❑	❑	❑	❑
Knowledge of Job	❑	❑	❑	❑	❑
Reliability/Punctuality	❑	❑	❑	❑	❑
Impact on Coworkers	❑	❑	❑	❑	❑
Safety	❑	❑	❑	❑	❑
Interpersonal Relationships	❑	❑	❑	❑	❑
Acceptance of Responsibility	❑	❑	❑	❑	❑
Initiative	❑	❑	❑	❑	❑
Appearance of Work Area	❑	❑	❑	❑	❑

Part C

Would you re-employ?   _____ YES   _____ YES, with reservations   _____ NO

If no, or with reservations, please explain. _____

Why is employee leaving? _____

Additional Comments: _____

TO BE COMPLETED BY EMPLOYEE LEAVING [COMPANY NAME]

_____ I understand that Part A will be released upon the request of a potential employer.

_____ I have read and give permission for Part B to be released for a job reference.

_____ I have read and give permission for Part C to be released for a job reference.
Initials

_____   _____

Employee's Signature   Date

_____   _____

Supervisor's Signature & Title   Date

Sample C.4.1 Departing Employee's Mailing Address

(For W-2 Forms and Other Correspondence)

Name: _____

Address: _____

_____

_____

Telephone: _____

Choose One:

❑ I do not wish to have my address or telephone number released to anyone without my permission.

❑ I give Company my permission to release my address and telephone number to anyone who requests it.

❑ I give Company my permission to release my address and telephone number to its employees.

Choose One:

I would like my Company email account to have an auto-reply:

❑ Yes   ❑ No

_____

Signature

_____

Date

Sample C.5.1 Early Exit Incentive Program Election Form

I understand that I am eligible to retire under the Company on or before June 30, 200_____. I acknowledge receipt of information on the Company's Early Exit Incentive Program.

I elect the following option for payment of $10,000 as part of the Early Exit Incentive Program (check one only):

1. _____ Pay one lump sum payment, paid October 15, 200——- or

2. _____ Pay one lump sum payment, paid January 15, 200——- or

3. _____ Pay multiple lump sum payments paid out over time. Specify dates/amounts:

Date	Amount
October 15, 200____	$_____
October 15, 200____	$_____
October 15, 200____	$_____

or

4. _____ Use money to establish a benefit allowance account to fund payment of _____ insurance premiums until the $10,000 is exhausted, or until July 31, 200____, whichever comes first.

If a participating retiree should die before receiving payment equivalent to the full amount of his/her individual $10,000, any remaining payments will be made to his/her estate.

_____   _____
Printed Name   Signature (must be notarized below)

_____
Date

State of _____

County of _____

Before me, the undersigned authority on this day personally appeared _____, known to me to be the person whose name subscribed to the foregoing instrument, and acknowledged to me that he executed the same for the purposes and consideration therein expressed.

Subscribed and sworn to before me this _____ day of _____, 20____, to certify which witness my hand and seal of office.

_____
Notary Public

My Commission Expires: _____

Sample C.6.1 Receipt of Early Exit Incentive Program Materials Acknowledgement Form

Spring, 200_____

I understand that I am eligible to retire under the Company's Early Exit Incentive Program on or before June 30, 200_____. I acknowledge receipt of information on the Company's Early Exit Incentive Program.

This package includes:

■ A document entitled Company's Early Exit Incentive Program;

■ A list of job titles and ages of persons employed by the Company who are and are not eligible for the Early Exit Incentive Program; and

■ A General Release Agreement and Waiver of Claims.

I understand I must elect to participate in the Program <u>no later than 4:30 PM on June 20, 200_____</u>.

_____   _____

Employee Signature   Date

SECTION D
Checklists

Checklists and timelines are useful to ensure that all termination-related steps are taken in a timely manner. This section contains a variety of checklists, including different timelines for voluntary and involuntary terminations.

Sample D.1.1   Separation Process Checklist

Name of Separating Employee: _____

Separating Employee's SSN: _____

Separating Employee's Supervisor: _____

Task	Dept. Responsible	Completed By	Date Completed
Notify HR of impending separation, reason for separation	Separating E's Supervisor		
Notify Management above separating employee of impending separation	Separating E's Supervisor		
Collect separating employee's final expense report and deliver to Payroll	Separating E's Supervisor		
Notify Payroll of impending separation	HR		
Notify Information Systems of impending separation	HR		
Calculate regular hours worked	Payroll		
Calculate overtime hours worked	Payroll		
Calculate wages owed	Payroll		
Calculate bonuses/commissions owed	Payroll		
Calculate unused vacation owed	Payroll		
Obtain final check(s) from Payroll Dept.	HR		
Collect company property & complete form	HR		
Deliver final paycheck (on final day for involuntary separation; next regular payday for voluntary separation)	HR		
Issue benefits letter to employee	HR		
Obtain letter of resignation from employee	HR		
Obtain signature on reference consent form	HR		
Follow up with Information Systems to confirm termination of passwords, access code	HR		
Delete voice mail	HR		
Conduct exit interview	HR		
Complete Record of Termination form	HR		
Reassign parking space	HR		
Obtain signed separation agreement	HR		
Obtain signed termination certificate	HR		
Place Separation Process Checklist in personnel file	HR		
Archive personnel file	HR		
Other:			

Sample D.1.2 Associate Termination Checklist

To be stapled inside personnel file.

Associate Name _____   Position _____

Date of Hire _____/_____/_____   Date of Termination _____/_____/_____

Last Day Worked _____/_____/_____

Reason for Termination _____

Eligible for rehire? _____ Yes _____ No

Exit interview conducted by _____

Forwarding address/information _____

Payroll

	Due YTD	Taken YTD	Owed YTD
Vacation Days	_____	_____	_____

Date Final Time Sheet received _____/_____/_____   Last Pay Date _____/_____/_____

❑ Severance Agreement Signed
Severance Payment Amount $ _____

❑ File to Payroll

❑ Check Issued and Mailed

❑ Termination date entered into employee file

Benefits

Tuition Reimbursement Program:

401(k) Participant:

Health and Life Insurance:

Balance of advance due to company $ _____

Date Mailed Distribution/
Withdrawal Request packet   _____/_____/_____

Coverage termination date   _____/_____/_____
(generally last day of last pay cycle)

Notification sent to Health Carrier   _____/_____/_____

COBRA notification sent   _____/_____/_____

Life conversion notice sent   _____/_____/_____

I/S Dept.

❑ Computer Log-In disabled

❑ Root passwords changed

❑ Word processing files transferred to _____

❑ Emails/Phones forwarded to _____

❑ Disk with Desktop items/Emails received and added to file

Return of Supplies

Verify before mailing final check.

❏ Check file for inventory control sheet

❏ Office keys/key card

❏ Credit cards

❏ Cellular phone

❏ Pager

❏ Computer equipment/laptop

❏ Library/Text books

❏ Course materials

❏ Other _____

Misc.

❏ Internal Announcement Sent Out

❏ External Job Postings: _____

❏ Copy of resignation letter and/or disciplinary documentation added to file

❏ Other: _____

Notes:

Sample D.1.3 Voluntary Separation Process Timeline

Name of Separating Employee: _____

Separating Employee's SSN: _____

Separating Employee's Supervisor: _____

Day of Notification of Resignation:

Task	Dept. Responsible	Completed By	Date Completed
Notify HR of impending separation, reason for separation	Separating E's Supervisor		
Notify Management above separating employee of impending separation	Separating E's Supervisor		
Notify Payroll of impending separation	HR		
Notify Information Systems of impending separation	HR		
Obtain letter of resignation from employee	HR		
Other:			

Before Resigning Employee's Last Day of Employment:

Task	Dept. Responsible	Completed By	Date Completed
Collect separating employee's final expense report and deliver to Payroll	Separating E's Supervisor		
Calculate regular hours worked	Payroll		
Calculate overtime hours worked	Payroll		
Calculate wages owed	Payroll		
Calculate bonuses/commissions owed	Payroll		
Calculate unused vacation owed	Payroll		
Schedule exit interview	HR		
Other:			

On Resigning Employee's Last Day of Employment:

Task	Dept. Responsible	Completed By	Date Completed
Collect company property and complete form	Separating E's Supervisor		
Obtain final check(s) from Payroll Dept.	HR		
Deliver final paycheck (on final day for involuntary separation; next regular payday for voluntary separation)	HR		
Issue benefits letter	HR		
Obtain signature on reference consent form	HR		
Follow up with Information Systems to confirm termination of passwords, access code	HR		
Delete voice mail	HR		
Conduct exit interview	HR		
Complete Record of Termination form	HR		
Reassign parking space	HR		
Obtain signed termination certificate	HR		
Provide and review copy of previously signed non-disclosure and non-compete agreements	HR		
Other:			

After Resigning Employee's Last Day of Employment:

Task	Dept. Responsible	Completed By	Date Completed
Follow up on employee signing separation agreement, if applicable	HR		
Process any COBRA elections	HR		
Call employee to wish well	HR		
Place Separation Process Checklist in personnel file	HR		
Archive personnel file	HR		
Other:			

Sample D.1.4 Involuntary Separation Process Timeline

Name of Separating Employee: _____

Separating Employee's SSN: _____

Separating Employee's Supervisor: _____

Prior to Notifying Employee of Involuntary Separation:

Task	Dept. Responsible	Completed By	Date Completed
Notify HR of decision to initiate separation process and reasons for the separation	Separating E's Supervisor		
Notify Management above separating employee of decision to initiate separation and reasons for the separation	Separating E's Supervisor		
Review facts, documentation, company policy to determine that termination is appropriate	HR and Separating E's Supervisor		
Contact legal counsel as necessary about any potential legal issues	HR		
Notify Payroll of impending separation	HR		
Notify Information Systems of impending separation	HR		
Prepare necessary disciplinary and termination documentation for employee's personnel file	Separating E's Supervisor and HR		
If appropriate, prepare separation agreement and have agreement reviewed by legal counsel	HR		
Prepare termination meeting script or outline	HR and Separating E's Supervisor		
Determine and arrange termination meeting logistics	HR and Separating E's Supervisor		
If necessary, arrange for appropriate workplace security measures during and after the termination meeting	HR		
Other:			

Day Employee is Notified of Involuntary Separation:

Task	Dept. Responsible	Completed By	Date Completed
Collect separating employee's final expense report and deliver to Payroll	Separating E's Supervisor		
Calculate regular hours worked	Payroll		
Calculate overtime hours worked	Payroll		
Calculate wages owed	Payroll		
Calculate bonuses/commissions owed	Payroll		
Calculate unused vacation owed	Payroll		

Obtain final check(s) from Payroll Dept.	HR		
Collect company property and complete form	HR		
Deliver final paycheck	HR		
Issue benefits letter	HR		
Review any confidentiality or non-disclosure agreements executed by the employee with him or her and provide employee with copy(ies)	HR		
Obtain signature on reference consent form	HR		
Follow up with Information Systems to confirm termination of passwords, access code	HR		
Delete voice mail	IT		
Conduct exit interview	HR		
If applicable, deliver to, and review with, employee separation agreement	HR		
Complete Record of Termination form	HR		
Other:			

After Employee's Last Day of Employment:

Task	Dept. Responsible	Completed By	Date Completed
If applicable, follow up on employee signing separation agreement	HR		
Process any COBRA elections	HR		
Place Separation Process Checklist in personnel file	HR		
Archive personnel file	HR		
Other:			

SECTION E

Termination Process Worksheets and Records

The samples in this section can be used to document various activities related to termination.

Every employer should use a form to record the conditions of separation: the date of the separation; whether it was voluntary or involuntary; and, if it was involuntary, whether it was a discharge or layoff. This section contains a variety of such forms.

In the period leading up to termination for poor performance or a violation of company policy, the employer should document any warnings, counseling, or progressive discipline the employee has received. Several such forms are collected here.

If the termination is the result of a RIF, it is important for the employer to assess whether the RIF has a disparate impact on any protected class of employees. The adverse impact worksheet provided in this section is a useful tool. Additionally, successful implementation of a RIF requires performing certain tasks at certain times, including, in some instances, issuing notices under the Worker Adjustment and Retraining Notification (WARN) Act. The RIF timeline included here will help employers stay on track.

In the post-termination period (and sometimes before termination if the termination is part of a RIF), employers will be asked to provide references. This section includes a form to record when an employer has provided a reference about a current or former employee.

Sample E.1.1   Employee Counseling Form

Employee Name _____   Property Name _____

Employee Position _____   Supervisor Name _____

Level of Counseling
❏ Verbal   ❏ Written   ❏ Suspension

Details of Behavior

Date of Most Recent Occurrence   **Time of Occurrence**   **Location of Most Recent Occurrence**

____/____/____   ____:____ ❏ AM ❏ PM   _____

Type(s) of Behavior Observed

Absenteeism/Tardiness

❏ Absent or tardy to work without a valid reason

❏ Absent from assigned area during working hours

❏ Excessive or chronic absenteeism or tardiness

❏ Failure to follow proper reporting procedures

Performance

❏ Quality of work performed is below expectations

❏ Quantity of work performed is below expectations

❏ Duties were not performed as instructed

Other

❏

[Company Name] Policy Violation

❏ Violation of Workplace Harassment Policy

❏ Violation of Electronic Communications Policy

❏ Violation of Safety Policy

Attitude

❏ Insubordination

❏ Undermining supervisor authority

❏ Poor teamwork

Frequency of This Behavior

Is this the first occurrence of this behavior?   ❏ Yes   ❏ No (Please describe below)

Date of Previous Occurrence	**Brief Description of Prior Behavior**	**When the employee was reevaluated, did he/she meet your expectations?**	
		Yes	No
____/____/____	_____	❏	❏
____/____/____	_____	❏	❏
____/____/____	_____	❏	❏
____/____/____	_____	❏	❏

Narrative of Most Recent Occurrence

_____

_____

_____

_____

_____

_____

Correct Behavior/Expectations

1. _____
2. _____
3. _____
4. _____

Employee's adherence to these expectations will be reevaluated on: _____/_____/_____

Supervisor's Signature _____   **Date** _____/_____/_____

Employee's Response (To be used for written counseling and suspension)

(Please check only one)

❏ I agree with my supervisor's comments and agree to comply with his/her expectations listed above

❏ I disagree with my supervisor's comments but agree to comply with his/her expectations listed above*

❏ I disagree with my supervisor's comments and will not comply with his/her expectations listed above*

*You must attach an explanation as to why you disagree and either give it to your supervisor or send it to the [Company Name] Corporate Office, ATTN HR: [Company Address]

My signature below indicates that I have been given a copy of this form and does not necessarily represent agreement with my supervisor's comments above. I am aware that my failure to comply with my supervisor's expectations (as defined above) will lead to further disciplinary action up to and including termination.

Employee Signature: _____   **Date** _____/_____/_____

Initial Review: [HR Manager] _____/_____/_____   Cc: [HR Assistant][Company Name]

Copy Distribution: Employee Personnel File

Final Review: [HR Manager] _____

Sample E.1.2 Employee Counseling Form

Name: _____   Date: _____

Reason for Action:

❑ **Excessive Absence or Lateness**

❑ **Violation of Safety Rules or Company Policy**

❑ **Unsatisfactory Work Performance**

❑ **Insubordination**—refusal to do assigned work

❑ **Other:** _____

Action Taken:

❑ **Verbal Warning,** employee may or may not be asked to sign to acknowledge receipt of counseling and be given a copy; it will **not** be placed in employee's file, but should be filed in supervisor's files.

❑ **Written Warning,** employee should sign to acknowledge receipt and be given a copy. A copy will be placed in the employee's file.

❑ **Suspension,** employee should sign to acknowledge receipt and be given a copy. A copy should be placed in the employee's file.

❑ **Termination,** formal action taken, employee should sign to acknowledge receipt and be given a copy. A copy should be placed in the employee's file.

Note: Disciplinary actions should be kept confidential with need-to-know access.

Description of Incident: (Be as specific as possible, including names and dates.)

_____

_____

_____

Important Note: Additional violations will result in further disciplinary action up to and possibly including termination.

Corrective Action To Be Taken:

What steps will employee take to correct inappropriate work behavior?

_____

_____

_____

Employee's Signature _____   Date: _____

(Indicates employee's receipt of corrective counseling; does not necessarily indicate employee's agreement.)

Supervisor Signature _____   Date: _____

Sample E.1.3 Record of Employee Discipline

Employee _____

Date and Time of Infraction _____

Nature of Infraction _____

_____

_____

_____

_____

_____

_____

Witnesses to Infraction _____

_____

_____

Discipline Imposed

    ❑ Verbal Warning

    ❑ Written Warning

    ❑ Suspension   Dates _____

    ❑ Termination

Performance Improvement Plan _____

_____

_____

_____

_____

_____

_____

_____

Signature of Supervisor _____

Signature of Employee Acknowledging Receipt _____

(Refusal of Employee to sign to acknowledge receipt is deemed insubordination, and is grounds for immediate termination of employment.)

Sample E.1.4 Documented Warning

Employee's Name _____

Department _____

Date of Documented Warning _____

Purpose of the Documented Warning:

❑ Absence

❑ Dishonesty

❑ Failure to follow instructions

❑ Falsifying records

❑ Further disciplinary action

❑ Insubordination

❑ Leaving work without approval

❑ Performance

❑ Tardiness

❑ Violation of policy

❑ Working overtime without approval

❑ Other _____

Describe the purpose of the Documented Warning:

_____

Prior discussion or warnings on this subject, whether verbal or written: xx **Not Applicable**

_____

Describe the impact that the behavior is having on any of the following: individual, team members/department, customer, and organization:

_____

Summary of corrective action to be taken:

_____

Consequences if failure to correct behavior:

_____

Follow-up Date(s):

_____

Employee's Comments _____

_____

_____

_____

_____

_____

Notice to Employee:

It is expected that the behavior noted above will be corrected as stated and/or that you will immediately perform all aspects of your responsibilities at a satisfactory level. Further disciplinary action, up to and including termination, will result if you fail to correct the noted behavior or perform your duties in a satisfactory manner whether or not those behaviors and/or responsibilities are noted above.

If you wish to appeal the corrective action noted above, you may do so under the grievance procedure available to all employees.

Employee Acknowledgement:

My supervisor has discussed the above with me. My signature is intended only to acknowledge receipt of this notice; it does not imply agreement or disagreement with the notice itself. If I refuse to sign, someone in a supervisory position within the organization will be asked to initial the form indicating that I received a copy of this form.

Employee's Signature _____   Date Signed _____

Supervisor's Signature _____   Date Signed _____

Department Head's Signature _____   Date Signed _____

Human Resources' Signature _____   Date Signed _____

Distribution:
1. Original to personnel file
2. Copy to employee
3. Copy to supervisor

Sample E.2.1 Employee Separation Form

Employee Name _____   Department Name _____

Employee Position _____   Supervisor Name _____

Last Day Worked _____/_____/_____   Date of Separation _____/_____/_____

Reason for Separation

❑ Voluntary Quit: (Select from list)

    ❑ Accepted Other Work*
    ❑ Job Abandonment
    ❑ No Reason Given
    ❑ Relocation*
    ❑ Returned to School*
    ❑ Other*

    *Additional Details: _____

(If the employee voluntarily quit, please skip to the narrative section of this form.)

❑ Involuntary Discharge: (Select from List)

    ❑ Assault or Threatened Assault
    ❑ Breach of Confidential Information
    ❑ Conduct Endangering an Employee or Resident
    ❑ Falsification of Company Document(s)
    ❑ Gross Neglect on Performing Assigned Duties
    ❑ Insubordination
    ❑ Position Eliminated
    ❑ Sleeping on the Job
    ❑ Theft or Destruction of Company or Tenant Property
    ❑ Unsatisfactory Attendance
    ❑ Unsatisfactory Performance
    ❑ Violation of Drugfree Workplace Policy
    ❑ Violation of Workplace Harassment Policy
    ❑ Other*

    *If other, please describe: _____

Additional Information on an Involuntary Discharge

Frequency of Behavior that Led to Discharge

Was the employee previously counseled for the behavior that led to his/her discharge?

❑ Yes (Please describe below)

❑ No

Date of Previous Occurrence	Brief Description of Prior Behavior Related to This Discharge	Level of Counseling		
		Verbal	Written	Suspension
_____/_____/_____		❑	❑	❑
_____/_____/_____		❑	❑	❑
_____/_____/_____		❑	❑	❑
_____/_____/_____		❑	❑	❑

Narrative of Circumstances Leading to Employment Separation

Supervisor Signature: _____ Date: _____/_____/_____

Initial Review: [HR Director] _____/_____/_____

Cc: [HR Assistant] and [Company Name] Property File

Copy Distribution: Central Personnel File On-site Employee File

Final Review: [HR Director]

Date Payroll Notified: _____/_____/_____

Sample E.2.2 **Employee Separation Report**

Name _____   Employee ID# _____

Position _____   Dept/Div _____

Hire Date _____   Last Day Worked _____   Separation Date _____

Status: ❑ Full-time   ❑ 3/4 Time   ❑ Part-time
         ❑ Exempt   ❑ Hourly

Separation Meeting Date _____   By: _____

Details of Separation

Type of Separation:

❑ Resignation   ❑ Retirement   ❑ End of Appointment
❑ Dismissal   ❑ No return from leave of absence   ❑ Other _____

Comments _____

Final Pay

Regular pay for period _____   Amount $ _____

Accumulated Vacation Pay* _____ hours @ $ _____   Amount $ _____

Accumulated Personal Time* _____ hours @ $ _____   Amount $ _____

Health Deduction   Amount $ _____

Annuity Deduction   Amount $ _____

Dental Deduction   Amount $ _____

Disability Ins Deduction   Amount $ _____

Gifts Deduction   Amount $ _____

Other Deductions _____   Amount $ _____

Date Payable _____   Total Payable Amount $ _____

❑ Direct Deposit**

❑ Mail check to: _____

* Turn in final slips for vacation & personal time so remaining accumulation can be calculated & paid.
**If closing bank account, ensure forwarding address is indicated.

Separation Details Covered During Meeting

❑ COBRA Rights   Medical Insurance Terminates on: _____

❑ HIPPA information

❑ Personal Phone Bills   *paid* _____

❑ Keys   *returned* _____ (Office, entrances, files, desk, others)

❑ Library Books   *returned* _____   ❑ Calling Card   *returned* _____

❑ ID Card   *returned* _____   ❑ Credit Card   *returned* _____

❑ Company equipment _____

❑ Clean out office/work space by _____

Administrative Processing

❑ COBRA notification requested

❑ Benefit providers notified:

_____ Health

_____ Life

_____ STD/LTD

_____ Dental

❑ Address Updated

_____ HR/Payroll System

_____ President's Office

Forwarding Address: _____

_____

❑ Final Pay Processed

❑ Employee file archived *(pull I-9, move file to terminations by year)*

Processed by: _____   Date: _____

Sample E.2.3 | Employee Separation Record

Employee Data

Last Name _____ First _____ Middle _____

Dept. _____ Job Title _____ EE # _____

❑ **Voluntary Separation**
(Attach Voluntary Quit Form)

❑ Another Job
❑ Relocation/School
❑ No Call/No Show
❑ Never Started
❑ Dissatisfaction w/job or Supervisor
❑ Dissatisfaction w/pay-benefits
❑ Domestic/Personal/Medical
❑ Temporary Employee
❑ Other _____
_____

❑ **Involuntary Separation**
(Attach Disciplinary Documentation if applicable)

❑ Misconduct
❑ Tardiness/Absenteeism
❑ Poor Performance
❑ Failed Drug Screen
❑ Lack of work
❑ Seasonal
❑ Other _____
_____

❑ **Leave of Absence**
(Attach Personal Leave request form)

❑ Educational
❑ Family Medical Leave Act
❑ Personal
❑ Military
❑ Pregnancy-related disability leave
Begin Leave _____
Return from leave _____
Notes _____
_____

Separation Date: _____/_____/_____   **Last Day Worked:** _____/_____/_____

Eligible for re-employment   ❑ Yes ❑ **No, please explain** _____
_____

Co. Items Returned: ❑ Uniform Items   ❑ Radio   ❑ Keys   ❑ Pager   ❑ Other _____

Additional Comments _____
_____

Final Paycheck:

❑ Please hold check for Employee pick-up

❑ I have received my final paycheck _____   Date _____

❑ Please mail my final check to the following address:

_____

Address   City   State   Zip

Employee (Optional) _____		**Date** _____
Manager _____		**Date** _____
Payroll _____		**Date** _____
Human Resources _____		**Date** _____

HR Use Only:

Election of COBRA:

COBRA Notice provided _____   Election: ❑ Yes ❑ No

Start date of Coverage _____   Type of COBRA Elected _____

❑ Medical   ❑ Life   ❑ Vacation   ❑ 401(K)   ❑ Dental   ❑ STD   ❑ LTD   ❑ AD&D

Sample E.3.1 HR-Accounting Final Pay Checklist

EE# _____   Dept _____   Name _____

Pay:

❑ Per hour pay _____

❑ Time sheet attached

❑ Total Reg. Hours _____   2nd Dept. _____

❑ Total Overtime Hours _____   2nd Dept. _____

❑ Accrued Vacation Hours _____

❑ Product Sales _____

❑ Product Commission _____   Commission Rate _____

❑ Service Sales/Commissions/Tips for piece workers   _____

Total Pay Hours _____

Comments: _____

_____

_____

Deductions:

❑ Medical _____ $ _____

❑ Dental _____ $ _____

❑ Vision _____ $ _____

❑ Total Premium $ _____

   Minus $ _____

   Total: $ _____ X 12 ÷ 26 = _____

Total Deductions to be taken out of pay $ _____

Comments: _____

Need By _____   Return Check to _____

_____   Date_____

HR Signature

_____   Date _____   Check#_____   Net $_____

Accounting Signature

Sample E.4.1 Benefits Upon Termination Worksheet

Last Day Worked:

Health Insurance:

Medical   Expires: _____

Dental   Expires: _____

Prescription   Expires: _____

Vision   Expires: _____

Life   Expires: _____

Disability   Expires: _____

Vacation Accrual:

Paid on last paycheck

Sick Time Accrual:

Not Paid

COBRA:

Paperwork will be sent by third party administrator within two weeks of termination

HIPAA:

Certificate will be sent by _____

Sample E.4.2   COBRA Payment Form

Name: _____   Social Security #: _____

Last Workday: _____   Termination Effective Date: _____

Notification To Cancel Benefits

Item	Done	As of	N/A	Comments
Medical				
Dental				
401(k)				
Life				
Voluntary Life				
Disability				
COBRA: Qualifying Event				❏ 18 months ❏ 29 months ❏ 36 months
Employee Discount				

COBRA – Activated

Election Expires: _____

Date Elected: _____

Type Elected: _____   ❏ Medical ❏ Dental ❏ Vision ❏ Other: (specify)_____

Who Elected: _____

Monthly Charge: _____

M	Month	Date Due	Date Paid	Amount Due	Amount Paid	Check #	Balance
1							
2							
3							
4							
5							
6							
7							
8							
9							
10							
11							
12							
13							
14							
15							
16							
17							
18							
19-36, if applicable							

Sample E.5.1 Position Reduction and Severance Process Timeline

Date	Action
November 15, 200___	Department budget cuts due to Budget and Research
	Review budget cuts
December 11, 200___	Severance proposal to Board of Directors
January 7, 200___	Distribute position reduction resource manual to department/function heads
January 9, 200___	Personnel Officers/liaisons meeting—Distribute resource manual
January 16, 200___	Proposed budget sent to Board of Directors Meet with Unions—Update
Mid – late February 200___	Board of Directors approves budget and position cuts
Mid – late February 200___	Begin position reduction process
Late February 200___	Training for supervisors who are directly affected
Late February 200___	If appropriate, send specific employees severance offers
March 200___	Evaluate success of first round of severance offers
March 200___	Continue position reduction, seniority determinations, etc., if necessary
March 200___	Department communication with affected employees
March 200___	If necessary, establish list of employees to be laid off, refer to employment services for outplacement, and generate severance package data
March 200___	Training for affected employees
April 200___	Position reductions and staff changes effective

Sample E.5.2   RIF Adverse-Impact Worksheet

Authors' Comments

Purpose:

The purpose of this worksheet is to facilitate examination of a proposed reduction in force for possible adverse-impact upon protected classes of employees. Significant disparities revealed by the examination may warrant closer scrutiny of selection criteria and processes in order to eliminate disparities that may be considered evidence of adverse-impact (or even intentional) discrimination.

Methodology:

The worksheet presents two types of analyses, one specifically for age, and one suitable for all protected classes (e.g., race, sex, national origin, age, and religion). More sophisticated statistical analyses can be conducted with the assistance of a qualified expert.

Confidentiality:

The information compiled in this worksheet should not be shown to managers making RIF selection decisions, as doing so could permit an employee to argue that protected status was taken into account in selecting persons for the RIF. Rather, this information should be utilized by Human Resources, preferably in concert with legal counsel (so as to attain status as attorney-client privileged), in order to ensure compliance with applicable anti-discrimination laws in terms of adverse impact upon protected classes of employees.

Significance:

Note that if the size of the groups being measured is too small, disparities may be statistically insignificant. However, even though a population is too small to allow the use of mathematical statistical tools, disparities revealed by this kind of testing may nevertheless be admissible and probative in the event of litigation. If completion of this worksheet reveals to Human Resources what appears to be a significant disparity, then the numbers may well strike a jury the same way.

Average/Median Age Test

Relevant Workgroup Being Tested: _____

[State the workgroup(s) in which reduction in force will be carried out, for example exempt employees, non-exempt employees, technical employees, hourly employees, administrative employees, or functional departments or workgroups used by employer. Where a RIF covers multiple workgroups, or workgroups within workgroups, employers may want to perform multiple tests.]

Number of Persons In Entire Workforce	Number of Persons Within Workgroup Being Tested	Number of Persons Subject to RIF

Number of Persons Age 40 and Older Within Entire Workforce	Number of Persons Age 40 and Older Within Workgroup Being Tested	Number of Persons Age 40 and Older Subject to RIF

	Average (Mean) Age of Entire Workforce	Average (Mean) Age of Relevant Workgroup	Median Age of Entire Workforce	Median Age of Relevant Workgroup
Before RIF				
After RIF				
Total Increase <Decrease>				
Percentage Increase <Decrease>				

Proportionality Test

Relevant Workgroup Being Tested: _____

[State the workgroup(s) in which reduction in force will be carried out, for example exempt employees, non-exempt employees, technical employees, hourly employees, administrative employees, or functional departments or workgroups used by employer. Where a RIF covers multiple workgroups, or workgroups within workgroups, employers may want to perform multiple tests.]

Protected Class Being Tested: _____

[State the particular protected class being tested, for example, persons age 40 and older, African-Americans, Hispanics, or females.]

Number of Persons in Entire Workforce	Number of Persons Within Workgroup Being Tested	Number of Persons Subject to RIF

Number of Persons in Protected Class Being Tested Within Entire Workforce	Number of Persons in Protected Class Being Tested Within Workgroup Being Tested	Number of Persons in Protected Class Subject to RIF

Percentage of Persons in Protected Class Being Tested With Entire Workforce	Percentage of Persons in Protected Class Being Tested Within Workgroup Being Tested	Percentage of Persons in Protected Class Subject to RIF

Sample E.6.1   Record of Employee Reference Form

This form must be completely filled out and delivered to the Human Resources Department within 24 hours of providing any references on current or former employees.

No information about current or former employees may be disclosed unless and until an originally signed Employee Consent/Release Form has been filed with the human resources department.

See Policy No. XX, or consult human resources, for any questions regarding the use of this form.

Record of Employment Reference for: _____
(Name of Employee)

Date Information Provided: _____

Person Requesting Information: _____

Name: _____

Title: _____

Company: _____

Address: _____

_____

Telephone: _____

Job for Which Employee Is Being Considered: _____

Form Completed By: _____

Title: _____

Signature: _____

State below any job-related reference information provided or not provided.

Provided	Not Provided	
❏	❏	Hire/termination date: _____
❏	❏	Titles: _____
❏	❏	Compensation: _____
❏	❏	Reason for leaving: _____
❏	❏	Evaluation of performance _____
		_____
❏	❏	Other: _____

Reprinted with permission, *Legal Effective References: How to Give and Get Them,* p. 47, Wendy Bliss: Alexandria, VA: Society for Human Resource Management, 2001.

SECTION F

Termination Notices and Letters

Even if an involuntarily terminated employee is notified verbally, the employer should provide written notice to the employee to eliminate any question as to what the employee was told, and when. This section contains forms that can be used to provide such notice in a variety of circumstances, including job abandonment, discharge, layoff, and failure to provide required I-9 information. The section also contains forms for documenting employee resignations.

Employers should consider formalizing the process by which other employees learn that an employee is departing; otherwise, the information will be disseminated through ad hoc disclosures by managers and through the rumor mill. A sample employee departure announcement is provided.

Finally, departing employees or their potential new employers may sometimes request a service letter documenting basic information about the employee's employment. In some states, service letters are required by law; employers in those states may need to modify the forms in this section to make sure all the legally required information is being provided.

Sample F.1.1   Employee Resignation Form and Company Confirmation of Resignation Form

Employee Resignation

I, _____ [print name] hereby give Company notice of my voluntary resignation of employment with Company effective _____ [insert employee's intended last day of employment]. The reason(s) for my resignation are as follows: [Optional. Attach additional sheets if necessary.]

_____

_____

_____

_____

_____

_____

_____

_____   _____
Employee Signature   Date

* *

Company Confirmation of Resignation

I, the undersigned duly authorized representative of Company, hereby confirm the voluntary resignation of the above-named employee.

_____   _____
Signature   Date

_____   _____
Printed Name

_____
Title

Sample F.1.2   Voluntary Resignation Notice

Name: _____   Dept: _____   Job Title: _____

I voluntarily resign my position as: _____
                                        Position

Effective: _____   _____   _____
              Month   Day   Year

My reasons for leaving are:

_____

_____

_____

Forwarding Address: _____   _____   _____   _____   _____
                          Address   City   State   Zip   Phone

_____   _____   _____   _____
Employee Signature   Date   Manager Signature   Date

Sample F.2.1   Confirmation of Employment Separation

To: [Employee Name]   **Date:** _____

Date of Hire: [Hire Date]

Status: [Status]

Location: [Location]

We hereby confirm that your employment with [Company Name] will be terminated effective [Termination Date] for the following reason:

❏ Resignation

❏ Retirement   ❏ Involuntary discharge

❏ Transfer   ❏ Involuntary discharge for cause

❏ Mutual Agreement   ❏ Temporary Layoff

❏ Other: _____   ❏ Permanent Layoff

As of your termination date you had accrued vacation as detailed below. Unused vacation hours will be included with your last payroll dated [Last Payroll Date].

200__ Vacation Accrual   [Vacation Accrual Rate] Hours

Earned vacation through [Term. Date]   [Vacation Earned 200__] Hours

200__ Vacation Used   [Vacation Used 200__] Hours

Balance due employee _____   **[Vacation Balance] Hours** _____

It is agreed that all marketing and promotional materials used and/or developed by the employee or by [Company Name] will remain the exclusive property of [Company Name] and that confidentiality stipulations, as agreed in the employment offer, will be adhered to.

Company Name

_____   _____

[Name]   [Employee Name]
Human Resource Manager

Sample F.3.1   Job Abandonment Letter

[Date]

Re: Termination of Employment Effective [Termination Date]

[First Name] [Last Name]

[Address]

[City], [State] [Zip]

Dear [First Name],

You failed to report for duty, and failed to call your supervisor, on [No Show Date], [No Show Date], and [No Show Date], as required by the Company Employee Handbook. You did not return phone calls from your supervisor on [Call Date] and [Call Date] concerning your failure to report for duty.

Per our Employee Handbook, "if you fail to report for work without any notification to your supervisor, you may be deemed to have abandoned your employment." Therefore, [Company] is terminating your employment effective [Termination Date].

Please find enclosed the following:
■ Final paycheck
■ COBRA Letter and Election Forms

If you have any questions, please feel free to contact me at [Phone Number]. [Employee], I wish you the very best.

Sincerely,

[Human Resources Manager]

Sample F.3.2   Job Abandonment Letter (for incarceration)

[Date]

Re: Termination Effective [Termination Date]

[First Name] [Last Name]

[Address]

[City], [State] [Zip]

Dear [First Name],

You did not report to work on [Missed Work Date], [Missed Work Date], and [Missed Work Date] because you were incarcerated. You have no paid time off remaining. Thus, [Company] is terminating your employment effective [Termination Date].

Please find enclosed the following:
■ Final paycheck
■ COBRA Letter and Election Forms

If you have any questions, please feel free to contact me at [Phone Number]. [Employee], I wish you the very best.

Sincerely,

[Human Resources Contact]

[Title]

Sample F.4.1   Termination Letter (leave of absence)

[Date]

Re: Termination of Employment Effective [Termination Date]

[First Name] [Last Name]

[Address]

[City], [State] [Zip]

Dear [First Name],

On [Notification Date], I received a phone call from you notifying me that your treating physician will not release you to return to work on [Original Return Date].

As you know, you do not have enough sick leave or unused vacation to cover any additional time off. Based on your length of service with the Company, you are not eligible for leave under the Family Medical Leave Act nor the State of _____ counterpart. Under the Company's leave policies, the only type of leave for which you are eligible to apply is unpaid personal leave. This type of leave is granted at the discretion of the Company, and must be approved by the Director of your Department and the Company's President. As you know, you were previously granted an unpaid personal leave up through [Original Return Date].

Unfortunately, based on the Company's business needs, we are unable to extend your leave beyond [Original Return Date]. Therefore, the Company is denying your request for additional unpaid personal leave, and is thus terminating your employment with the Company effective today. If you desire to re-apply for a position when you are available for work, we welcome you to do so.

Please find enclosed the following:
- Final paycheck
- COBRA Letter and Election Forms

If you have any questions, please feel free to contact me at [Phone Number]. [Employee], [The Company] wishes you the very best.

Sincerely,

[Human Resources Director]

[Title]

Enclosures

`Sample F.4.2` Termination Letter (leave of absence)

[Date]

[Employee's name]

[Address]

[City], [State] [Zip]

Dear [Employee],

In accordance with [Company's] policy regarding Leave of Absence, employees on any leave of absence for more than one year are terminated from our system. Your Workers' Compensation leave began on [date]; therefore, your employment status will change to terminated effective [date]. [Employee], because you are in good standing with the company but terminated for this reason, you are eligible to apply for rehire in the future.

You currently maintain medical, dental, and vision benefits through [Company]. These benefits will end on [date]. You will be eligible for COBRA benefits. Information on COBRA benefits will be mailed separately to your home.

Information regarding distribution of your 401(k) account will be sent to you directly from _____ within 30 days of your inactive effective date.

Please contact me if you have any questions.

Sincerely,

[Sr. HR Generalist, PHR]

`Sample F.4.3` Termination Letter (proof of U.S. employability)

[Date]

Re: Termination of Employment Effective [Termination Date]

[First Name] [Last Name]

[Address]

[City], [State] [Zip]

[First Name],

Please find enclosed a copy of the letter you received from [Company] on [Date of Notice to Provide Proof of U.S. Employability]. This letter stated in conclusion that you were "notified that we cannot allow you to continue to work for the company unless you provide proof of valid employment authorization by [Due date on Notice]." As of this due date, you have failed to provide this proof of valid employment authorization.

Therefore, [Company] is terminating your employment with the company effective today.

Please find enclosed the following:
- Final paycheck
- Notice of Right to Elect COBRA Continuation Coverage
- COBRA Election Form

If you have any questions, please feel free to contact me at [Phone Number]. Good luck with everything, [First Name].

Sincerely,

[Human Resources Director]

Enclosures

Sample F.4.4 Termination Warning Letter (incorrect Social Security Number)

[Date]

Re: Social Security Number

[First Name] [Last Name]

[Address]

[City], [State] [Zip]

Dear [First Name],

The Social Security Administration office of central records operations has advised us that the Social Security number which you have provided is not consistent with Social Security records.

After reviewing the documentation we have on file, Company has determined that the documents that you have provided to us as evidence of your ability to legally work in the United States may not be satisfactory. If so, the Immigration Nationality Act prohibits us from legally continuing to employ persons who cannot legally work in the U.S. unless they were hired and continuously employed since before November 6, 1986.

You are therefore notified that we cannot allow you to continue to work for the company unless you provide proof of valid employment authorization by [Two Weeks From Notification Date].

This is a very serious matter that requires your immediate attention. Should you have any questions please contact [Human Resources Contact] at [Phone Number].

Sincerely,

[Human Resources Contact]

[Title]

I understand the contents of this letter which I have read and which have been explained to me. I have been provided with a copy.

_____   _____

Employee Signature   Date

Sample F.5.1 **Layoff Memorandum**

Memorandum

Date: [Date]

To: [Name of terminated Employee]

From: [Name of manager responsible for handling termination]

Re: Termination of Employment and Separation Agreement

This is to advise you that effective [date], your employment as [state all applicable positions] [in all capacities] is being terminated by [Name of Employer] ("Company"). The reason for this action is layoff due to lack of work.

The Company desires to provide for a smooth and amicable termination of your employment and transition to new employment. Therefore, [and in recognition of your valuable service to the Company,] the Company is offering you a Separation Agreement in the form attached hereto. This severance pay [and these benefits] [is] [are] being offered to you in addition to any compensation and benefits to which you are otherwise entitled under the terms of your employment. Additionally, because your employment is being terminated for no fault of your own, you may be eligible for unemployment insurance benefits if you choose to file a request for them.

In exchange for severance pay [and these benefits], the Separation Agreement contains a standard release of claims and confidentiality agreement. Please be sure that you fully understand the terms of the Separation Agreement before signing it. You should direct any questions regarding the Separation Agreement to [name].

Our records reflect that you have been paid in full for all work performed through the effective date of the termination, and that you [do] [do not] have [any] accrued but unused vacation time [in the amount of _____] [for which you will be paid on [date]]. (If you disagree with our records, please advise [name] in writing no later than [date].)

The Company greatly appreciates your service on its behalf, and greatly regrets that business conditions have necessitated this change. We wish you all the best in your future endeavors.

Sample F.6.1 **Employee Departure Announcement**

Please be advised that _____ [date] will be [or "was"] the final date of employment of _____ [name of employee] from [his] [her] position as _____ [insert job title].

_____ [name of employee] started with Company on _____ . [Describe course of employee's career with Company, including dates and nature of positions held].

Company wishes _____ [name of employee] the best of luck in [his] [her] future endeavors.

Sample F.7.1 Service Letter

Authors' Note: Service letter requirements vary by state. Consult an employment attorney to determine the applicability of service letter laws to your organization, and the necessary content and other requirements for service letters.

[Date]

[Former Employee's Name]

[Address]

[City], [State] [Zip]

Re: Service Letter

Dear [Employee]:

You were originally hired on [Date]. In [Year], you were promoted to [Job Title] and on [Date], you were again promoted to [Job Title]. Your termination was made due to [Reason].

Sincerely,

[Name]

[Title]

SECTION G

Separation Agreements and Releases

Separation agreements and releases of claims are an effective way to manage the risk of lawsuits arising from the termination of employment and events that preceded the termination. This section contains a variety of forms reflecting different approaches to drafting separation agreements.

It is critical when using a separation agreement that employers use the appropriate form for the particular situation. If a separating employee is 40 years or older, the Older Worker Benefit Protection Act (OWBPA) regulates the content of the agreement. If the OWBPA requirements are not satisfied, the agreement will not be effective in extinguishing claims based on the Age Discrimination in Employment Act (ADEA). The OWBPA requirements differ depending on whether there is a single termination or a group termination. Always make sure to use the correct OWBPA-compliant form for the situation.

Sample G.1.1 **Employee Separation Agreement [Non-OWBPA release form]**

This Agreement, made and entered into between [employee name], employee of [company name] (hereinafter referred to as "Employee"), and [company name] (hereinafter referred to as "Company").

A. Employee is employed for Company.

B. Employee is willing to tender his/her voluntary resignation from employment with Company and to waive all rights with respect to any matter connected with his/her employment with Company or its affiliates.

C. Company is willing to accept such resignation, and will give consideration to Employee as set forth below, which is in addition to anything of value to which Employee is already entitled.

Now, therefore, in consideration of the mutual covenants of the parties hereto, **it is agreed:**

1. Employee herewith voluntarily resigns from employment with Company effective [date].

2. Employee expressly waives any and all rights with respect to all matters relating to or connected with his/her employment at or separation from Company which he/she has, did, or may have against Company and agrees not to initiate any action, legal or otherwise, against Company or any successor or assign or any other employee, agent or representative of Company. Employee agrees that in the event such action is initiated, he/she will repay the consideration listed in 3.b. below to Company as liquidated damages and not as a penalty and will indemnify Company for all costs incurred by Company in any such action, including attorneys' fees, litigation costs and expenses.

3. Company agrees to pay Employee, minus all applicable tax withholdings, and Employee hereby acknowledges receipt of same:

   a. PTO $_____
   b. Consideration for release $_____

4. Employee agrees to the return of all company property, including property keys and access card at the time of separation.

5. Employee agrees not to discuss matters of Company business with those outside the Company. Furthermore, Employee agrees not to contact any Company employee or Company vendor with the intention of injuring the reputation or operation of said Company. If employee violates this provision of the Agreement, he/she agrees to repay the consideration listed in 3.b. above as liquidated damages and not as a penalty. Employee will also pay all attorneys' fees and costs incurred by Company in seeking a court order to stop the violation or in seeking damages for any prior, ongoing, or future violation of this provision.

Company and Employee intend this document to contain all of the details of their agreement. The document is a complete and accurate integration of their agreement and no evidence of prior or contemporaneous agreements or negotiations will be offered to either contradict or supplement said agreement. This Agreement will be binding upon Company and Employee and upon their heirs, administrators, representatives, executors, and successors.

Signed this _____ day of _____, 200___

Employee: _____   Company, by: _____

                                                 Title: _____

Sample G.1.2 Separation Agreement [Non-OWBPA release form]

This Separation Agreement ("Agreement") is entered into effective this _____ day of _____, 200___, by and between [Company] ("Employer") and _____ ("Employee"). This Agreement is entered for the benefit of Employer, and any or all of its subsidiaries, affiliates, and divisions, and the officers, directors, agents, employees, and attorneys of each of them (collectively, the "Releasees").

Employer has advised Employee that her employment with Employer is being terminated effective _____ 200___.

In consideration of the mutual promises and covenants contained herein, Employer and Employee, therefore, agree as follows:

1. Commencing _____, 200___, Employer shall pay Employee _____ weeks of severance pay at the rate of Employee's regular salary, less withholding authorized or required by law.

2. If Employee elects to obtain continuation coverage on employee's group health insurance, then Employer shall pay the premiums therefore for a period of up to _____ months.

3. Employer hereby retains Employee as an independent contractor to perform certain consulting services related to the transition of Employee's duties to other personnel.

In consideration of the severance pay, payment of insurance premiums, retention of Employee as a consultant, and the other mutual promises contained in this Separation Agreement, which Employee warrants to be good and valuable consideration for this Agreement, Employee for [himself] [herself] and [his][her] heirs, assigns, and personal representatives hereby forever waives and releases the Releasees from any and all claims, demands, rights, liabilities, causes of action, and grievances ("claims"), known or unknown, statutory or at common law, arising out of Employee's employment or termination of employment. By way of example only and without limitation, this waiver and release is applicable to any claims under Title VII of the Civil Rights Act of 1964, the Age Discrimination in Employment Act, the Older Workers Benefit Protection Act, the Rehabilitation Act of 1973, the Americans With Disabilities Act, the Civil Rights Act of 1991, the Equal Pay Act of 1963, the Pregnancy Discrimination Act, the Family and Medical Leave Act, the Fair Labor Standards Act, _____
[insert names of applicable state employment laws], any and all applicable state anti-discrimination statutes, laws or regulations, and local laws and ordinances, or of wrongful discharge, implied or express contract, covenant of good faith and fair dealing, intentional or negligent infliction of emotional distress, defamation and any other claim in contract or tort.

Employee further agrees to return promptly all Employer property of any kind or character. This shall include employee identification cards, any Employer equipment, books, keys, journals, records, publications, files, memoranda and documents of any kind or description, or any other Employer property which may be in [his] [her] possession.

Employee agrees to make [himself] [herself] available on reasonable notice and after regular working hours as a consultant to the Company for the purpose of assisting in the transfer of [his] [her] duties to other personnel. Upon execution of this Agreement, Employee shall be paid a total of $_____ for such consulting services not to exceed a total of _____ hours. Employee shall be responsible for paying all taxes including income tax and FICA tax associated with such consulting payment.

Employee understands, and it is [his] [her] intent, that in the event this Agreement is ever held to be invalid and unenforceable (in whole or in part) as to any particular type of claim or as to any particular circumstances, it shall remain fully valid and enforceable as to all other claims and circumstances.

The parties have entered into this Agreement knowingly and voluntarily and have carefully read its contents and clarified any point not fully understood. Employee acknowledges that in executing this Agreement [he] [she] has not relied upon any representation or statement not set forth in this Agreement and that this Agreement may not be modified orally.

Employee agrees that [he] [she] shall keep this Agreement and its terms strictly confidential; provided, however, that Employee may disclose this Agreement and its terms to [his] [her] immediate family, accountants, attorneys, and any state or federal agency.

Employee

_____

Date of Execution

[Company]

_____

By

_____

Title

_____

Date of Execution

Sample G.2.1 Confidential Separation and Release Agreement [OWBPA release form for single terminations]

This Confidential Separation And Release Agreement ("Agreement") is made and entered into by and between _____ ("Employer") and _____ ("Employee") (collectively, the "parties") as of the Effective Date of this Agreement defined in paragraph 5 below.

I. Recitals

Whereas, _____ [state reason for termination of employment, for example, layoff, resignation, job elimination]; and

Whereas, the parties wish to make the separation amicable but conclusive on the terms and conditions set forth herein; and

Whereas, Employee accepts the benefits of this Separation and Release Agreement with the acknowledgment that by its terms Employee has been fully and satisfactorily compensated.

II. Covenants

Now, Therefore, in consideration of the mutual promises and covenants contained in this Agreement, it is hereby agreed by and between the parties hereto as follows:

1. **Termination.** Employee's employment as _____ [insert job title], and any and all other positions Employee may have held with Employer, is terminated effective as of _____ (the "Separation Date").

2. **Consideration.** Although Employer has no policy, practice, or procedure requiring payment of any severance benefits, Employer agrees to the following:

   (a) **Lump Sum Payment.** Employer agrees to pay Employee _____ Dollars ($_____), less all legally required deductions and withholdings (the "Payment"). The Payment shall be made by check, and shall be delivered to Employee's home address within _____ business days after the expiration of the Deliberation and Revocation Period as defined below. Employee acknowledges and agrees that Employee is solely responsible to inform Employer in writing of any change in Employee's current mailing address should Employee change Employee's residence and that failure to do so may result in Employee not receiving this payment under this Agreement.

   (b) **Outplacement Services.** Employer shall provide Employee with outplacement services through the outplacement firm of _____, for a period not to exceed _____ months and a total expenditure not to exceed _____ ($_____), commencing on the Effective Date of this Agreement.

   (c) **Insurance.** To the extent permitted by the federal COBRA law and the insurance policies and rules applicable to Employer, Employee will be eligible to continue health insurance benefits at Employee's own expense. Employee acknowledges that Employer has provided Employee with a COBRA notification form setting forth Employee's rights and responsibilities with regard to COBRA coverage. As additional consideration for the mutual promises and covenants contained herein, Employer shall pay Employee's COBRA health and dental insurance premiums for a period of _____ months from the Separation Date, or until Employee becomes insured under another insurance plan, whichever date occurs first. Employee agrees to inform Employer immediately upon Employee becoming reinsured. All COBRA premium payments for which Employer has agreed to pay shall be paid directly by Employer to Employer's health and dental insurance carrier.

   (d) **No Other Compensation.** Employee acknowledges and agrees that Employee will not receive (nor is Employee entitled to receive) any additional consideration, payments, reimbursements, incentive payments, commission payments, bonuses, stock, stock options, equity interests or other benefits or compensation of any kind. Employee further acknowledges and agrees that Employer has paid in full any and all wages, salary, accrued but unused vacation, paid time off, commission payments, bonuses, stock, stock options, incentive payments or other compensation due and owing to Employee as of the Separation Date.

3. **Covenant Not To Sue and Release of Claims by Employee.** In consideration for the consideration set forth in this Agreement and the mutual covenants of Employer and Employee, Employee hereby covenants not to sue Employer and hereby releases and forever discharges Employer, its affiliated corporations and entities, its and their officers, directors, agents, representatives, attorneys, employees, shareholders, successors and assigns of and from any and all claims, liabilities, demands, causes of action, costs, expenses, attorneys' fees, damages, indemnities and obligations of every kind and nature, in law, equity, or otherwise, whether known or unknown, whether suspected or unsuspected, whether disclosed or undisclosed, and whether liquidated or contingent, including, but not limited to: claims arising out of or in any way related to agreements, events, acts or conduct at any time prior to and including the Effective Date, including, but not limited to, any and all such claims and demands directly or indirectly arising out of or in any way connected with Employee's employment with Employer or the termination of Employee's employment; claims or demands related to salary, bonuses, commissions, incentive payments, stock, stock options, or any ownership or equity interests in Employer, vacation pay, personal time off, fringe benefits, expense reimbursements, severance benefits, or any other form of compensation; claims pursuant to: federal, state or any local law, statute, common law causes of action,

including, but not limited to, claims under the Federal Civil Rights Act of 1964, the federal Age Discrimination in Employment Act of 1967, the Federal Americans with Disabilities Act of 1990, the Family and Medical Leave Act, _____ [insert names of applicable state employment laws], or other similar state or federal statutes or regulations; or claims under tort law or contract law or other common law claims, including but not limited to claims of wrongful discharge, breach of implied contract, promissory estoppel, fraud, defamation, libel, emotional distress, and/or breach of an express or implied covenant of good faith and fair dealing.

4. **ADEA/OWBPA Waiver and Release by Employee.** Employee acknowledges that Employee has been given this Agreement on _____, and that under this Agreement Employee is knowingly and voluntarily waiving and releasing any rights that Employee may have under the federal Age Discrimination in Employment Act of 1967, as amended ("ADEA Waiver and Release"), among other claims. Employee acknowledges that the consideration given for this ADEA Waiver and Release is in addition to anything of value to which Employee was already entitled. The parties agree and acknowledge that Employee has been advised by this writing that:

   (a) notwithstanding anything to the contrary contained in this Agreement, this ADEA Waiver and Release does not apply to any claims under ADEA that may arise after the date that Employee signs this Agreement;

   (b) Employee has the right to and is advised to consult with an attorney prior to executing this Agreement;

   (c) Employee has twenty-one (21) days within which to consider this ADEA Waiver and Release (although Employee may choose to voluntarily execute this ADEA Waiver and Release earlier) (the "Deliberation Period"); and

   (d) Employee has seven (7) days following the execution of this Agreement to revoke his ADEA Waiver and Release by sending, via certified United States mail, written notice of revocation to the attention of _____ (the "Revocation Period").

   The parties acknowledge and agree that revocation by Employee of the ADEA Waiver and Release shall not be effective to revoke Employee's waiver or release of any other claims pursuant to this Agreement.

5. **Effective Date.** This Agreement is effective on the expiration of the Deliberation Period and Revocation Period (the "Effective Date"). If not executed by Employee on or before the close of business on _____, the first business day following the end of the twenty-one (21) day Deliberation Period afforded Employee, the terms and provisions of this Agreement shall be null and void.

6. **Acknowledgment of Release.** Employee represents that Employee understands and agrees that this Agreement contains a release of all known and unknown claims.

7. **Denial of Liability.** The parties acknowledge that the consideration given by Employer and the release of claims by Employee pursuant to this Agreement are made in compromise of any potential disputes, and, that Employer and Employee in no way admit any liability to each other, but rather that the parties expressly deny any such liability to each other.

8. **Tax Consequences.** Employee acknowledges that Employer has made no representations or warranties to Employee as to the tax treatment of the consideration provided for in this Agreement, and that Employee is solely responsible for ascertaining such tax consequences.

9. **Confidentiality.** The provisions of this Agreement shall be held in strictest confidence by Employee and shall not be publicized or disclosed in any manner whatsoever. Notwithstanding the prohibition in the preceding sentence, Employee may disclose this Agreement in confidence to Employee's attorneys, accountants, auditors, tax preparers, and financial advisors, provided that such persons shall be informed of the existence of this confidentiality obligation and shall agree to be bound thereby to the same extent as Employee.

10. **Non-Disparagement.** Employee agrees that Employee will not at any time disparage or speak ill of Employer, or any employee, officer or director thereof, or make any statement or take any action that tends to cast any such person or entity in a false or negative light.

11. **References.** To coordinate Employer's response to any inquiries from prospective employers seeking employment references concerning Employee, Employee agrees to direct such prospective employers exclusively to _____. Should _____ receive an inquiry, _____ (or an authorized agent acting on behalf of _____) shall provide Employee's dates of employment with Employer, the position(s) Employee held, and, if requested, the salary Employee received as an employee. Also, if asked the reason for Employee's termination, Employer shall indicate that Employee's position with Employer was terminated due to _____ [insert brief description of reason for termination; for example "a job elimination"].

12. **Employer Property.** Employee represents and warrants that Employee has returned to Employer all of Employer's property in Employee's possession, custody or control, including, but not limited to, financial information, customer information, customer lists, employee lists, Employer's files, Employee's business cards, notes, cellular telephones, contracts, drawings, records, business plans and forecasts, specifications, computer-recorded information, software, computer equipment, tangible property, credit cards, entry cards, identification badges and keys, and any other materials, documents or things of any kind which contain or embody any proprietary or confidential material of Employer.

13. **Proprietary Information.** Employee agrees and acknowledges that Employee continues to be bound by the Proprietary Information Agreement between Employer and Employee that Employee dated _____.

14. No Third Party Rights. The parties agree that by making this Agreement they do not intend to confer any benefits, privileges or rights to any person who is not a party to this Agreement. The Agreement is strictly between the parties hereto, subject to the terms of paragraph 3 above, and it shall not be construed to vest in any other the status of third-party beneficiary.

15. Duty To Effectuate. The parties agree to perform any lawful additional acts, including the execution of additional agreements, as are reasonably necessary to effectuate the purpose of this Agreement.

16. Entire Agreement. This Agreement constitutes the complete, final and exclusive embodiment of the entire agreement between Employee and Employer with regard to the subject matter hereof. Employee represents and agrees that this Agreement is entered into without reliance on any promise or representation, written or oral, other than those expressly contained herein. This Agreement may not be modified except in a writing signed by Employee and a duly authorized officer of Employer.

17. Successors and Assigns. This Agreement shall bind the heirs, personal representatives, successors, assigns, executors and administrators of each party, and inure to the benefit of each party, its heirs, successors and assigns.

18. Applicable Law. The parties agree that this Agreement is entered into in the State of _____, and that the parties agree and intend that it be construed and enforced in accordance with the laws of the State of _____.

19. Forum Selection. Any controversy arising out of or relating to this Agreement or the breach thereof, or any claim or action to enforce this Agreement or portion thereof, or any controversy or claim requiring interpretation of this Agreement must be brought in a forum located within the State of _____.

20. Severability. If any provision of this Agreement is determined to be invalid, void or unenforceable, in whole or in part, such determination shall not affect any other provision of this Agreement, and the provision in question shall be modified so as to be rendered enforceable.

21. Section Headings. The section and paragraph headings contained in this Agreement are for reference purposes only and shall not affect in any way the meaning or interpretation of this Agreement.

22. Counterparts. This Agreement may be executed by facsimile and in two or more counterparts, each of which shall be deemed an original, and all together shall constitute one and the same instrument.

23. Voluntary and Knowing. Employee represents and agrees that in executing this Agreement, Employee has reviewed it, understands its terms, has had an opportunity and was advised to seek guidance from counsel of Employer's own choosing, and acted knowingly and voluntarily.

In Witness Whereof, the parties have duly authorized and caused this Agreement to be executed as follows:

Employee:

_____, an individual

_____
[Signature]

Date: _____

Employer:

_____ [insert Company name]

By: _____
[Signature]

Title: _____

Date: _____

Approved As To Form:

Counsel for Employee:

_____
[Signature]

Date: _____

Counsel for Employer:

_____
[Signature]

Date: _____

Sample G.2.2 Employee Separation Agreement [OWBPA release form for single terminations]

This Agreement, made and entered into between [employee name] (hereinafter referred to as "Employee"), employee of [Company], and [company name] (hereinafter referred to as "Company").

A. Employee is employed for Company.

B. Employee is willing to tender his/her voluntary resignation from employment with Company and to waive all rights with respect to any matter connected with his/her employment with Company or its affiliates.

C. Company is willing to accept such resignation, and will give consideration to Employee as set forth below, which is in addition to anything of value to which Employee is already entitled.

D. Employee is advised to consult with an attorney of his/her choice before signing this Agreement and has a period of 21 calendar days in which to consider this Agreement after he/she receives it. After Employee signs this Agreement, he/she has 7 calendar days in which to revoke it. Revocation must be in writing addressed to [HR Manager], [Company Address]. This Agreement will not become effective or enforceable until after the revocation period has expired.

Now, Therefore, in consideration of the mutual covenants of the parties hereto, **It Is Agreed:**

1. Employee herewith voluntarily resigns from employment with Company effective [date].

2. Employee expressly waives any and all rights with respect to all matters relating to or connected with his/her employment at or separation from Company which he/she has, did, or may have against Company, including any claims under the Age Discrimination and Employment Act (ADEA), 29 U.S.C. § 621 et seq. Employee agrees not to initiate any action, legal or otherwise, against Company or any successor or assign or any other employee, agent or representative of Company. Employee agrees that in the event such action is initiated, he/she will repay the consideration listed in 3.b. below to Company as liquidated damages and not as a penalty and will indemnify Company for all costs incurred by Company in any such action, including attorneys' fees, litigation costs and expenses.

3. Company agrees to pay Employee, minus all applicable tax withholdings, and Employee hereby acknowledges receipt of same:

	Gross Pay
a. PTO	$_____
b. Consideration for release	$_____

4. Employee agrees to the return of all company property, including property keys and card at the time of separation.

5. Employee agrees not to discuss matters of Company business with those outside the Company. Furthermore, Employee agrees not to contact any Company employee or Company vendor with the intention of injuring the reputation or operation of said Company. If employee violates this provision of the Agreement, he/she agrees to repay the consideration listed in 3.b. above as liquidated damages and not as a penalty. Employee will also pay all attorneys' fees and costs incurred by Company in seeking a court order to stop the violation or in seeking damages for any prior, ongoing, or future violation of this provision.

Company and Employee intend this document to contain all of the details of their agreement. The document is a complete and accurate integration of their agreement and no evidence of prior or contemporaneous agreements or negotiations will be offered to either contradict or supplement said agreement. This Agreement will be binding upon Company and Employee and upon their heirs, administrators, representatives, executors, and successors.

Signed this _____ day of _____, 200___

Employee: _____   Company, by: _____

Title: _____

Sample G.2.3   Separation and Release Agreement [OWBPA release form for single terminations]

This Separation and Release Agreement ("Agreement") is entered into this _____ day of _____, 200___, by and between _____, its directors, officers, employees, agents, attorneys, insurers, representatives, affiliates, assigns, and successors, past and present (hereinafter collectively referred to as "_____"), and _____, his/her heirs, successors, and assigns.

1. _____ resigns his/her position as _____ and as an employee of _____ in any other capacity effective _____, 200___. _____'s last day to report for work at _____ will be _____, 200___, and any claims by _____ for reimbursement of expenses must be submitted by that date.

2. (a) _____ and _____ agree that _____ shall receive a severance payment in the amount of $_____ (less federal and state withholding and authorized deductions) that shall be paid no later than _____, 200___. (_____ will continue to receive salary and benefits and will accrue benefits until _____, 200___.) The date of termination of _____'s employment with _____ shall be _____, 200___.

   (b) This Agreement does not alter any rights or benefits that _____ may have under _____'s profit sharing or 401 (k) plans that are vested as of the date of the termination of _____'s employment with _____. _____ shall direct _____ within 60 days of his/her termination regarding any transfer of disposition of these funds.

3. Except for those obligations created by or arising out of this Separation and Release Agreement, _____ hereby fully releases and discharges _____ with respect to any and all claims, causes of action, obligations, attorneys' fees, damages, and liabilities of whatever kind or nature, including claims asserted or adjudicated through administrative agencies, in law or equity, whether now known or unknown, which _____ now owns or holds or has at any time owned, possessed, or held against _____, arising out of or in any way connected with _____'s employment relationship with _____. Furthermore, _____ hereby releases and discharges _____ from any other damage or injury whatsoever, known or unknown, suspected or unsuspected, resulting from any act or omission by or on the part of _____ committed or omitted before the date of this Agreement, including but not limited to Title VII of the Civil Rights Act of 1964; state, county, or municipal human rights laws; laws against wrongful discharge or termination; or the Americans with Disabilities Act. _____ warrants that [he] [she] has not filed any charges arising from the above-mentioned acts of law.

4. The parties agree that the terms hereof are confidential and neither the terms hereof nor the existence of the Agreement shall be disclosed to any third party without the consent of all parties to the Agreement.

5. _____ agrees to forever refrain from making any disparaging remarks or other negative or derogatory statements, written or oral, to any third party relating to _____ or its affiliates, officers, directors, employees, and agents.

6. The parties recognize that, during their employment relationship, _____ may have had access to certain confidential information and materials, including but not limited to trade secrets, software programs, source codes, object codes, data, formulas, processes, know-how, designs, documentation, program files, flow charts, specifications, developments, improvements, inventions, techniques, customer information, prospective client and customer lists, accounting and other financial data, statistical data, research projects, development and marketing plans, promotional ideas, strategies, budgets, projections, licenses, prices, costs, new products, and supplier lists, originated by _____ or disclosed to _____ by others ("Confidential Information"). Failure to mark any of the Confidential Information as confidential or proprietary does not affect its status as Confidential Information under this Agreement.

   _____ agrees to keep in confidence and trust all Confidential Information, and will not, without the written consent of _____, use or disclose to any person any Confidential Information or anything relating to it, whether in written, electronic, or oral form, or permit any person to examine and/or make copies of any Confidential Information or reports or other material containing Confidential Information prepared by _____ or that came into _____'s possession or under [his] [her] control by reason of the parties' employment relationship.

7. All documents, records, photocopies, notes, drawings, manuals, computer programs, data, documentation, disks, diskettes, computer tapes, apparatus, equipment, voice mail, and other materials, whether or not pertaining to Confidential Information, furnished to _____ by _____ or produced by _____ in connection with the parties' employment relationship, with exception of the computer and printer kept at _____'s residence, shall remain the sole property of _____ and shall be returned to _____ upon execution of this Agreement.

8. For a period of 5 years from the date of this Agreement, _____ shall not divert, take away, call upon, contact, induce, or otherwise solicit or attempt to solicit, directly or indirectly, any clients of _____, nor will _____ contact or communicate with such clients by offering, providing, selling, or licensing any program, product, or service that is competitive with _____. The term "client" shall include, without limitation, all providers, labor unions, and trust funds with which _____ has a contract.

9. For a period of 5 years from the date of this Agreement, _____ shall not divert, take away, call upon, contact, induce, or otherwise solicit or attempt to solicit, directly or indirectly, any employee of _____ or any of _____'s clients, to leave the employ of _____.

10. The parties agree and acknowledge that the restrictions contained in Paragraphs 8 and 9 of this Agreement are fair and reasonable in that they are reasonably required for the protection of _____. If, however, for any reason, a court should determine that any or all of the restrictions therein are overly broad or otherwise not reasonable, then such restriction(s) shall be interpreted, modified, or rewritten to the minimum extent necessary to render the restriction(s) valid and enforceable.

11. _____ agrees that _____ will suffer irreparable harm in the event that _____ breaches any of his/her obligations under this Agreement, and that it is impossible to measure in money the damages that will accrue to _____ in the event of such a breach or threatened breach. Accordingly, if any action or proceeding is commenced by or on behalf of _____ to enforce any of the provisions contained in this Agreement, _____ hereby waives the claim or defense that _____ has an adequate remedy at law or has not been or is not being irreparably injured by such breach or threatened breach, and _____ agrees not to raise such claim or defense in any such action or proceeding. _____ further agrees that _____ shall be entitled to temporary and permanent injunctive relief to restrain any breaches or further violations of this Agreement, without the posting of any bond, and that this right to injunctive relief shall be in addition to any and all of _____'s other remedies and damages, including but not limited to costs and reasonable attorneys' fees incurred as a result of said breach or threatened breach.

12. In the event that either party breaches this Agreement, the prevailing party shall be entitled to its costs, including reasonable attorneys' fees, from the other party that are incurred as a result of such breach.

13. Except as otherwise provided herein, all of the covenants, conditions, and provisions of this Agreement shall be binding upon and shall inure to the benefit of the parties hereto and their respective heirs, personal representatives, successors, and assigns.

14. This Agreement shall be governed by the laws of the state of _____, without reference to the choice of law provisions thereof.

15. The provisions of this Agreement are severable, and it is the intention of the parties hereto that in the event a court of competent jurisdiction holds that any one or more provisions of this Agreement are unenforceable, the remaining provisions of the Agreement shall be given full force and effect as if the part or parts held invalid had not been included.

16. The section and paragraph headings are inserted only as a matter of convenience and reference and in no way define, limit, or proscribe the scope or intent of this Agreement.

17. This Agreement constitutes the entire agreement and understanding of the parties hereto and supersedes any prior agreements, understandings, representations, and warranties concerning the subject matter hereof, and no provision herein may be waived, changed, or modified except in a writing signed by both parties. The Employment Agreement is hereby terminated effective as of the date of this Agreement, and this Agreement supersedes the terms thereof.

18. _____ acknowledges the following: (a) This Agreement waives, among other claims, any claims [he] [she] may have under the Age Discrimination in Employment Act; (b) _____ advises that _____ consult with an attorney prior to signing this Agreement; (c) _____ may consider the terms of this Agreement for a period of 21 days, and the execution of this Agreement is not required before expiration of the 21-day period; (d) _____ may revoke [his] [her] acceptance of this Agreement within 7 days of signing it; and (e) payment of the first lump-sum payment set forth in Paragraph 2(a) above shall be made to _____ on the 8th day following the date of execution of this Agreement by _____.

In Witness Whereof, the parties have affixed their hands and seals as of the dates indicated below.

_____

Reprinted with permission. *Ending the Employment Relationship without Ending Up in Court*, pp. 106–111, Francis t. Coleman, Esq.: Alexandria, VA: Society for Human Resource Management, 2001.

Sample G.2.4 Separation Agreement and Release
[OWBPA release form for single terminations]

[Date]

[Title] [First Name] [Last Name]
[Address Line 1]
[Address Line 2]
[City], [State] [ZIP Code]

Dear [First Name]:

Note: The following examples of a first paragraph are examples of the kinds of things you would want to say in the opening paragraph. It will need to be customized to each situation.

As we have discussed, recent changes in our customers' requirements have caused us to need to rethink the structure of the technical side of the organization. Unfortunately, given what we now know, we do not see an ongoing role for you at [Company Name]. Consequently, your employment at [Company Name] will end as of [Last Day of Employment].

As we have discussed, [Company Name] has decided to exercise its option to end your employment relationship with the Company. Consequently, your last day of employment at [Company Name] is [Last Day of Employment].

Out of appreciation for your efforts on behalf of the Company, and recognizing that we may have differing views regarding the circumstances leading to this decision, the following Separation Agreement and Release details the proposed terms of your departure from [Company Name].

1. Your last day of employment at [Company Name] is [Last Day of Employment]. On your last day, you will receive all compensation earned through that date, including any accrued vacation time, less withholding.

2. Within ten (10) days of executing this Agreement (providing you have not subsequently revoked the Agreement) [Company Name] will provide you with [Weeks of Severance] weeks of severance pay, minus withholding.

3. (*Choose a or b.*) *a)* You should feel free to use us as an employment reference. Please refer all potential employers to [Contact Name] at [Contact Phone] or [Contact Email Address]. *b)* As far as employment references are concerned, we will adhere to the policy of providing only dates of employment, title of position, and salary.

4. Your health care benefits have been paid for through [Last Day of Benefits]. You are eligible to purchase an additional eighteen (18) months of health insurance benefits at your own expense through the provisions outlined in COBRA. Your separation packet includes a letter detailing your rights and the procedures for electing COBRA coverage.

5. On [Last Day of Employment], you will return to [Company Name] all files, records, reports, data, correspondence, memoranda and other documents (including handwritten notes and drafts), computer equipment, pager, keys and all other physical or personal property you received from the Company and which are Company property.

6. (*Choose a or b.*) *a)* You are, of course, welcome to apply for available positions in the future. We would be pleased to have you back when circumstances improve. *b)* You agree that our employment agreement permanently ends here. You will not seek employment at [Company Name] or any of its affiliated companies in the future.

7. You agree that you will strictly abide by the terms of your Non-Disclosure Agreement. Your signature below confirms that you have reviewed this agreement to be certain you are aware of all responsibilities and prohibitions it contains.

8. You also acknowledge that this Agreement and all matters relating to negotiating and carrying out this Agreement are confidential and will not be disclosed to any third party except your spouse, legal advisor and tax advisor to the extent necessary to perform services, or as required by law.

9. You further agree not to malign or denigrate the Company to anyone including but not limited to any employee, contractor, vendor or customer of [Company Name], just as we will not malign or denigrate you to potential employers. Should you violate this non-denigration clause, any severance payments that may have been made to you must be reimbursed to [Company Name]. Furthermore, [Company Name] may pursue all available equitable remedies including damages and injunctive relief.

10. Our offer to you, described above, depends on your agreement that you fully release the Company from any liability, claim, damages, or cause of action arising out of your employment relationship with the Company or the termination of that employment. This includes, but is not limited to, any claim for additional salary or bonus, or any claim relating to any local, state or federal labor regulations, or equal employment laws, wage laws, ordinances, regulations or orders, such as claims under Title VII of the Civil Rights Act of 1964, or the Age Discrimination in Employment Act. It also includes any claim that you might wish to assign or transfer to a third party.

You likewise will not assist in or encourage the pursuit of litigation against the Company by any other person or entity. The Company, in this instance, includes its officers, directors, partners, employees, parent companies, subsidiaries, affiliates, shareholders, representatives and agents.

11. Your signature below confirms your understanding that if you initiate, participate in, or in any manner seek relief through any suit or Claim, you must not only repay any severance provided, but must also pay to [Company Name], and any of its agents covered by this release, all attorneys' fees incurred by those who must defend or otherwise respond to the suit or Claim.

12. Both you and [Company Name] understand and agree that neither paying severance, nor executing this release is an admission of any liability whatsoever.

13. Both you and [Company Name] hereby acknowledge that no promise or inducement has been offered or made except as stated in this Agreement and that this Agreement and your Non-Disclosure Agreement contain all the terms and conditions by which each party agrees to be bound. If any individual provision of this Agreement is found to be invalid or unenforceable then only that provision shall be removed. All other provisions and the remainder of the Agreement will remain in force.

14. You have twenty-one (21) days in which to consider our offer; however, your services will no longer be required after [Last Day of Employment]. No payments or benefits described in this Agreement will be due or payable until you have executed the agreement. Executing the agreement prior to the conclusion of the twenty-one (21)-day review period indicates your intentional waiver of the remaining portion of the review period and a willingness to enter into this agreement voluntarily.

15. Once you have signed the agreement, you have seven (7) days to revoke the Agreement. To be effective, this revocation must be in writing, and received by [Company Name] within seven (7) days after you have executed the Agreement.

16. If these terms are not acceptable, [Company Name] does nonetheless need to terminate your employment. Should you decide not to sign this letter, you will be terminated as of [Last Day of Employment], and receive only your earned wages and accrued vacation pay as provided by the "at-will" terms of your employment. You will continue to be bound by the terms of your Non-Disclosure and Agreement.

[First Name], we encourage you to consult with an attorney before signing this Agreement. Your signature below confirms that you have had the opportunity to carefully review and consider this Confidential Separation Agreement and Release and are knowingly, freely and voluntarily entering into this Agreement.

If the above terms and conditions are agreeable to you, kindly acknowledge your agreement by signing in the space provided below and return it to [Return Document To]. You may mail it to [Mail Document to] or fax it to [Fax Document to].

Again, [First Name], we thank you for your efforts on behalf of [Company Name] and wish you well in your future endeavors.

Respectfully,

[Signed by]
[Signed by Title]
[Company Name]

Agreed and Accepted:

_____   _____
[First Name] [Last Name]   Date

Sample G.2.5 Resignation Agreement
[OWBPA release form for single terminations]

_____ ("Company") and _____ ("Employee"), in consideration of the mutual promises set forth herein, agree as follows:

Company Agrees:

1. To accept Employee's resignation of employment effective _____ [date].

2. To pay Employee _____ weeks severance pay in the amount of $_____ which Employee would not otherwise be entitled to receive.

3. To keep the circumstances of Employee's termination and terms of this Agreement confidential for prospective employment inquiries unless Employee breaches Employee's confidentiality obligation or directs full disclosure of the circumstances of Employee's departure from employment. Unless one of these conditions is met, any inquiries concerning Employee's departure from Company will reflect Employee's "resignation" as opposed to "termination" from Company, with no specifics as to the nature of the departure or the cause of the resignation. To ensure maximum confidentiality all prospective employment inquiries must be directed to _____.

4. To allow Employee twenty-one (21) days to consider and accept this Agreement and, once signed, seven (7) days to revoke Employee's acceptance.

5. By entering into this Agreement, the parties do not admit any wrongdoing and the terms of the Agreement should not be so construed. The parties also agree that if any part of this Agreement is deemed invalid the rest of the Agreement shall continue in full force and effect.

Employee agrees:

1. To tender Employee's resignation effective _____ [date].

2. That Employee has received, or will receive, under the terms of this Agreement, all sums to which Employee is in any way entitled from Employee's employment or the termination thereof by Company, and that Employee has received additional amounts to which Employee would not otherwise be entitled.

3. To forever release and discharge Company, its parent or subsidiary companies, its officers, agents, and employees, from any and all manner of claims by himself, chose in action, or suit, whether asserted under statute, contract, tort, or other civil or criminal basis, including but not limited to claims under all federal and state statutes including, without limitation, the Age Discrimination in Employment Act, arising out of or relating to Employee's employment with Company or the termination of such employment.

4. Not to bring any action in court or against Company.

5. To keep confidential the details of Employee's resignation, this Agreement, and the payment made under this Agreement, except that Employee may disclose these matters to attorneys and tax advisors who agree to be similarly bound, or pursuant to a valid subpoena. In the event that Employee violates this confidentiality provision, Employee agrees to pay $_____ to Company as liquidated damages.

6. That Employee will return all property of Company by _____ [date].

7. That Employee understands the terms and effects of this Agreement, and that Employee is not relying upon any statement or representation by Company other than those set forth in this Agreement.

8. That Employee has had sufficient time to deliberate about this Agreement before signing it.

9. That Company has advised Employee to consult with an attorney of Employee's own choosing prior to executing this Agreement.

10. That Employee is entering this Agreement knowingly and voluntarily.

11. By entering into this Agreement, the parties do not admit any wrongdoing and the terms of the Agreement should not be so construed. The parties also agree that if any part of this Agreement is deemed invalid the rest of the Agreement shall continue in full force and effect.

Signed and Agreed To This _____ Day of _____, 20____

Company

By: _____

Title: _____

Employee

_____

[Signature]

Sample G.3.1   Confidential Separation and Release Agreement [OWBPA release form for group terminations]

This Confidential Separation And Release Agreement ("Agreement") is made and entered into by and between _____ ("Employer") and _____ ("Employee") (collectively, the "parties") as of the Effective Date of this Agreement defined in paragraph 5 below.

I. Recitals

Whereas, _____ [state reason for termination of employment, for example, layoff, resignation, job elimination]; and

Whereas, the parties wish to make the separation amicable but conclusive on the terms and conditions set forth herein; and

Whereas, Employee accepts the benefits of this Separation and Release Agreement with the acknowledgment that by its terms Employee has been fully and satisfactorily compensated.

II. Covenants

Now, Therefore, in consideration of the mutual promises and covenants contained in this Agreement, it is hereby agreed by and between the parties hereto as follows:

1. **Termination.** Employee's employment as _____ [insert job title], and any and all other positions Employee may have held with Employer, is terminated effective as of _____ (the "Separation Date").

2. **Consideration.** Although Employer has no policy, practice, or procedure requiring payment of any severance benefits, Employer agrees to the following:

   (a) Lump Sum Payment. Employer agrees to pay Employee _____ Dollars ($_____), less all legally required deductions and withholdings (the "Payment"). The Payment shall be made by check, and shall be delivered to Employee's home address within _____ business days after the expiration of the Deliberation and Revocation Period as defined in sections 4(c) and 4(d). Employee acknowledges and agrees that Employee is solely responsible to inform Employer in writing of any change in Employee's current mailing address should Employee change Employee's residence and that failure to do so may result in Employee not receiving this payment under this Agreement.

   (b) Outplacement Services. Employer shall provide Employee with outplacement services through the outplacement firm of _____, for a period not to exceed _____ months and a total expenditure not to exceed _____ ($_____), commencing on the Effective Date of this Agreement.

   (c) Insurance. To the extent permitted by the federal COBRA law and the insurance policies and rules applicable to Employer, Employee will be eligible to continue health insurance benefits at Employee's own expense. Employee acknowledges that Employer has provided Employee with a COBRA notification form setting forth Employee's rights and responsibilities with regard to COBRA coverage. As additional consideration for the mutual promises and covenants contained herein, Employer shall pay Employee's COBRA health and dental insurance premiums for a period of _____ months from the Separation Date, or until Employee becomes insured under another insurance plan, whichever date occurs first. Employee agrees to inform Employer immediately upon Employee becoming reinsured. All COBRA premium payments for which Employer has agreed to pay shall be paid directly by Employer to Employer's health and dental insurance carrier.

   (d) No Other Compensation. Employee acknowledges and agrees that Employee will not receive (nor is Employee entitled to receive) any additional consideration, payments, reimbursements, incentive payments, commission payments, bonuses, stock, stock options, equity interests or other benefits or compensation of any kind. Employee further acknowledges and agrees that Employer has paid in full any and all wages, salary, accrued but unused vacation, paid time off, commission payments, bonuses, stock, stock options, incentive payments or other compensation due and owing to Employee as of the Separation Date.

3. **Covenant Not To Sue and Release of Claims by Employee.** In consideration for the consideration set forth in this Agreement and the mutual covenants of Employer and Employee, Employee hereby covenants not to sue Employer and hereby releases and forever discharges Employer, its affiliated corporations and entities, its and their officers, directors, agents, representatives, attorneys, employees, shareholders, successors and assigns of and from any and all claims, liabilities, demands, causes of action, costs, expenses, attorneys' fees, damages, indemnities and obligations of every kind and nature, in law, equity, or otherwise, whether known or unknown, whether suspected or unsuspected, whether disclosed or undisclosed, and whether liquidated or contingent, including, but not limited to: claims arising out of or in any way related to agreements, events, acts or conduct at any time prior to and including the Effective Date, including, but not limited to, any and all such claims and demands directly or indirectly arising out of or in any way connected with Employee's employment with Employer or the termination of Employee's employment; claims or demands related to salary, bonuses, commissions, incentive payments, stock, stock options, or any ownership or equity interests in Employer, vacation pay, personal time off, fringe benefits, expense reimburse-

ments, severance benefits, or any other form of compensation; claims pursuant to: federal, state or any local law, statute, common law causes of action, including, but not limited to, claims under the Federal Civil Rights Act of 1964, the federal Age Discrimination in Employment Act of 1967, the Federal Americans with Disabilities Act of 1990, the Family and Medical Leave Act, _____ [insert names of applicable state employment laws], or other similar state or federal statutes or regulations; or claims under tort law or contract law or other common law claims, including but not limited to claims of wrongful discharge, breach of implied contract, promissory estoppel, fraud, defamation, libel, emotional distress, and/or breach of an express or implied covenant of good faith and fair dealing.

4. **ADEA/OWBPA Waiver and Release by Employee.** Employee acknowledges that Employee has been given this Agreement on _____, and that under this Agreement Employee is knowingly and voluntarily waiving and releasing any rights that Employee may have under the federal Age Discrimination in Employment Act of 1967, as amended ("ADEA Waiver and Release"), among other claims. Employee acknowledges that the consideration given for this ADEA Waiver and Release is in addition to anything of value to which Employee was already entitled. The parties agree and acknowledge that Employee has been advised by this writing that:

(a) notwithstanding anything to the contrary contained in this Agreement, this ADEA Waiver and Release does not apply to any claims under ADEA that may arise after the date that Employee signs this Agreement;

(b) Employee has the right to and is advised to consult with an attorney prior to executing this Agreement;

(c) Employee has forty-five (45) days within which to consider this ADEA Waiver and Release (although Employee may choose to voluntarily execute this ADEA Waiver and Release earlier) (the "Deliberation Period"); and

(d) Employee has seven (7) days following the execution of this Agreement to revoke his ADEA Waiver and Release by sending, via certified United States mail, written notice of revocation to the attention of _____ (the "Revocation Period").

(e) The individuals who are eligible to participate in this program are shown on the attached spreadsheet, **Exhibit A.**

(f) Employee and the other individuals are eligible for participation in this program because their employment is being terminated in this _____ [job restructuring] [layoff] [plant closing].

(g) The job titles of the individuals eligible to participate in this program are shown on the attached spreadsheet.

(h) The ages of the persons eligible, and ineligible, to participate in this program are shown on the attached spreadsheet.

The parties acknowledge and agree that revocation by Employee of the ADEA Waiver and Release shall not be effective to revoke Employee's waiver or release of any other claims pursuant to this Agreement.

5. **Effective Date.** This Agreement is effective on the expiration of the Deliberation Period and Revocation Period (the "Effective Date"). If not executed by Employee on or before the close of business on _____, the first business day following the end of the forty-five (45) day Deliberation Period afforded Employee, the terms and provisions of this Agreement shall be null and void.

6. **Acknowledgment of Release.** Employee represents that Employee understands and agrees that this Agreement contains a release of all known and unknown claims.

7. **Denial of Liability.** The parties acknowledge that the consideration given by Employer and the release of claims by Employee pursuant to this Agreement are made in compromise of any potential disputes, and, that Employer and Employee in no way admit any liability to each other, but rather that the parties expressly deny any such liability to each other.

8. **Tax Consequences.** Employee acknowledges that Employer has made no representations or warranties to Employee as to the tax treatment of the consideration provided for in this Agreement, and that Employee is solely responsible for ascertaining such tax consequences.

9. **Confidentiality.** The provisions of this Agreement shall be held in strictest confidence by Employee and shall not be publicized or disclosed in any manner whatsoever. Notwithstanding the prohibition in the preceding sentence, Employee may disclose this Agreement in confidence to Employee's attorneys, accountants, auditors, tax preparers, and financial advisors, provided that such persons shall be informed of the existence of this confidentiality obligation and shall agree to be bound thereby to the same extent as Employee.

10. **Non-Disparagement.** Employee agrees that Employee will not at any time disparage or speak ill of Employer, or any employee, officer or director thereof, or make any statement or take any action that tends to cast any such person or entity in a false or negative light.

11. **References.** To coordinate Employer's response to any inquiries from prospective employers seeking employment references concerning Employee, Employee agrees to direct such prospective employers exclusively to _____. Should _____ receive an inquiry, _____ (or an authorized agent acting on behalf of _____) shall provide Employee's dates of employment with Employer, the position(s) Employee held, and, if requested, the salary Employee received as an employee. Also, if asked the reason for Employee's termination, Employer shall indicate that Employee's position with Employer was terminated due to _____ [insert brief description of reason for termination; for example "a job elimination"].

12. Employer Property. Employee represents and warrants that Employee has returned to Employer all of Employer's property in Employer's possession, custody or control, including, but not limited to, financial information, customer information, customer lists, employee lists, Employer's files, Employee's business cards, notes, cellular telephones, contracts, drawings, records, business plans and forecasts, specifications, computer-recorded information, software, computer equipment, tangible property, credit cards, entry cards, identification badges and keys, and any other materials, documents or things of any kind which contain or embody any proprietary or confidential material of Employer.

13. Proprietary Information. Employee agrees and acknowledges that Employee continues to be bound by the Proprietary Information Agreement between Employer and Employee that Employee dated _____.

14. No Third Party Rights. The parties agree that by making this Agreement they do not intend to confer any benefits, privileges or rights to any person who is not a party to this Agreement. The Agreement is strictly between the parties hereto, subject to the terms of paragraph 3 above, and that it shall not be construed to vest in any other the status of third-party beneficiary.

15. Duty To Effectuate. The parties agree to perform any lawful additional acts, including the execution of additional agreements, as are reasonably necessary to effectuate the purpose of this Agreement.

16. Entire Agreement. This Agreement constitutes the complete, final and exclusive embodiment of the entire agreement between Employee and Employer with regard to the subject matter hereof. Employee represents and agrees that this Agreement is entered into without reliance on any promise or representation, written or oral, other than those expressly contained herein. This Agreement may not be modified except in a writing signed by Employee and a duly authorized officer of Employer.

17. Successors and Assigns. This Agreement shall bind the heirs, personal representatives, successors, assigns, executors and administrators of each party, and inure to the benefit of each party, its heirs, successors and assigns.

18. Applicable Law. The parties agree that this Agreement is entered into in the State of _____, and that the parties agree and intend that it be construed and enforced in accordance with the laws of the State of _____.

19. Forum Selection. Any controversy arising out of or relating to this Agreement or the breach thereof, or any claim or action to enforce this Agreement or portion thereof, or any controversy or claim requiring interpretation of this Agreement must be brought in a forum located within the State of _____.

20. Severability. If any provision of this Agreement is determined to be invalid, void or unenforceable, in whole or in part, such determination shall not affect any other provision of this Agreement, and the provision in question shall be modified so as to be rendered enforceable.

21. Section Headings. The section and paragraph headings contained in this Agreement are for reference purposes only and shall not affect in any way the meaning or interpretation of this Agreement.

22. Counterparts. This Agreement may be executed by facsimile and in two or more counterparts, each of which shall be deemed an original, and all together shall constitute one and the same instrument.

23. Voluntary and Knowing. Employee represents and agrees that in executing this Agreement, Employee has reviewed it, understands its terms, has had an opportunity and was advised to seek guidance from counsel of Employer's own choosing, and acted knowingly and voluntarily.

In Witness Whereof, the parties have duly authorized and caused this Agreement to be executed as follows:

Employee: **Employer:**

_____, an individual   _____ [insert Company name]

                                                                     By: _____
[Signature]   [Signature]

                                                                     Title: _____

Date: _____   Date: _____

Approved As To Form:

Counsel for Employee: **Counsel for Employer:**

_____   _____
[Signature]   [Signature]

Date: _____   Date: _____

Exhibit A
[Attach spreadsheet containing information required by the OWBPA, 29 U.S.C. 626(f)(1)(H).]

Sample G.3.2 General Release Agreement and Waiver of Claims [OWBPA release form for group terminations]

Notice: Various state and federal laws and regulations prohibit employment discrimination based on age, race, color, religion, sex, national origin, disability, citizenship, and veteran status. These laws are enforced through the Equal Employment Opportunity Commission, U.S. Department of Labor, and other federal and state agencies. If you feel that your agreement to participate in the Company Early Exit Incentive Program ("EEIP") and signing of this General Release Agreement and Waiver of Claims was coerced or is discriminatory, you are encouraged to speak with the Company's Director of Human Resources and/or an attorney about your concerns. **You are advised to consult with an attorney regarding your legal rights and obligations under the General Release Agreement and Waiver of Claims and the Early Exit Incentive Program. You are advised to consult with an attorney prior to making an election to participate in the Early Exit Incentive Program. You are advised to consult with an attorney prior to signing this General Release Agreement and Waiver of Claims.** *You should thoroughly review and understand the effect of this document before signing it. Therefore, please take this General Release Agreement and Waiver of Claims, along with all the documents provided in the Early Exit Incentive Program packet, and carefully consider it forty-five (45) days before signing it. Additionally, after you have executed this form, you have seven (7) days (until [Date]) to reconsider and revoke your agreement. Any revocation of this agreement must be made in writing and submitted to the Director of Human Resources no later than 4:30 p.m. on [Date].*

General Release: I acknowledge that in the document entitled "Company Early Exit Incentive Program," I have been provided with notice of the ages of the class, unit, or group of individuals covered by the EEIP, and the time limits applicable to the EEIP. I further acknowledge that in the document entitled "Company Early Exit Incentive Program," I have been provided with notice of the job titles and ages of all individuals eligible or selected for the EEIP, and the ages of all individuals in the same job classification or organizational unit who are not eligible or selected for the program. In consideration of my acceptance of the payments and benefits offered to me as described in the document entitled "Company Early Exit Incentive Program," (attached hereto as Exhibit "A" and incorporated by reference), I, individually and on behalf of my spouse, family members, heirs, executors, administrators, legal representatives, beneficiaries and assigns (collectively the "Releasing Parties"), hereby release, waive and discharge Company and its affiliates, organizations, current and former officers, directors, trustees, employees, agents, successors, and assigns of such persons or entities (collectively the "Released Parties") from any and all claims, liabilities, demands and causes of action, and demands of whatever kind or character known or unknown, fixed or contingent, arising out of my employment relationship or the termination or resignation of my employment with Company, including but not limited to: claims arising under federal, state, or local constitutions, charters or laws; any claims of race, sex, ethnicity, color or religious or other discrimination under state and/or federal constitutions and/or laws; any claim of age discrimination under the Age Discrimination in Employment Act (29 U.S.C. § 621-634) and/or state law; any claim of disability discrimination under the Americans with Disabilities Act and/or state law; any claim for benefits by me or payment of benefits to me under any employee benefit plan; or any other act, conduct, omission, or negligence of any of the Released Parties, whether vicarious, derivative, or direct, including, as required by the Age Discrimination in Employment Act (29 U.S.C. § 621-634), any claims arising under the Act before this Agreement is executed. This General Release Agreement does not have any effect on any claim that may arise after the date this General Release Agreement is executed and/or reaffirmed. I do hereby agree not to file a lawsuit or charge of discrimination to assert such claims. I further acknowledge and agree that by accepting the EEIP benefits, I have given up my right to file any complaint, lawsuit, or other legal action against any of the Released Parties growing out of, connected with, or relating in any way to my employment, or the termination or resignation of my employment, with Company. Further in consideration of the payments and benefits offered to me, I acknowledge and agree that the Released Parties may recover from me any loss, including attorneys' fees and costs of defending against any claim brought by me or the Releasing Parties, that they may suffer arising out of my breach of this General Release Agreement and Waiver of Claims.

Additionally, in further consideration of the promises and undertakings of Company, I hereby agree that I will not ever apply for or otherwise seek regular employment with Company and that my forbearance to seek future employment is purely contractual and is in no way involuntary, discriminatory, or retaliatory. I understand that nothing in this Agreement prevents me from applying for employment with Company on a temporary or substitute basis.

I understand and agree that this General Release Agreement and Waiver of Claims is final and binding. If I challenge the enforceability of this General Release Agreement and Waiver of Claims, I agree initially to tender to Company all benefits received pursuant to the EEIP, and invite Company to retain such money and agree with me to cancel this General Release Agreement and Waiver of Claims. In the event Company accepts this offer, Company shall retain such money and this General Release Agreement and Waiver of Claims will be void. In the event Company does not accept such offer, Company shall so notify me, and shall place such money in an interest bearing escrow account pending the resolution of any dispute as to whether this General Release Agreement and Waiver of Claims shall be set aside and/or otherwise be tendered unenforceable. I understand and agree that if I do challenge the enforceability of this General Release Agreement and Waiver of Claims, Company is not obligated to continue to pay me any EEIP benefits still outstanding.

I warrant and represent to Company that: (i) I have the authority to execute this General Release Agreement and Waiver of Claims individually and on behalf of all the Releasing Parties; (ii) neither I nor any other Releasing Party individually, collectively, or otherwise, has assigned to any other person any part of any claim or cause of action against Company or any Released Party, whether vicarious, derivative, or direct, and that no person is or may be entitled to any portion of the EEIP benefits I will receive, either by subordination or otherwise; and (iii) I will return to Company any and all items of Company's property which I had access to or control over during my employment no later than the last day of my employment.

I acknowledge and agree that Company has no legal obligation to provide the EEIP benefits except as described herein, and my acceptance of the obligations and attendant additional compensation as described herein constitutes my agreement to all terms and conditions set forth in this General Release Agreement and Waiver of Claims, and are in consideration of the promises and undertakings of Company. I understand that I cannot receive the EEIP benefits unless and until I have fully complied with the notice requirements stated in the EEIP Document, and until the revocation period has expired. I further acknowledge that the EEIP payments will be paid to me as described in the document entitled "Company Early Exit Incentive Program" provided to me with this waiver. This General Release Agreement and Waiver of Claims does not have any effect on any claim that may arise after the date this General Release Agreement and Waiver of Claims is executed and/or reaffirmed.

I acknowledge and agree that: (1) this General Release Agreement and Waiver of Claims will be construed and enforced in accordance with the laws of the State of _____; (2) if any provision of this General Release Agreement and Waiver of Claims is held unenforceable, such provision shall be considered separate, distinct, and severable from the other remaining provisions of the General Release Agreement and Waiver of Claims and shall not affect the validity or enforceability of such other remaining provisions; and that, in all other respects, this General Release Agreement and Waiver of Claims shall remain in full force and effect.

I have carefully read and fully understand all of the provisions of this General Release Agreement and Waiver of Claims. I further acknowledge that this General Release Agreement and Waiver of Claims is signed knowing and voluntary on my part, that I have had at least forty-five (45) days to deliberate regarding its terms, that I have been advised to consult with an attorney before signing this General Release Agreement and Waiver of Claims, and that I have been advised to consult with an attorney before electing to participate in the EEIP. *I further acknowledge that I have been informed that I have seven (7) days after signing (until [Date]) to revoke this General Release Agreement and Waiver of Claims,* and that my election to retire will be effective [Date].

Date Signed: _____

_____
Signature of Employee

_____
Printed Name

State of _____

County of _____

Before me, the undersigned authority on this day personally appeared _____, known to me to be the person whose name subscribed to the foregoing instrument, and acknowledged to me that he executed the same for the purposes and consideration therein expressed.

Subscribed and Sworn to before me this _____ day of _____, 20___, to certify which witness my hand and seal of office.

_____

Notary Public in and for the State of _____

My Commission Expires: _____

Sample G.3.3 Separation Agreement [OWBPA release form for group terminations]

This Separation Agreement ("Agreement") is entered into by and between _____ ("Employer") and _____ ("Employee").

The waivers and releases contained in this Agreement are for the benefit of Employer, and any or all of its subsidiaries, affiliates, and divisions, and the officers, directors, agents, employees, and attorneys of each of them (collectively, the "Releasees").

Recitals

Employer has notified Employee that Employee's employment will be terminated effective [Date] as part of a job restructuring.

In recognition of, and appreciation for, Employee's valuable service to Employer, Employer desires to provide for a smooth and amicable termination of Employee's employment and for the speedy transition of Employee to alternative employment.

Therefore, Employer and Employee now agree as follows:

Covenants

Employer shall provide Employee with _____ weeks of severance pay at Employee's regular salary. Such severance pay shall be paid by Employer in a single lump sum as soon as practicable after the expiration of the seven (7) day revocation period described below, and shall be subject to all withholding authorized or required by law.

Employee acknowledges that, but for this Agreement, Employee would not otherwise be entitled to receive such severance pay from Employer.

In consideration of Employer's payments to Employee as described above, Employee for Employee and Employee's heirs, assigns, and personal representatives hereby forever waives and releases the Releasees from any and all claims, demands, rights, liabilities, causes of action, and grievances ("claims"), known or unknown, statutory or at common law, arising out of Employee's employment or termination of employment which exist or may exist as of the effective date of this Agreement.

By way of example only and without limitation, this waiver and release is applicable to any claims under Title VII of the Civil Rights Act of 1964, the Age Discrimination in Employment Act, the Older Workers Benefit Protection Act, the Rehabilitation Act of 1973, the Americans With Disabilities Act, the Civil Rights Act of 1991, the Equal Pay Act of 1963, the Pregnancy Discrimination Act, the Family and Medical Leave Act, the Fair Labor Standards Act, _____ [insert names of applicable state employment laws], any and all applicable state anti-discrimination statutes, laws or regulations, and local laws and ordinances, or of wrongful discharge, implied or express contract, covenant of good faith and fair dealing, intentional or negligent infliction of emotional distress, defamation and any other claim in contract or tort.

Employee understands, and it is Employee's intent, that in the event this Agreement is ever held to be invalid and unenforceable (in whole or in part) as to any particular type of claim or as to any particular circumstances, it shall remain fully valid and enforceable as to all other claims and circumstances.

Employee acknowledges and represents that Employee has entered into this Agreement knowingly and voluntarily and has carefully read its contents and clarified any point not fully understood.

Employee acknowledges and represents that in executing this Agreement Employee has not relied upon any representation or statement not set forth in this Agreement and that this Agreement may not be modified orally.

Employee acknowledges and represents that Employee has had the opportunity to review this Agreement with legal counsel. Employee is encouraged to consult with legal counsel and a tax advisor to review this Agreement, and shall have forty-five (45) days from the date on which Employee received this Agreement, in which to perform said review. After execution of this Agreement, Employee shall have seven (7) days in which to revoke this Agreement.

This Agreement shall not become effective or enforceable until expiration of the seven (7) day revocation period.

Employee agrees that Employee shall keep this Agreement, its terms, and all circumstances leading to this Agreement strictly confidential; provided, however, that Employee may disclose this Agreement and its terms to Employee's immediate family, accountants, attorneys, and any state or federal agency; provided further that such persons do not disclose this Agreement or its terms to any other person. In the event of a breach of this confidentiality obligation by Employee, Employee shall be liable to Employer for all amounts paid under this Agreement as liquidated damages, together with all reasonable attorney fees and costs incurred in the enforcement of this Agreement.

Employee:

_____

_____
Date of Execution

Employer:

_____
By

_____
Title

_____
Date of Execution

Sample G.4.1 OWBPA Group Disclosure Memorandum (with exhibit)

Memorandum

[OWBPA Group Disclosure Memorandum]

Date: _____

To: _____ [insert employee name]

From: _____ [Company]

Re: Termination of Employment and Separation Agreement

Please be advised that your employment with [Company] will be terminated effective _____. [Company] greatly appreciates your service on its behalf over the period of your employment.

In recognition of, and appreciation for, your valuable service, [Company] desires to provide for a smooth and amicable termination of your employment and for your speedy transition to alternative employment. Therefore, [Company] is prepared to offer you a Separation Agreement in the form attached hereto. In addition, upon the termination of your employment, you will be paid for any earned but unpaid salary and any accrued but unused Paid Time Off hours.

As required by federal law, 29 U.S.C. § 626(f)(1)(H), you are hereby advised of the following information pertinent to the Separation Agreement:

1. The individuals who are eligible to participate in this program are shown on the attached spreadsheet. You and the other individuals are eligible for participation in this program because your employment is being terminated due to _____ [insert a brief description for the reason for the group termination; for example "the plant closure," "mass layoff," or "job restructuring."].

2. The time limits applicable to this program are from the date of the termination of your employment through the time periods described in the Separation Agreement, i.e., forty-five (45) days within which to consider and sign the Separation Agreement and a seven (7) day period within which to revoke the Separation Agreement after it has been signed.

3. The job titles of the individuals eligible to participate in this program are shown on the attached spreadsheet.

4. The ages of the persons eligible, and ineligible, to participate in this program are shown on the attached spreadsheet.

5. If you desire to participate in this program, please return your signed Separation Agreement to: _____ no later than forty-five (45) days from the date of this Memorandum.

6. If you have any questions about the Separation Agreement, please contact _____ at _____.

Exhibit A

Employees Not Eligible to Receive Benefits Under This Plan

Employee	Department	Position	Age

Employees Eligible to Receive Benefits Under This Plan

Employee	Department	Position	Age

Sample G.4.2 Early Exit Incentive Program Disclosure

Background:

The Company has developed an Early Exit Incentive Program ("EEIP") under which eligible employees may elect to accept benefits in exchange for the signing and execution of a General Release Agreement and Waiver of Claims ("Release Agreement") relating to various terms and conditions. This document will provide employees with information regarding: (1) the class, unit and/or groups of individuals covered by the EEIP; (2) the eligibility factors for the EEIP; (3) the time limits applicable to the EEIP; and (4) the benefits offered under the EEIP. In accordance with the Older Workers Benefit Protection Act, the job titles and ages of all individuals potentially eligible for the EEIP, and the ages of all individuals in the same job classification or organizational unit who are not eligible are set forth in the EEIP Disclosure Document attached hereto as Appendix 1. The EEIP will provide opportunities to realign staffing levels and redirect financial resources. The EEIP is voluntary. *This is a one-time program offering that will not be repeated.*

Employees Covered by the EEIP:

All full-time Company employees who meet the eligibility factors defined below are eligible for the EEIP. All employees who are eligible for the EEIP who elect to participate are selected for the EEIP. **Eligibility Factors:**

To qualify for the EEIP, the Company employee must:

1. Be eligible for retirement through the Company Retirement Program ("CRP") as of June 30, 20___;

2. Elect to retire through the CRP;

3. Submit a completed application and all required forms to CRP for retirement in sufficient time to obtain approval from CRP of a retirement date no later than June 30, 20___;

4. Sign and notarize the Release Agreement and return it to the Human Resources Office within forty-five (45) days after receiving the Release Agreement. The Release Agreement acknowledged before a notary public provides to the Company a written release and waiver of all pre-retirement claims against the Company, its officers, agents and/or employees, including without limitation to claims of race, sex, ethnicity, color, religious or other discrimination under state or federal law; age discrimination under the Age Discrimination in Employment Act (29 U.S.C. §§ 621-634) and state law; disability discrimination under the Americans with Disabilities Act and state law; and that provides that the employee agrees not to seek reemployment in the future with the Company without the consent of the Company. If the Release Agreement is completed and returned to the Human Resources Office, the employee will have until June 28, 20___ to revoke the Release Agreement in writing;

5. Elect and sign the Election Form for the [$ Amount] payment (attached as Exhibit B to the Release Agreement) for payout of the [$ Amount] payment. Not revoke the Release Agreement; and

6. Not revoke their election to retire through the CRP.

Compliance with all of the requirements set forth above is necessary for participation in the EEIP. Any employee who elects to participate in the EEIP but fails to timely and properly comply with the foregoing requirements will not be eligible for participation in the EEIP.

Time Limits Applicable to the EEIP:

All EEIP packets will be distributed between April 30, 20___ and May 3, 20___ only. Eligible employees who voluntarily participate in the EEIP must elect to participate in the EEIP no later than 4:30 p.m. on June 20, 20___. Once the Release Agreement is returned to the Human Resources Office, the employee has until June 28, 20___ to revoke the Release Agreement. If the employee so elects, the employee will not be eligible for the EEIP. If the employee does not elect to revoke the Release Agreement and has satisfied all other EEIP requirements, the employee's election to retire and the Release Agreement will be effective and enforceable on June 28, 20___.

Benefits Provided Under the EEIP:

Eligible employees that elect to participate in the EEIP and timely comply with all requirements of the EEIP will receive the following benefits from the Company:

1. Upon retirement no later than June 30, 20___, the participating employee will be paid $1,000.00 plus up to thirty (30) days of previously accumulated but unused sick leave. All previously accrued but unused vacation leave will also be paid.

2. The participating employee will receive an amount equivalent to the payment of sixty (60) days of the employee's remaining total balance of previously accumulated but unused sick leave, as of the retirement date less the payment amount set forth in section 1 above, to be paid on January 15, 20___; and until the employee's individual sick leave accumulation is exhausted, an amount equivalent to the payment of thirty (30) days of previously accumulated but unused sick leave on April 15, 20___, July 15, 20___, October 15, 20___, January 15, 20___, April 15, 20___, and July 15, 20___. In summary, and *only to the extent the participating employee has sufficient previously accumulated but unused sick leave,* payments equivalent to the following will be made:

At retirement on June 30, 20___:	30 days of accumulated but unused sick leave
January 15, 20___	60 days (with 2% interest from 7-1-___)
April 15, 20___	30 days
July 15, 20___	30 days
October 15, 20___	30 days
January 15, 20___	30 days
April 15, 20___	30 days
July 15, 20___	30 days

If a participating retiree should die before receiving payment equivalent to the full amount of his/her individual previously accrued but unused sick leave, remaining payments will be made to his/her estate.

3. A payment of [$ Amount] will be issued to the participating employee, with one of the following options for payment:

    ■ one lump sum payment, paid either October 15, 20___ or January 15, 20___; or

    ■ multiple payments totaling [$ Amount] paid out over time, on October 15, 20___, October 15, 20___, and/or October 15, 20___; or insurance premiums until [$ Amount] is exhausted, or until July 31, 20___, *whichever comes first.*

    If a participating retiree should die before receiving payment equivalent to the full amount of his/her individual [$ Amount], remaining payments will be made to his/her estate.

4. The participating employee will receive interest on the payment amount equivalent to a maximum of sixty (60) days of previously accumulated but unused sick leave, at the rate of two percent (2%) per annum calculated from July 1, 20___ until January 15, 20___. The participating employee will not be entitled to receive any interest on the payment amounts, if any, for previously accrued but unused sick leave in excess of a total of sixty (60) days of accumulated but unused sick leave.

5. The Company will make its regular contribution to the participating employee's TMRS account for the amount equivalent to a maximum of ninety (90) days of previously accumulated but unused sick leave at the time of retirement on June 30, 20___. The employee contribution (at seven percent (7%)) will also be made on a maximum of thirty (30) days of previously accumulated but unused sick leave at the time of retirement on June 30, 20___; the Company *will prepay for the employee an amount to CRP equivalent to the employee's seven percent (7%) contribution on a maximum of sixty (60) days of previously accumulated but unused sick leave at the time of the employee's retirement on June 30, 20___ and will withhold an equal amount from the amount paid to the employee on January 15, 20___.*

Election To Participate in the EEIP

Your acceptance of the terms and conditions of the Release Agreement will become effective and enforceable on June 28, 20__.

If you have any questions relating to the EEIP or the EEIP benefits please contact the Human Resource Office at [Phone Number]. You are advised to consult with an attorney regarding your legal rights and obligations under the Release Agreement and this EEIP prior to making an election to participate in the EEIP and prior to signing the Release Agreement.

The terms and conditions of the EEIP including the Release Agreement are final and non-negotiable, and may not be modified, amended or altered. Please carefully read this letter and ensure that you fully understand the effect of your participation in the EEIP.

_____   _____
Company President   Date

Employee

The undersigned employee hereby elects to participate in the Early Exit Incentive Program, and does by the signature below represent that the undersigned employee: (1) has been given at least forty-five (45) days to review the General Release Agreement and Waiver of Claims; and (2) has read and fully understands the Early Exit Incentive Program.

_____
(Signature)

_____
Printed Name

_____
Date

Completed form received by Human Resource Office: _____, 20___ (date and time) by _____ (signature).

SECTION H

Employee Separation Packet Materials

It is a good idea to prepare separation packets for departing employees to provide information about benefits, policies on references, rehire, access to personnel records, severance pay, and persons to contact with questions. Separation packets are especially useful in implementing RIFs. This section contains samples of materials that could be included in an employee's separation packet.

▇▇▇▇▇▇▇▇ Termination Benefits Information
Sample H.1.1

- ▇ Health, Dental, Life, and Disability Insurance continues until midnight on _____, 200___.

- ▇ You are eligible for COBRA: continuation of healthcare insurance.

- ▇ You will receive a COBRA notification from our third party administrator, _____.

- ▇ You have sixty (60) days to respond to our third-party administrator that you want to continue the insurance.

- ▇ You then have forty-five (45) days to send in your payment.

- ▇ Read the COBRA document very carefully as it will outline all the dates that you need to respond to for completing the COBRA process. The cost of coverage continuation should be about $[XXX.XX] per month.

Sample H.1.2 Voluntary Resignation Incentive Benefit Package Letter

Date

Dear Company Employee:

This is not a layoff notice. *This letter describes the Voluntary Resignation Incentive Benefit Package offered to eligible employees. It offers those employees an incentive to resign to help the Company avoid employee layoffs.*

You are in a job classification that has positions identified for elimination in the upcoming budget cuts. This action may result in the layoff of one or more Company employees. While you may have enough seniority within your classification to avoid layoff or bumping actions, other employees in the classification may be laid off.

To minimize the number of employees laid off, we are offering a one-time Voluntary Resignation Incentive Benefit Package to eligible employees. The specifics of the package are set forth in _____. In general terms, it provides the following benefits:

Severance pay—An employee receiving the package will get severance pay in an amount equal to 2% of the employee's annual base salary for each full year of full-time Company service. The amount paid will be no less than two (2) weeks of the employee's base salary at the time of separation. Only the time worked since the employee's most recent date of hire will count towards this calculation.

Example: 2% of annual base salary for every full year of service:

Salary	Years of Service	Severance
$42,000	7	$5,880.00

Calculation: $42,000 x 2% x 7 = $5,880

Health benefits—In addition, the Company would pay the Company portion of the premium on health/dental insurance for the first two months following voluntary separation of the resigning employee.

If you voluntarily resign you agree to give up your recall rights in any Company classification to which you have bumping rights. However, you may apply for reinstatement to eligible lists in accordance with Personnel Rule 18.

How to Apply—If you would like to volunteer to accept the Voluntary Resignation Incentive Benefit Package, return the enclosed response to the Personnel Director's Office *by 12:00 noon on* _____, *200___*. The number of employees who will be granted this incentive package depends upon the number of potential layoffs in each class. If more employees volunteer than are necessary, seniority within the classification will be used to determine which employees will receive the incentive package. If you have any questions, please call the Personnel Hotline at [Phone Number].

Sincerely,

Personnel Director

Enclosure

Sample H.2.1 Unemployment Benefits from the State of Arizona

Company employees that are laid off may consider filing for unemployment benefits with the State of Arizona. The following information from the State of Arizona - Department of Economic Security is provided for your convenience:

All initial claim applications for Unemployment Insurance Benefits are filed by telephone, regardless of whether you are living in Arizona or in another state. ARRA is the acronym for the Arizona Re-employment Rapid Access. ARRA is the telephone method used to file an Arizona claim for Unemployment Insurance Benefits. It is a computer-based, interactive voice response system. It can only be used with a touch-tone telephone and you can choose to have the instructions read in English or Spanish. Phone numbers are listed below (as well as walk-in office information for those without touch-tone phones).

You should have the following information ready before making your call:

Your Social Security Number; your residence address, Company, state and ZIP Code; County of residence; the name, mailing address and ZIP Code of your last employer; your Alien Registration Number if you are not a citizen of the United States; forms SF-8 and SF-50 if you have worked as a Federal Civilian Employee in the past 18 months; your DD-214 (Member 4 copy) if you have served in the US Military in the past 18 months; a Personal Identification Number (PIN) (your PIN is a 4-digit, secret number you make up before you place your call).

ARRA Phone Numbers
(to file a claim for unemployment benefits):

Metro Phoenix Area [###-####]
Metro Tucson Area [###-####]
All Other Areas [###-####]
TDD/TTY [###-####]

The ARRA System is available Monday - Friday from 7:00 a.m. - 4:30 p.m. (Mountain Standard Time-MST).

If do not have access to a touch-tone phone, you may report to the Arizona Job Service Office nearest to your home and ask for assistance. The downtown Phoenix office is located at:

438 West Adams Street, Phoenix

Telephone: [###-####]

The following State of Arizona-DES web site contains this and much more information, including Frequently Asked Questions:

http://www.de.state.az.us/esa/faq.asp

Sample H.3.1 Severance Package Questions and Answers

1. What is a severance package and what is the purpose?

A severance package is a cash payment to an employee to entice the employee to leave Company employment, or, in the case of a layoff, a severance package provides financial assistance. Severance packages are important to ensure that employees who may have to leave Company employment have compensation to help them and their families as they transition to new employment. Also, in the past, voluntary or resignation severances and retirement incentives have been shown to be an effective way to reduce staffing.

2. Who will be offered a severance and what is the timeframe?

Severance packages will be used only to prevent a layoff. In February 2006, the Company will adopt a final budget. Once the budget is adopted, Personnel will review those positions identified for elimination and will look at vacancies within the same classifications. This includes seniority determinations and "bumping" actions. After this process, if there are still employees in eliminated positions, severance offers will be used in an attempt to prevent layoffs. In late February or March, severance letters will be sent to employees only in classifications that would be impacted. A severance offer will be accepted only if it will prevent a layoff.

3. Who decides which severance offers will be accepted?

If more employees offer to take a severance than are needed to prevent a layoff, seniority will determine whose offer is accepted. Seniority is determined by time in classification. Company service time is used as a tiebreaker.

4. What are the different types of severances?

There are three types: retirement, resignation, and layoff. A retirement severance is only for employees who are currently eligible to retire. The Company does not allow "early retirement." A resignation severance is for an employee who willingly leaves Company employment. A layoff severance is given to an employee whose employment ends involuntarily.

5. How much is the severance package?

For resignation and layoff, the severance is 2% of annual base salary for every full year of full-time Company of service. The retirement severance is based on a graduated percent of annual base salary for every full year of Company service at a rate of 2% for the first $40,000 of salary, 1% for the next $40,000, and 0.5% of additional salary.

6. Am I likely to receive severance?

It's difficult to predict. In the early 1990s during the last Company-wide position reduction process, 470 positions were eliminated. A total of 68 severances resulted: 51 retirement, 13 resignations, and 4 layoffs.

7. Why is the retirement severance offer different than the other two?

The retirement severance takes into account the added value to retirees who will receive an increase in their retirement income and receive medical benefits upon separation. As a percentage of annual salary, the retirement severance provides the greatest economic assistance to employees who earn the least. The plan is designed with total cost in mind—the more the Company pays in severance, the more that departments have to cut out of their budgets.

8. I'm eligible and was planning to retire in December. Should I wait and see if I can get a good severance package next year to boost my retirement income?

When to retire is entirely an employee's choice. However, it's important for employees to make informed decisions; you may want to consult with the Retirement Office. Things to consider:

- When longevity is paid;
- When is your next salary increase;
- In order to be eligible for cost of living adjustments (COLA) to a retiree's monthly pension, a retiree has to be retired for a full 36 months, effective January 1. Retiring in January instead of December impacts the three full calendar year waiting period; and
- Retiring close to month-end lessens the time to receiving the first pension check.

9. When am I eligible to retire?

You are eligible to retire if you are 60 years old and have 10 or more years of credited service; if you are 62 years old and have 5 or more years of credited service; or if your age and years of credited service combined equal 80.

10. Whom can I talk to about retirement?

Contact the Retirement Office at [Retirement Office phone number]

11. If I was able to buy additional years of service from the military or a previous employer for retirement purposes, does that change my Company seniority date?

No. Company seniority dates are based on Company service alone.

Sample H.4.1 Severance Pay Examples

(Please note the different years of service in each example)

Retirement Severance—Example

First $0 – $40,000 of salary at 2%

$40,001 – $80,000 of salary at 1%

$80,001 + at 0.5%

Salary	Years of Service	Severance
$42,000	28	$22,960

Calculation: $40,000 x 2% + $2,000 x 1% = $820

$820 x 28 (years of service) = $22,960

Voluntary Severance—Example

2% of annual base pay for every full year of service

Salary	Years of Service	Severance
$42,000	7	$5,880

Calculation: $42,000 x 2% x 7 = $5,880

Involuntary Severance—Example

2% of annual base pay for every full year of service

Salary	Years of Service	Severance
$42,000	2	$1,680

Calculation: $42,000 x 2% x 2 = $1,680

Sample H.5.1 Reduction in Force (Bumping) Frequently Asked Questions

(as of _____, 200___)

---

1. When bumping or severance offers occur, how is seniority determined and what is it based on?

Seniority is based primarily on an employee's time spent in a particular classification. If two or more employees are "tied" for time in a classification, then years with the Company are used to determine seniority. For example, if two employees both have three years in their current classification, but one has been with the Company for 10 years and the other for five, the person with 10 years is considered senior. However, if the 10-year employee has only one year in the current classification, then the employee who has three years in the classification (even though she has fewer years with the Company) would be the senior employee.

2. What can employees do now to prepare for this upcoming change?

It will be difficult for employees to predict how upcoming budget cuts may impact them. Employees should continue to perform their best during these uncertain times, and keep informed by reading the Company's written communications about the ongoing process. We will make every effort to provide information, as it becomes available.

3. My position is on my department's list to be eliminated; does that mean that I will be laid off?

Not all of the positions identified by departments will be cut. If filled positions are cut, then layoffs are determined by seniority within a classification. If you have more time in your current classification than someone else in your department in the same classification, you can normally expect to remain in your current department. The employee in your department with the least amount of full-time service in your classification would displace (bump) the person in that class with the lowest seniority in the Company.

4. There are no positions in my department's list of reductions in my classification; does that mean that I will not be affected by the layoffs?

Not necessarily. A position in your classification in a different department may be scheduled for elimination. If the incumbent employee is more senior than other employees in the class, he or she may bump a junior employee in the same class. In addition, an employee from a higher level class may bump back to your class.

5. I have been promoted several times since my initial employment with the Company. What are my seniority rights if I am the junior person in my current classification?

If you are bumped from your current classification because you have the lowest seniority, you have rights to bump into the classification from which you were promoted. Your seniority time in the lower class would be a combination of the time you served in the lower classification, plus the time you served in the higher classification. There are some exceptions to this policy; specifically, non-classified positions do not accrue seniority rights, nor do part-time or temporary positions.

6. Must I have completed probation in a classification to have rights to bump back to that class?

No. If you have full-time classified (not considered exempt) service in the class, your seniority rights will be calculated.

7. I have been in my current classification for four years. The classification from which I was promoted no longer exists in the Company. Do I have rights to bump back to something if I am the junior employee in my current class?

No. The class in which you have previous service must still exist and be funded to be used for bumping.

8. If I am laid off or reduced to a lower job, what are my rights to return to my classification in the future?

Your name will be placed on a recall list. This will be good for three years. When vacancies occur in a class with a recall list, only the highest seniority name will be sent to the department for selection. If you are offered a job in your classification from a recall list and you don't accept it, your name will be removed from the recall list, and you will forfeit any further entitlements. Please note that your recall rights are to a classification, not to a particular department.

9. Do employees take a pay cut if they are bumped back to a lower classification?

Personnel will transfer employees laterally when possible, within the employee's current classification in another Company department. Also if a lateral transfer to an equivalent classification for which he or she is qualified is available, the employee may be placed in a vacant position without a pay cut. However, if an employee is bumped back to a lower classification there will usually be a pay cut associated with the transaction.

10. How will bumped employees be notified?

Employees will be personally notified by their department management of when and where they will report to their new assignment.

11. There is a change coming up in my life in the next two months (e.g., moving to another state, planning to retire, etc.). I have enough seniority to stay in my job. Should I tell someone about this future change?

Yes. It will not affect your ability to stay in your job, but it is a factor that the Company can consider when it is preparing to release another employee. So, please tell your supervisor or personnel officer.

12. What happens to my employee benefits if I am laid off?

Orientation classes will be held to discuss benefits with employees to be laid off. In general terms, you have the right to continue your current health and dental plans for 18 months. The Company will make its current monthly payment for the first two months. After that, you will be responsible for the full monthly premium. You will receive a more detailed explanation at the orientation meeting.

13. If I am attending school and would have requested tuition reimbursement when the semester ends, can I still get reimbursed?

Yes. If you were eligible for reimbursement when you started the class, you may be reimbursed at the completion of the course, even if you have been laid off.

14. Will the Company offer incentive packages to encourage employees to resign or retire early?

On December 11, 2002, the Company adopted a severance package. The package will be offered to employees only when filled positions in their classification are being cut or bumped and their vacancy would assist the Company in preventing a layoff.

Sample H.6.1 Retirement Benefits

If you are retiring, schedule an appointment to discuss medical, dental, and life insurance coverage, or deferred compensation.

What to consider:

Medical Insurance

- Company group medical insurance coverage stops on the last day of the month in which you cease employment.

- A benefit-eligible retiree can enroll in retiree medical coverage within 31 days of retirement.

- As a retiree, you will receive a Company contribution toward the cost of medical coverage based on your years of Company service.

- If you "defer" your retirement when you separate from employment, you will not be eligible for the Company's retiree medical coverage, unless you requalify through future Company employment.

Dental Insurance

- A retiree can continue existing dental coverage for up to 18 months through COBRA coverage if application is made within 60 days. Premium is 102% of the total monthly cost.

Life Insurance

- Occupational AD&D (Accidental Death and Dismemberment) and Life Insurance stop on the last day of employment. Basic Life, Basic AD&D, and Voluntary Supplemental Life Insurance coverage stop on the last day of the month in which you cease employment.

- You have 31 days from the date coverage ceases to apply for conversion of Basic Life and/or Basic AD&D, or continuation of Voluntary Supplemental Life coverage.

For questions on Medical, Dental, or Life, call [Name] at [Phone Number].

Deferred Compensation (DCP)

- As a retiree, you are eligible to receive benefit payments from your DCP account. If you want to receive payment, complete a Benefit Withdrawal Application and send it to [Name]. You should receive your payment approximately 15 days after receipt of the application by [Name]. Staff in the Benefits Office can assist you with this process during your scheduled retiree benefits meeting.

- If you wish, you may leave your money in your DCP account. However, your beginning payment date must be no later than April 1 of the calendar year following the year in which you reach age 70.5.

- You can also transfer part or all of your balance to a 457 plan, a 401 plan, a 403(b) plan, or a traditional IRA.

- You have the flexibility to choose a beginning payment, or transfer date at any time after leaving employment.

- To obtain forms, please contact the Benefits Office at [Phone Number].

If you have questions on DCP, call [Name] at [Phone Number]

Questions & Answers

Medical

- **How much will my medical premiums cost?**

  Currently, single coverage is $_____/month. Family coverage is $_____/month. The medical premium is reduced if you and/or your spouse are Medicare eligible. The Company provides $_____/month toward family coverage, reducing family coverage to $_____. This amount is applied directly to your premium deduction.

- **Does the Company further contribute toward retiree medical coverage?**

  Yes, the Company, through its Medical Expense Reimbursement Plan (MERP) provides a monthly contribution based upon years of service. This contribution comes to you as a separate check each month. It is not based on the type of coverage (single or family) you elect.

How much MERP do I get?

MERP is paid according to the number of years of credited Company service.

Less than 5 years of active credited Company service—$_____
5–14 years— $_____
15–24 years— $_____
25 or more years—$_____

If I move out of state, what medical coverage do I have?

You are covered under the Out-of-Network benefit level of the Company's plan. You will have a $_____ annual deductible per family member (up to 3 members) after which covered expenses will be paid at ____% of reasonable and customary charges. If you are on Medicare Parts A&B, your Medicare will pay first and the Company's coverage will pay as secondary.

If I drop my Company retiree coverage, can I come back into the Company's retiree medical plan?

You can apply for the Company's medical coverage during the annual open enrollment period, or within 31 days of the loss of other group coverage. You must show proof of continuous, comparable coverage for the time you were not covered under the Company's plan.

Dental

What are the dental benefits for retirees?

Dental insurance is not a retiree benefit. However, a retiree can continue existing coverage through COBRA for up to 18 months or convert to the Dental Health (prepaid) plan on an individual basis.

Life Insurance

How do I continue my life insurance? How much is that?

You can convert your Basic Life and Basic AD&D insurance within 31 days of the date of retirement. The cost is based on the amount of coverage in effect and your age. You can continue your Voluntary Supplemental Life insurance by enrolling within 31 days of the date of retirement. The cost is greater than active employee rates. Please contact the Benefits Office for more details.

Deferred Compensation Program

How and when do I get my DCP?

Once you have retired, you may request that DCP be paid to you. You have many options for receiving the money from [Name]. You must complete a Benefit Withdrawal Application and mail it to: [Address]. Payment should be received about 15 days after receipt of the application.

Why would I want to leave my contributions in the DCP account?

You may want to consider leaving your money in the 457 plan. If you do not need the money immediately, it will continue to be tax deferred and accrue interest while it is in the 457 account. Upon retirement, you have access to the entire account at your discretion with no early withdrawal penalty. However, you will pay regular income taxes on the amount of the distribution.

Can I transfer my money to another plan?

You can roll your funds into a traditional IRA or 401 plan, or, if you obtain other employment, their 457, 401, or 403(b) plan. The receiving plan must agree to this transfer of funds. The Company allows this transfer at any time after you retire.

Can I use this money to "buy back" service time and increase my pension?

You can use your 457 funds to buy back time. However, the Retirement Office must approve your eligibility. For more information, call the Retirement Office at [Phone Number].

SECTION I

Exit Interview Tools

Most employers conduct exit interviews or ask separating employees to complete an exit survey. As discussed in Chapter 4, there are many good reasons to do so. The topics covered vary according to organizational needs. Several different exit interview tools are provided in this section.

Exit interviews are more flexible than exit surveys, because they allow a properly trained questioner to add a personal touch to how questions are asked and responses are recorded. In some situations, the employee may be more comfortable with an interview format; in other situations, a questionnaire is better. This choice can depend as much on the personality of the employee as on the nature of the termination (e.g., resignation, disciplinary dismissal, or layoff). Each method has its advantages and disadvantages, depending on the circumstances of the particular termination.

Employers should design an exit interview/survey process that works for them and that can be consistently maintained long enough to establish benchmark data. Employers may want to consider outsourcing exit interviews to increase the likelihood that departing employees will give candid feedback or if company staff do not have the time or expertise necessary to conduct effective interviews.

Sample I.1.1   Termination and Exit Interview Schedule

Employee _____   Date _____

You are scheduled to meet with me on [Last Day Scheduled to Work] for your exit interview.

Please bring the following with you:

❏ Keys: door, cabinets, files

❏ Any Company business cards in your name

❏ Company-issued credit cards

❏ Company-issued telephone card

❏ Notebooks

❏ Computer

❏ Calculators

❏ Any other Company-owned equipment you may have in your possession.

❏ $$$ to pay outstanding phone or postage expenses

❏ Passwords for computer access, protected files, e-mail and voice mail

❏ Other

During this meeting, you can expect to:

❏ Have an exit discussion

❏ Sign a termination certificate

❏ Give a forwarding address for mailing your W-2 at the end of the year

❏ Receive your final paycheck

❏ Receive information about your HIPAA certificate

❏ Receive an explanation of your COBRA rights

❏ Receive information on insurance portability

❏ Receive information on your participation in the 401(k) retirement plan

❏ Receive information on _____

We can discuss anything you need or would like to discuss, or any benefit you may need information on, during this exit interview. If you need to speak with me prior to the exit interview, please stop by at any time.

Human Resources Manager

Sample I.2.1 Exit Interview Template

Associate Name: _____

Title: _____

Division: _____

Length of Service with Company: _____

Length of Service in Current Position: _____

Termination Date: _____

Amount of Notice Given: _____

Interviewer's Notes: To be kept in a separate, confidential file. Explain to associate that these comments may be passed along to upper management.

Division/Position

Throughout your interview/hiring process, how accurately was your job described/presented to you?

| |
| |
| |
| |
| |

What did you think of the amount of work expected of you?

| |
| |
| |
| |
| |

How important do you feel your position is to the organization?

| |
| |
| |
| |
| |

Please evaluate your work environment. Did you have the necessary equipment to do your job? When you needed information to do your job, were you able to get it easily?

| |
| |
| |
| |
| |

How is the morale in your Division/Department? How do people feel about their jobs, management, the company, etc.?

How do you feel about your co-workers? Do you feel that they were easy to work with and supportive of you?

Pay

How would you evaluate your pay in comparison to the work that you performed? Was pay a factor in your decision to leave?

Safety

Were the working conditions satisfactory? Was there anything that made you feel unsafe or uncomfortable in your work environment?

Benefits

What do you think of the company's benefits program? Is there anything that you feel the program is lacking?

Training and Development

How would you evaluate the initial training you received?

How would you evaluate the ongoing training you have received? Is there any necessary training that you would recommend, but were not provided?

Have you had sufficient opportunities to develop your capabilities in your present job?

Management

Do you think you were fairly rated on your performance reviews? Was the performance review process useful/beneficial to you?

What is your opinion of the direction you received? Did you receive adequate coaching, support, feedback, etc., from your manager?

Do you feel your work was appreciated by your manager?—By Company, in general?

Was overall treatment both fair and impartial?

General

Why did you originally come to work for Company? What attracted you to this role?

What, specifically, made you decide to leave your job? Do you have any personal comments regarding the company? Feel free to elaborate openly and honestly—your comments will be appreciated.

What could have been done to prevent your leaving?

Would you consider applying for work at Company in the future?

Do you have any suggestions for change or improvement?

Interviewer signature: **Date:**

❏ **Go through Termination Checklist**

Sample I.2.2   **Exit Interview**

1. How long were you employed with [Company Name]? *(Interview notes: full-time employment, last continuous employment period).*

Years: _____   Months: _____

2a). What are the main reasons you left [Company Name]?

❑ Benefits

❑ Career change

❑ Compensation

❑ Co-worker

❑ Job responsibilities

❑ Job stress

❑ Location

❑ Personal/family reasons

❑ Promotion

❑ Relocation

❑ Retirement

❑ Schedule

❑ School

❑ Supervisor

❑ Other: _____

2b). If more than one answer for 2a:

➔ Of these reasons you mentioned, which would you say is the primary reason?
(Interviewer, please circle their answer from the possible answers in 2A).

3. If you were a consultant to the department you are leaving, what recommendations would you make for improvements in the department?

_____

_____

_____

_____

_____

_____

_____

_____

_____

_____

4. **What factors were most important in choosing your new job?**

❏ Benefits

❏ Career change

❏ Compensation

❏ Job responsibilities

❏ Location

❏ Promotion

❏ Schedule

❏ Other: _____

❏ Not Applicable

5. **Under what conditions would you have stayed?**

_____

_____

_____

_____

_____

_____

_____

_____

_____

_____

_____

6. **I'm going to read to you a series of statements. Please answer with one of the following responses: Strongly Agree, Agree, Disagree, Strongly Disagree, or Unable to Rate.**

a) My job-related talents/skills were used effectively.

❏ Strongly Agree   ❏ Agree   ❏ Disagree   ❏ Strongly Disagree   ❏ Unable to Rate

b) My physical working conditions were reasonable for my type of work.

❏ Strongly Agree   ❏ Agree   ❏ Disagree   ❏ Strongly Disagree   ❏ Unable to Rate

c) I was given a fair opportunity to attend [Company Name]-sponsored training programs.

❏ Strongly Agree   ❏ Agree   ❏ Disagree   ❏ Strongly Disagree   ❏ Unable to Rate

d) The Company pays as well as most other employers in the area for similar work.

❏ Strongly Agree   ❏ Agree   ❏ Disagree   ❏ Strongly Disagree   ❏ Unable to Rate

e) The people who got promoted were generally well qualified.

❏ Strongly Agree   ❏ Agree   ❏ Disagree   ❏ Strongly Disagree   ❏ Unable to Rate

f) I was kept informed about issues facing my department that affected me.

❏ Strongly Agree   ❏ Agree   ❏ Disagree   ❏ Strongly Disagree   ❏ Unable to Rate

g) I received the training needed to do my job.

❏ Strongly Agree   ❏ Agree   ❏ Disagree   ❏ Strongly Disagree   ❏ Unable to Rate

7. Using the following scale, how would you rate your own performance on the job?

❏ Excellent   ❏ Above Average   ❏ Average   ❏ Below Average   ❏ Poor

8. What did you like the most about working for [Company Name]?

_____
_____
_____
_____
_____
_____
_____
_____
_____
_____

9. What did you like the least about working for [Company Name]?

_____
_____
_____
_____
_____
_____
_____
_____
_____
_____
_____

10. Of the following five Vision and Values statements, which do you think [Company Name] is the best on? Which do you think needs the most improvement?

Vision and Values Statements	Best	Improvement
We are dedicated to serving our customers		
We work as a team		
We learn, change, and improve		
We focus on results		
We work with integrity		

11. In your opinion, what are some things that supervisors and managers in your department did well?

_____
_____
_____
_____
_____
_____
_____
_____
_____
_____

12. In your opinion, what are some things that supervisors and managers in your department can improve?

_____
_____
_____
_____
_____
_____
_____
_____
_____
_____
_____

13. Again, I'm going to read to you a series of statements. Please answer using the same responses as before: Strongly Agree, Agree, Disagree, Strongly Disagree, or Unable to Rate.

a) Overall, my immediate supervisor did a good job.

❑ Strongly Agree   ❑ Agree   ❑ Disagree   ❑ Strongly Disagree   ❑ Unable to Rate

b) [Company Name]'s employee benefits are as good as most employers in the area.

❑ Strongly Agree   ❑ Agree   ❑ Disagree   ❑ Strongly Disagree   ❑ Unable to Rate

c) Ideas and suggestions for improvements were encouraged in my department.

❑ Strongly Agree   ❑ Agree   ❑ Disagree   ❑ Strongly Disagree   ❑ Unable to Rate

d) My department treated all employees fairly regardless of race, age, religion, disability, gender, sexual orientation, or ethnic background.

❑ Strongly Agree   ❑ Agree   ❑ Disagree   ❑ Strongly Disagree   ❑ Unable to Rate

e) [Company Name] values diversity and differences in the workplace.

❑ Strongly Agree   ❑ Agree   ❑ Disagree   ❑ Strongly Disagree   ❑ Unable to Rate

f) Employees in my department were encouraged to support diversity in working with each other and serving our customers.

❑ Strongly Agree   ❑ Agree   ❑ Disagree   ❑ Strongly Disagree   ❑ Unable to Rate

g) Employees in my work group treated each other with respect.

❑ Strongly Agree   ❑ Agree   ❑ Disagree   ❑ Strongly Disagree   ❑ Unable to Rate

h) Supervisors in my department took the time to encourage and assist employees to help them reach their career goals.

❑ Strongly Agree   ❑ Agree   ❑ Disagree   ❑ Strongly Disagree   ❑ Unable to Rate

14. Are there any issues you would like to address that we may not have asked about?

_____

_____

_____

_____

_____

_____

_____

_____

_____

_____

The next series of questions covers demographic information. This is captured for statistical purposes and will help identify trends.

15. Gender (filled in by interviewer)

❑ Male

❑ Female

16. Which ethnicity group do you most identify with?

❑ African American   ❑ Asian   ❑ Caucasian   ❑ Hispanic   ❑ Native American   ❑ Other

17. Which age group do you belong in?

❑ Under 18   ❑ 18 – 25   ❑ 26 – 35   ❑ 36 – 45   ❑ 46 – 55   ❑ 55 +

18. Which department are you/did you work for?

> ❑ AAA
>
> ❑ BBB
>
> ❑ CCC
>
> ❑ DDDD
>
> ❑ Other: _____
>
> ❑ Decline to answer

Sample I.3.1   Exit Survey

We are interested in what you have to say about your work experience with [Company]. Please complete this form; be frank in your responses. Your thoughtful answers can be helpful to everybody in the effort to keep [Company] a very special place to work. Thank you for your time and efforts. We wish you the best in your future endeavors.

Name _____   Employment Date _____

Position _____   Last Work Day _____

Department _____   Separation Date _____

Supervisor _____

Briefly indicate why you are leaving [Company]: _____

_____

_____

Please check any of the following items that may have contributed to the decision to leave and **circle the primary reason:**

❑ Better job opportunity   ❑ Relationship with supervisor

❑ Working conditions   ❑ Family circumstances

❑ Content of work   ❑ Returning to school

❑ Compensation   ❑ Lack of recognition

❑ Health   ❑ Self-employment

❑ Commuting distance   ❑ Lack of opportunity for advancement

❑ Moving from area   ❑ Better fringe benefit package

❑ Moving closer to family   ❑ Distance from urban center

❑ Other (please explain) _____

What did you think of your supervision with regard to the following?

	Always	Usually	Sometimes	Never
Demonstrated fair and equal treatment				
Provided recognition on the job				
Developed cooperation and teamwork				
Encouraged/listened to suggestions				
Resolved complaints and problems effectively				
Followed policies and practices				
Communicated well with others in the department				

Comments on supervision: _____

_____

_____

How would you rate the following in relation to your job?

	Excellent	Good	Fair	Poor
Cooperation within department				
Cooperation with other departments				
Communications in your department				
Communications within the company as a whole				
Communications between you and your leadership				
Morale in your department				
Friendliness of fellow staff or faculty				
Job satisfaction				
Training you received or orientation to the job				
Growth potential				

Comments: _____

_____

_____

How did you feel about your pay and benefits?

	Excellent	Good	Fair	Poor	No Opinion
Rate of Pay					
Health Insurance					
Life Insurance					
Dental Insurance					
Paid Holiday					
Vacation					
Sick Leave					
Short Term Disability					
Long Term Disability					
Annuity Plan					
Wellness Services					
Professional Development					
Tuition Reimbursement					
Other benefits					

Comments on pay and benefits: _____

_____

Workload:

Was your workload usually: ☐ Too heavy ☐ Varied ☐ About right ☐ Too light

Comments: _____

_____

_____

General Questions:

1. What did you find:

    a. most satisfying about your job/work?

    b. most frustrating about your job/work?

2. Do you feel your job was important and significant in the overall operations of the company?

3. Were there any policies or procedures that made your work more difficult? If so, have you any suggestions on how to eliminate them?

4. Would you consider returning to the company in the future?

5. Would you recommend the company to a family member or friend as a good place to work?

6. Do you believe the company lives up to its Mission Statement? Why?

7. Do you have any suggestions for improvement either at the company or in your work area?

8. Is there anything the company could have done to prevent you from leaving?

9. Any other comments?

Sample I.3.2 Exit Interview Questionnaire

Name _____ Date _____

Branch _____ Dept. _____ Immediate Supervisor/Manager _____

Title _____ Hire Date _____

1. Do you have a new job? ❏ Yes ❏ No

    If yes, what kind of move is it in terms of:

    Responsibility: ❏ More ❏ Less ❏ Same

    Salary: ❏ More ❏ Less ❏ Same

2. Who initiated the contact leading to the new job?

    _____

3. Would you recommend the Company to a friend as a good place to work?

    ❏ Yes ❏ No ❏ Yes, with reservations

    If "Yes, with reservations," or "No," please offer some explanation: _____

    _____

    _____

    _____

4. Was separation: ❏ Employee initiated ❏ Company initiated?

    If "employee initiated": was your decision influenced by any of the following? (Please check all answers that are applicable.)

    ❏ Better Job Opportunity   ❏ Family Circumstances

    ❏ Type of Work   ❏ Self-Employment

    ❏ Rate of Pay   ❏ Illness or Physical Condition

    ❏ Commuting Distance   ❏ Return to School

    ❏ Supervision   ❏ Other: _____

5. If you have accepted another job, what does the new job offer you that your job here did not?

    _____

    _____

    _____

6. What do you think of the supervision you received from your management? (Circle the number under the appropriate heading.)

	Poor	Below Average	Average	Above Average	Excellent
a. Personal relationship with you	1	2	3	4	5
b. Technical knowledge	1	2	3	4	5
c. Leadership ability	1	2	3	4	5
d. Delegation of responsibility	1	2	3	4	5
e. Help and encouragement	1	2	3	4	5
f. Career path counseling/Development	1	2	3	4	5
g. Design of the job description	1	2	3	4	5
h. Follows policies and practices	1	2	3	4	5
i. Demonstrates fair and equal treatment	1	2	3	4	5
j. Provides recognition on the job	1	2	3	4	5
k. Develops cooperation	1	2	3	4	5
l. Resolves complaints, grievances and problems	1	2	3	4	5
m. Offers opportunities for achievement	1	2	3	4	5
n. Reception of new ideas	1	2	3	4	5

7. How would you rate the following about your job or department?

	Poor	Below Average	Average	Above Average	Excellent
a. Cooperation within your department	1	2	3	4	5
b. Cooperation with other departments	1	2	3	4	5
c. On-the-job training	1	2	3	4	5
d. Equipment provided	1	2	3	4	5
e. Communication	1	2	3	4	5
f. Physical working conditions	1	2	3	4	5
g. Friendliness of co-workers	1	2	3	4	5
h. Opportunity to use your skills	1	2	3	4	5
i. Your workload	1	2	3	4	5
j. Opportunity to do interesting work	1	2	3	4	5
k. Overtime policy	1	2	3	4	5
l. Salary review program	1	2	3	4	5
m. Performance appraisal program	1	2	3	4	5

8. With what specific conditions, if any, were you dissatisfied?

_____

_____

_____

9. How did you feel about the following?

	Poor	Below Average	Average	Above Average	Excellent
a. Your personal chances for advancement	1	2	3	4	5
b. Advancement in your department in general	1	2	3	4	5
c. Your supervisor's review of your performance	1	2	3	4	5

Did you ever feel overlooked? If so, when and under what circumstances?

_____

_____

_____

10. What do you feel are your department's major strengths and weaknesses?

_____

_____

_____

11. What changes or improvements would you recommend to make the Company a more satisfying and rewarding place to work?

_____

_____

_____

12. How did you feel about your rate of pay and the employee benefits provided by the Company?

	Poor	Below Average	Average	Above Average	Excellent
a. Rate of pay for your job	1	2	3	4	5
b. Paid holidays	1	2	3	4	5
c. Paid vacation	1	2	3	4	5
d. Retirement plan	1	2	3	4	5
e. Life insurance	1	2	3	4	5
f. Hospital and surgical insurance	1	2	3	4	5
g. Paid sick leave plan	1	2	3	4	5

13. When you started your job, were you informed of your duties, hours of work, pay rate, immediate supervisor, company policies and benefits, etc.?

_____

_____

14. Additional comments about your job, department or the company:

_____

_____

_____

_____

_____

_____

_____

_____

_____

_____

Immediate Supervisor/Manager's Signature	Human Resources Department Signature

Employee's Signature	Separation Date

Comments of Management:

_____

_____

_____

_____

_____

_____

_____

_____

_____

_____

_____

Sample I.3.3   Exit Interview Questionnaire

Instructions: Circle the number beside each statement that most accurately describes the degree of agreement or disagreement with the statement.

Number Key

1. Strongly Agree   2. Agree   3. Tend to Agree

4. Tend to Disagree   5. Disagree   6. Strongly Disagree

Example:

1. There is nothing I enjoy more than filling out questionnaires.	1	2	3	4	5	6

Name _____   **Position** _____

Should you choose to supply us with this information, it will be kept confidential.

---

1. My new position offers better pay.	1	2	3	4	5	6
2. My new position offers better benefits.	1	2	3	4	5	6
3. My new position offers better advancement opportunities.	1	2	3	4	5	6
4. My new position offers a better work environment.	1	2	3	4	5	6
5. My new position is closer to home.	1	2	3	4	5	6
6. I was compensated fairly for the work I performed.	1	2	3	4	5	6
7. The compensation I received for my position was competitive with other local companies.	1	2	3	4	5	6
8. The employee benefit package here is comparable with other local companies.	1	2	3	4	5	6
9. Opportunities for training were open to all employees.	1	2	3	4	5	6
10. The working conditions here were healthy, safe and pleasant.	1	2	3	4	5	6
11. Merit pay increases were directly related to performance.	1	2	3	4	5	6
12. I felt management appreciated me.	1	2	3	4	5	6
13. If I had a problem or concern, I always felt I could approach my supervisor, or other members of management, to discuss it.	1	2	3	4	5	6
14. My supervisor was always fair and consistent.	1	2	3	4	5	6
15. I enjoyed the quarterly Chat Sessions.	1	2	3	4	5	6
16. I felt I was well-informed about the company's goals and objectives.	1	2	3	4	5	6
17. I felt my input and opinions were valued.	1	2	3	4	5	6
18. Management demonstrated concern for the human factor, how people feel, etc.	1	2	3	4	5	6
19. Employees were made to feel as though their efforts were important.	1	2	3	4	5	6
20. Work assignments and projects were assigned fairly.	1	2	3	4	5	6
21. Performance expectations and standards were clearly defined and readily measurable.	1	2	3	4	5	6
22. My supervisor helped me to develop new skills and abilities.	1	2	3	4	5	6

Please use the following area for any comments you may have regarding your employment at [Company]. Use additional sheets if necessary. Thank you for your help.

_____

_____

_____

_____

_____

_____

_____

_____

_____

_____

_____

_____

_____

_____

_____

_____

_____

_____

_____

_____

_____

Sample I.4.1 Employee Separation—Supervisor Questionnaire

Employee Name: _____

Supervisor Name: _____

Department: _____

Separation Date: _____

Reason for Separation:

_____ Resigned, Verbal

_____ Resigned, Written (letter attached)

_____ Discharged, Reason: _____

Please rate this employee's performance in the following areas:

Category	Very Good	Good	Average	Unsatisfactory
Attendance				
Quality				
Quantity				
Relationships				
Culture Fit				

Rehire recommendation:

_____ Eligible without reservation

_____ Eligible with some reservation (please comment below)

_____ Not eligible (please comment below)

Comments:

_____

_____

Supervisor Signature: _____ Date: _____

SECTION J

COBRA Notices

The Consolidated Omnibus Budget Reconciliation Act (COBRA) requires that certain notices be given regarding the rights of employees and other qualified beneficiaries to continue insurance coverage.

A variety of notices are required, depending on the circumstances. In some instances, it is the employer or plan administrator who is required to provide notice; in others, it is the employee or other covered beneficiary.

This section includes a number of forms that can be used in these different situations. Forms are also included to elect to continue insurance coverage.

Sample J.1.1 Model General Notice of COBRA Continuation Coverage Rights (for use by single-employer group health plans)

Continuation Coverage Rights Under COBRA

Introduction

You are receiving this notice because you have recently become covered under a group health plan (the Plan). This notice contains important information about your right to COBRA continuation coverage, which is a temporary extension of coverage under the Plan. **This notice generally explains COBRA continuation coverage, when it may become available to you and your family, and what you need to do to protect the right to receive it.**

The right to COBRA continuation coverage was created by a federal law, the Consolidated Omnibus Budget Reconciliation Act of 1985 (COBRA). COBRA continuation coverage can become available to you when you would otherwise lose your group health coverage. It can also become available to other members of your family who are covered under the Plan when they would otherwise lose their group health coverage. For additional information about your rights and obligations under the Plan and under federal law, you should review the Plan's Summary Plan Description or contact the Plan Administrator.

What is COBRA Continuation Coverage?

COBRA continuation coverage is a continuation of Plan coverage when coverage would otherwise end because of a life event known as a "qualifying event." Specific qualifying events are listed later in this notice. After a qualifying event, COBRA continuation coverage must be offered to each person who is a "qualified beneficiary." You, your spouse, and your dependent children could become qualified beneficiaries if coverage under the Plan is lost because of the qualifying event. Under the Plan, qualified beneficiaries who elect COBRA continuation coverage *[choose and enter appropriate information:* must pay *or* are not required to pay]* for COBRA continuation coverage.

If you are an employee, you will become a qualified beneficiary if you lose your coverage under the Plan because either one of the following qualifying events happens:

- Your hours of employment are reduced, or
- Your employment ends for any reason other than your gross misconduct.

If you are the spouse of an employee, you will become a qualified beneficiary if you lose your coverage under the Plan because any of the following qualifying events happens:

- Your spouse dies;
- Your spouse's hours of employment are reduced;
- Your spouse's employment ends for any reason other than his or her gross misconduct;
- Your spouse becomes entitled to Medicare benefits (under Part A, Part B, or both); or
- You become divorced or legally separated from your spouse.

Your dependent children will become qualified beneficiaries if they lose coverage under the Plan because any of the following qualifying events happens:

- The parent-employee dies;
- The parent-employee's hours of employment are reduced;
- The parent-employee's employment ends for any reason other than his or her gross misconduct;
- The parent-employee becomes entitled to Medicare benefits (Part A, Part B, or both);
- The parents become divorced or legally separated; or
- The child stops being eligible for coverage under the plan as a "dependent child."

> *[If the Plan provides retiree health coverage, add the following paragraph:]*
>
> Sometimes, filing a proceeding in bankruptcy under title 11 of the United States Code can be a qualifying event. If a proceeding in bankruptcy is filed with respect to *[enter name of employer sponsoring the plan]*, and that bankruptcy results in the loss of coverage of any retired employee covered under the Plan, the retired employee will become a qualified beneficiary with respect to the bankruptcy. The retired employee's spouse, surviving spouse, and dependent children will also become qualified beneficiaries if bankruptcy results in the loss of the coverage under the Plan.

When is COBRA Coverage Available?

The Plan will offer COBRA continuation coverage to qualified beneficiaries only after the Plan Administrator has been notified that a qualifying event has occurred. When the qualifying event is the end of employment or reduction of hours of employment, death of the employee, [*add if Plan provides retiree health coverage:* commencement of a proceeding in bankruptcy with respect to the employer,] or the employee's becoming entitled to Medicare benefits (under Part A, Part B, or both), the employer must notify the Plan Administrator of the qualifying event.

You Must Give Notice of Some Qualifying Events

For the other qualifying events (divorce or legal separation of the employee and spouse or a dependent child's losing eligibility for coverage as a dependent child), you must notify the Plan Administrator within 60 days [*or enter longer period permitted under the terms of the Plan*] after the qualifying event occurs. You must provide this notice to: [*Enter name of appropriate party*]. [*Add description of any additional Plan procedures for this notice, including a description of any required information or documentation.*]

How is COBRA Coverage Provided?

Once the Plan Administrator receives notice that a qualifying event has occurred, COBRA continuation coverage will be offered to each of the qualified beneficiaries. Each qualified beneficiary will have an independent right to elect COBRA continuation coverage. Covered employees may elect COBRA continuation coverage on behalf of their spouses, and parents may elect COBRA continuation coverage on behalf of their children.

COBRA continuation coverage is a temporary continuation of coverage. When the qualifying event is the death of the employee, the employee's becoming entitled to Medicare benefits (under Part A, Part B, or both), your divorce or legal separation, or a dependent child's losing eligibility as a dependent child, COBRA continuation coverage lasts for up to a total of 36 months. When the qualifying event is the end of employment or reduction of the employee's hours of employment, and the employee became entitled to Medicare benefits less than 18 months before the qualifying event, COBRA continuation coverage for qualified beneficiaries other than the employee lasts until 36 months after the date of Medicare entitlement. For example, if a covered employee becomes entitled to Medicare 8 months before the date on which his employment terminates, COBRA continuation coverage for his spouse and children can last up to 36 months after the date of Medicare entitlement, which is equal to 28 months after the date of the qualifying event (36 months minus 8 months). Otherwise, when the qualifying event is the end of employment or reduction of the employee's hours of employment, COBRA continuation coverage generally lasts for only up to a total of 18 months. There are two ways in which this 18-month period of COBRA continuation coverage can be extended.

Disability extension of 18-month period of continuation coverage

If you or anyone in your family covered under the Plan is determined by the Social Security Administration to be disabled and you notify the Plan Administrator in a timely fashion, you and your entire family may be entitled to receive up to an additional 11 months of COBRA continuation coverage, for a total maximum of 29 months. The disability would have to have started at some time before the 60th day of COBRA continuation coverage and must last at least until the end of the 18-month period of continuation coverage. [*Add description of any additional Plan procedures for this notice, including a description of any required information or documentation, the name of the appropriate party to whom notice must be sent, and the time period for giving notice.*]

Second qualifying event extension of 18-month period of continuation coverage

If your family experiences another qualifying event while receiving 18 months of COBRA continuation coverage, the spouse and dependent children in your family can get up to 18 additional months of COBRA continuation coverage, for a maximum of 36 months, if notice of the second qualifying event is properly given to the Plan. This extension may be available to the spouse and any dependent children receiving continuation coverage if the employee or former employee dies, becomes entitled to Medicare benefits (under Part A, Part B, or both), or gets divorced or legally separated, or if the dependent child stops being eligible under the Plan as a dependent child, but only if the event would have caused the spouse or dependent child to lose coverage under the Plan had the first qualifying event not occurred.

If You Have Questions

Questions concerning your Plan or your COBRA continuation coverage rights should be addressed to the contact or contacts identified below. For more information about your rights under ERISA, including COBRA, the Health Insurance Portability and Accountability Act (HIPAA), and other laws affecting group health plans, contact the nearest Regional or District Office of the U.S. Department of Labor's Employee Benefits Security Administration (EBSA) in your area or visit the EBSA website at www.dol.gov/ebsa. (Addresses and phone numbers of Regional and District EBSA Offices are available through EBSA's website.)

Keep Your Plan Informed of Address Changes

In order to protect your family's rights, you should keep the Plan Administrator informed of any changes in the addresses of family members. You should also keep a copy, for your records, of any notices you send to the Plan Administrator.

Plan Contact Information

[*Enter name of group health plan and name (or position), address and phone number of party or parties from whom information about the plan and COBRA continuation coverage can be obtained on request.*]

This model form is available on the Department of Labor Web site at http://www.dol.gov/ebsa/modelgeneralnotice.doc.

Sample J.2.1 Employer's Notice to Plan Administrator of Occurrence of COBRA Qualifying Event

Name and Address of Plan Administrator:

_____

_____

_____

Name of Covered Employee:

_____

Qualifying Events:

The following qualifying events have occurred, on the dates stated, resulting in a loss of health coverage on _____ [insert date]:

❏ The covered employee experienced a reduction in work hours   Date: _____

❏ The employment of the covered employee has terminated for reasons other than "gross misconduct"   Date: _____

❏ Death of the covered employee   Date: _____

❏ The covered employee became entitled to Medicare   Date: _____

Please send a notice of COBRA continuation rights and a COBRA election form to the following individual(s) who is (are) a qualified beneficiary(ies) under COBRA, within 14 days of the day you receive this notice:

Name(s) of Qualified Beneficiary(ies) Whose Coverage Will Be Affected by the Qualifying Event:

Name   Relationship to Covered Employee

_____   _____

_____   _____

_____   _____

Name, Signature, and Title of Employer Representative:

_____

[Print name]

_____

[Signature]   Date:

_____

[Title]

Sample J.2.2 Qualified Beneficiary's Notice to Plan Administrator of Occurrence of COBRA Qualifying Event

Name and Address of Plan Administrator:

_____

_____

_____

Name of Covered Employee:

_____

Qualifying Events:

The following qualifying events have occurred, on the dates stated, resulting in a loss of health coverage

❑ Divorce or legal separation of the covered employee. Documentation is enclosed.   Date: _____

❑ Loss of "dependent child" status under group health plan rules   Date: _____

Extension of Coverage Duration Due To Disability:

❑ I received a determination of disability from the Social Security Administration, and have enclosed a copy   Date: _____

Name of Qualified Beneficiary:

_____

[Print full name]

Signature of Qualified Beneficiary:

_____   _____

                                                            Date:

Sample J.3.1 Model COBRA Continuation Coverage Election Notice (for use by single-employer group health plans)

[Enter date of notice]

Dear: *[Identify the qualified beneficiary(ies), by name or status]*

This notice contains important information about your right to continue your health care coverage in the [*enter name of group health plan*] (the Plan). Please read the information contained in this notice very carefully.

To elect COBRA continuation coverage, follow the instructions on the next page to complete the enclosed Election Form and submit it to us.

If you do not elect COBRA continuation coverage, your coverage under the Plan will end on [*enter date*] due to [*check appropriate box*]:

- ❏ End of employment
- ❏ Death of employee
- ❏ Entitlement to Medicare
- ❏ Reduction in hours of employment
- ❏ Divorce or legal separation
- ❏ Loss of dependent child status

Each person ("qualified beneficiary") in the category(ies) checked below is entitled to elect COBRA continuation coverage, which will continue group health care coverage under the Plan for up to _____ months [*enter 18 or 36, as appropriate and check appropriate box or boxes; names may be added*]:

- ❏ Employee or former employee
- ❏ Spouse or former spouse
- ❏ Dependent child(ren) covered under the Plan on the day before the event that caused the loss of coverage
- ❏ Child who is losing coverage under the Plan because he or she is no longer a dependent under the Plan

If elected, COBRA continuation coverage will begin on [*enter date*] and can last until [*enter date*]. You may elect any of the following options for COBRA continuation coverage: [*list available coverage options*].

COBRA continuation coverage will cost: [*enter amount each qualified beneficiary will be required to pay for each option per month of coverage and any other permitted coverage periods.*] You do not have to send any payment with the Election Form. Important additional information about payment for COBRA continuation coverage is included in the pages following the Election Form.

If you have any questions about this notice or your rights to COBRA continuation coverage, you should contact [*enter name of party responsible for COBRA administration for the Plan, with telephone number and address*].

COBRA Continuation Coverage Election Form

Instructions: To elect COBRA continuation coverage, complete this Election Form and return it to us. Under federal law, you must have 60 days after the date of this notice to decide whether you want to elect COBRA continuation coverage under the Plan.

Send completed Election Form to: [*Enter Name and Address*]

This Election Form must be completed and returned by mail [*or describe other means of submission and due date*]. If mailed, it must be postmarked no later than [*enter date*].

If you do not submit a completed Election Form by the due date shown above, you will lose your right to elect COBRA continuation coverage. If you reject COBRA continuation coverage before the due date, you may change your mind as long as you furnish a completed Election Form before the due date. However, if you change your mind after first rejecting COBRA continuation coverage, your COBRA continuation coverage will begin on the date you furnish the completed Election Form.

Read the important information about your rights included in the pages after the Election Form.

I (We) elect COBRA continuation coverage in the [*enter name of plan*] (the Plan) as indicated below:

Name	Date of Birth	Relationship to Employee	SSN (or other identifier)

a. _____

    [*Add if appropriate:* Coverage option elected: _____]

b. _____

    [*Add if appropriate:* Coverage option elected: _____]

c. _____

    [*Add if appropriate:* Coverage option elected: _____]

_____   _____
Signature   Date

_____   _____
Print Name   Relationship to individual(s) listed above

_____   _____

_____   _____
Print Address   Telephone number

Important Information About Your COBRA Continuation Coverage Rights

What is continuation coverage?

Federal law requires that most group health plans (including this Plan) give employees and their families the opportunity to continue their health care coverage when there is a "qualifying event" that would result in a loss of coverage under an employer's plan. Depending on the type of qualifying event, "qualified beneficiaries" can include the employee (or retired employee) covered under the group health plan, the covered employee's spouse, and the dependent children of the covered employee.

Continuation coverage is the same coverage that the Plan gives to other participants or beneficiaries under the Plan who are not receiving continuation coverage. Each qualified beneficiary who elects continuation coverage will have the same rights under the Plan as other participants or beneficiaries covered under the Plan, including special enrollment rights.

How long will continuation coverage last?

In the case of a loss of coverage due to end of employment or reduction in hours of employment, coverage generally may be continued only for up to a total of 18 months. In the case of losses of coverage due to an employee's death, divorce or legal separation, the employee's becoming entitled to Medicare benefits or a dependent child ceasing to be a dependent under the terms of the plan, coverage may be continued for up to a total of 36 months. When the qualifying event is the end of employment or reduction of the employee's hours of employment, and the employee became entitled to Medicare benefits less than 18 months before the qualifying event, COBRA continuation coverage for qualified beneficiaries other than the employee lasts until 36 months after the date of Medicare entitlement. This notice shows the maximum period of continuation coverage available to the qualified beneficiaries.

Continuation coverage will be terminated before the end of the maximum period if:

- any required premium is not paid in full on time,
- a qualified beneficiary becomes covered, after electing continuation coverage, under another group health plan that does not impose any pre-existing condition exclusion for a pre-existing condition of the qualified beneficiary,
- a qualified beneficiary becomes entitled to Medicare benefits (under Part A, Part B, or both) after electing continuation coverage, or
- the employer ceases to provide any group health plan for its employees.

Continuation coverage may also be terminated for any reason the Plan would terminate coverage of a participant or beneficiary not receiving continuation coverage (such as fraud).

[*If the maximum period shown on page 1 of this notice is less than 36 months, add the following three paragraphs:*]

How can you extend the length of COBRA continuation coverage?

If you elect continuation coverage, an extension of the maximum period of coverage may be available if a qualified beneficiary is disabled or a second qualifying event occurs. You must notify [*enter name of party responsible for COBRA administration*] of a disability or a second qualifying event in order to extend the period of continuation coverage. Failure to provide notice of a disability or second qualifying event may affect the right to extend the period of continuation coverage.

Disability

An 11-month extension of coverage may be available if any of the qualified beneficiaries is determined by the Social Security Administration (SSA) to be disabled. The disability has to have started at some time before the 60th day of COBRA continuation coverage and must last at least until the end of the 18-month period of continuation coverage. [*Describe Plan provisions for requiring notice of disability determination, including time frames and procedures.*] Each qualified beneficiary who has elected continuation coverage will be entitled to the 11-month disability extension if one of them qualifies. If the qualified beneficiary is determined by SSA to no longer be disabled, you must notify the Plan of that fact within 30 days after SSA's determination.

Second Qualifying Event

An 18-month extension of coverage will be available to spouses and dependent children who elect continuation coverage if a second qualifying event occurs during the first 18 months of continuation coverage. The maximum amount of continuation coverage available when a second qualifying event occurs is 36 months. Such second qualifying events may include the death of a covered employee, divorce or separation from the covered employee, the covered employee's becoming entitled to Medicare benefits (under Part A, Part B, or both), or a dependent child's ceasing to be eligible for coverage as a dependent under the Plan. These events can be a second qualifying event only if they would have caused the qualified beneficiary to lose coverage under the Plan if the first qualifying event had not occurred. You must notify the Plan within 60 days after a second qualifying event occurs if you want to extend your continuation coverage.

How can you elect COBRA continuation coverage?

To elect continuation coverage, you must complete the Election Form and furnish it according to the directions on the form. Each qualified beneficiary has a separate right to elect continuation coverage. For example, the employee's spouse may elect continuation coverage even if the employee does not. Continuation coverage may be elected for only one, several, or for all dependent children who are qualified beneficiaries. A parent may elect to continue coverage on behalf of any dependent children. The employee or the employee's spouse can elect continuation coverage on behalf of all of the qualified beneficiaries.

In considering whether to elect continuation coverage, you should take into account that a failure to continue your group health coverage will affect your future rights under federal law. First, you can lose the right to avoid having pre-existing condition exclusions applied to you by other group health plans if you have more than a 63-day gap in health coverage, and election of continuation coverage may help you not have such a gap. Second, you will lose the guaranteed right to purchase individual health insurance policies that do not impose such pre-existing condition exclusions if you do not get continuation coverage for the maximum time available to you. Finally, you should take into account that you have special enrollment rights under federal law. You have the right to request special enrollment in another group health plan for which you are otherwise eligible (such as a plan sponsored by your spouse's employer) within 30 days after your group health coverage ends because of the qualifying event listed above. You will also have the same special enrollment right at the end of continuation coverage if you get continuation coverage for the maximum time available to you.

How much does COBRA continuation coverage cost?

Generally, each qualified beneficiary may be required to pay the entire cost of continuation coverage. The amount a qualified beneficiary may be required to pay may not exceed 102 percent (or, in the case of an extension of continuation coverage due to a disability, 150 percent) of the cost to the group health plan (including both employer and employee contributions) for coverage of a similarly situated plan participant or beneficiary who is not receiving continuation coverage. The required payment for each continuation coverage period for each option is described in this notice.

The Trade Act of 2002 created a new tax credit for certain individuals who become eligible for trade adjustment assistance and for certain retired employees who are receiving pension payments from the Pension Benefit Guaranty Corporation (PBGC) (eligible individuals). Under the new tax provisions, eligible individuals can either take a tax credit or get advance payment of 65% of premiums paid for qualified health insurance, including continuation coverage. If you have questions about these new tax provisions, you may call the Health Coverage Tax Credit Customer Contact Center toll-free at 1-866-628-4282. TTD/TTY callers may call toll-free at 1-866-626-4282. More information about the Trade Act is also available at www.doleta.gov/tradeact/2002act_index.asp.

When and how must payment for COBRA continuation coverage be made?

First payment for continuation coverage

If you elect continuation coverage, you do not have to send any payment with the Election Form. However, you must make your first payment for continuation coverage not later than 45 days after the date of your election. (This is the date the Election Notice is postmarked, if mailed.) If you do not make your first payment for continuation coverage in full not later than 45 days after the date of your election, you will lose all continuation coverage rights under the Plan. You are responsible for making sure that the amount of your first payment is correct. You may contact [*enter appropriate contact information, e.g., the Plan Administrator or other party responsible for COBRA administration under the Plan*] to confirm the correct amount of your first payment.

Periodic payments for continuation coverage

After you make your first payment for continuation coverage, you will be required to make periodic payments for each subsequent coverage period. The amount due for each coverage period for each qualified beneficiary is shown in this notice. The periodic payments can be made on a monthly basis. Under the Plan, each of these periodic payments for continuation coverage is due on the [*enter due day for each monthly payment*] for that coverage period. If you make a periodic payment on or before the first day of the coverage period to which it applies, your coverage under the Plan will continue for that coverage period without any break. The Plan [*select one:* will *or* will not] send periodic notices of payments due for these coverage periods.

Grace periods for periodic payments

Although periodic payments are due on the dates shown above, you will be given a grace period of 30 days after the first day of the coverage period to make each periodic payment. Your continuation coverage will be provided for each coverage period as long as payment for that coverage period is made before the end of the grace period for that payment. However, if you pay a periodic payment later than the first day of the coverage period to which it applies, but before the end of the grace period for the coverage period, your coverage under the Plan will be cancelled as of the first day of the coverage period and then retroactively reinstated (going back to the first day of the coverage period) when the periodic payment is received. This means that any claim you submit for benefits while your coverage is suspended may be denied and may have to be resubmitted once your coverage is reinstated.

If you fail to make a periodic payment before the end of the grace period for that coverage period, you will lose all rights to continuation coverage under the Plan.

Your first payment and all periodic payments for continuation coverage should be sent to:

[*enter appropriate payment address*]

For more information

This notice does not fully describe continuation coverage or other rights under the Plan. More information about continuation coverage and your rights under the Plan is available in your summary plan description or from the Plan Administrator.

If you have any questions concerning the information in this notice or your rights to coverage, or if you want a copy of your summary plan description, you should contact [*enter name of party responsible for COBRA administration for the Plan, with telephone number and address*].

For more information about your rights under ERISA, including COBRA, the Health Insurance Portability and Accountability Act (HIPAA), and other laws affecting group health plans, contact the U.S. Department of Labor's Employee Benefits Security Administration (EBSA) in your area or visit the EBSA website at www.dol.gov/ebsa. (Addresses and phone numbers of Regional and District EBSA Offices are available through EBSA's website.)

Keep Your Plan Informed of Address Changes

In order to protect your and your family's rights, you should keep the Plan Administrator informed of any changes in your address and the addresses of family members. You should also keep a copy, for your records, of any notices you send to the Plan Administrator.

This model form is available on the Department of Labor Web site at http://www.dol.gov/ebsa/modelelectionnotice.doc.

Sample J.4.1   Plan Administrator's Notice to Applicant of Unavailability of COBRA Continuation Coverage

Name and Address of COBRA Coverage Applicant:

_____

_____

_____

Dear COBRA Coverage Applicant:

We received on _____ [date] your Notice of Election of COBRA Continuation Coverage (or Notice of Social Security Administration disability determination). We regret to inform you that you are not eligible for COBRA continuation coverage (or extended COBRA coverage) for the reason(s) indicated below. If you believe this Notice of Unavailability of COBRA Continuation Coverage is in error, please contact us immediately at [Phone Number].

Reason for Unavailability of COBRA Coverage or Extended COBRA Coverage:

❑ Your election form was submitted too late. The deadline was _____.

❑ Your notice of divorce or legal separation was submitted too late. A qualified beneficiary must notify the Plan Administrator within 60 days after divorce or legal separation. The deadline was _____.

❑ Your notice of ceasing to be covered as a dependent child was submitted too late. A qualified beneficiary must notify the Plan Administrator within 60 days after ceasing to be covered as a dependent child. The deadline was _____.

❑ You were not covered under the plan on the day before the claimed Qualifying Event.

❑ The employment of the covered employee was terminated for "gross misconduct."

❑ Your notice of determination of disability by the Social Security Administration was submitted too late. The disability determination must be provided to the Plan Administrator within 60 days of a disability determination and prior to the expiration of the initial 18-month term. Your disability determination was made on _____. The initial 18-month term expired on _____. Therefore, the deadline was _____.

❑ You waived COBRA coverage during the election period, and did not revoke your waiver until after the expiration of the election period. The deadline to revoke your waiver was _____.

❑ Other _____

_____

Name of Covered Employee:

_____

Qualifying Events:

Our records reflect that you relied upon the following Qualifying Event(s):

❑ The covered employee experienced a reduction in work hours   Date: _____

❑ The employment of the covered employee has terminated for reasons other than "gross misconduct"   Date: _____

❑ Death of the covered employee   Date: _____

❑ The covered employee became entitled to Medicare   Date: _____

❑ Divorce or legal separation of the covered employee   Date: _____

❑ Loss of "dependent child" status under the plan rules   Date: _____

Name, Signature, and Title of Plan Representative:

_____

[Print name]

_____

[Signature]   Date:

_____

[Title]

Sample J.5.1 # Plan Administrator's Notice To COBRA Beneficiary of Early Termination of COBRA Continuation Coverage

Name and Address of COBRA Coverage Beneficiary:

_____

_____

_____

Dear COBRA Coverage Beneficiary:

You are hereby notified that your COBRA continuation coverage will expire early due to _____ [insert valid reason per COBRA for early termination; for example, "your failure to pay the required premium by the applicable due date"]

Your COBRA continuation coverage will expire on _____.

If you believe this Notice of Early Termination of COBRA Continuation Coverage is in error, please contact us immediately at [Phone Number].

Please note that alternative group or individual coverage under the plan may be available to you as follows: [list any such alternative coverage that may exist, such as conversion rights].

Name, Signature, and Title of Plan Representative:

_____

[Print name]

_____   _____

[Signature]   Date:

_____

[Title]

SECTION K

HIPAA Certificate

The Health Insurance Portability and Accountability Act (HIPAA) entitles employees to documentation showing evidence of their prior health insurance coverage. Such documentation may be helpful to employees in obtaining insurance that does not contain an exclusion for pre-existing conditions.

The form in this section can be used to notify employees of their HIPAA portability rights; it shows the required content of the certificate.

Sample K.1.1 Certificate Of Group Health Plan Coverage

1. Date of this certificate: _____

2. Name of group health plan: _____

   _____

3. Name of participant: _____

4. Identification number of participant: _____

5. Name of individuals to whom this certificate applies: _____

   _____

6. Name, address, and telephone number of plan administrator or issuer responsible for providing this certificate: _____

   _____

7. For further information, call: _____

8. If the individual(s) identified in line 5 has (have) at least 18 months of creditable coverage (disregarding periods of coverage before a 63-day break), check here and skip lines 9 and 10: _____

9. Date waiting period or affiliation period (if any) began: _____

   _____

10. Date coverage began: _____

11. Date coverage ended (or if coverage has not ended, enter "continuing"): _____

[Note: separate certificates will be furnished if information is not identical for the participant and each beneficiary.]

Statement of HIPAA Portability Rights

Important—Keep This Certificate. This certificate is evidence of your coverage under this plan. Under a federal law known as HIPAA, you may need evidence of your coverage to reduce a preexisting condition exclusion period under another plan, to help you get special enrollment in another plan, or to get certain types of individual health coverage even if you have health problems.

Preexisting condition exclusions. Some group health plans restrict coverage for medical conditions present before an individual's enrollment. These restrictions are known as "preexisting condition exclusions." A preexisting condition exclusion can apply only to conditions for which medical advice, diagnosis, care, or treatment was recommended or received within the 6 months before your "enrollment date." Your enrollment date is your first day of coverage under the plan, or, if there is a waiting period, the first day of your waiting period (typically, your first day of work). In addition, a preexisting condition exclusion cannot last for more than 12 months after your enrollment date (18 months if you are a late enrollee). Finally, a preexisting condition exclusion cannot apply to pregnancy and cannot apply to a child who is enrolled in health coverage within 30 days after birth, adoption, or placement for adoption.

If a plan imposes a preexisting condition exclusion, the length of the exclusion must be reduced by the amount of your prior creditable coverage. Most health coverage is creditable coverage, including group health plan coverage, COBRA continuation coverage, coverage under an individual health policy, Medicare, Medicaid, State Children's Health Insurance Program (SCHIP), and coverage through high-risk pools and the Peace Corps. Not all forms of creditable coverage are required to provide certificates like this one. If you do not receive a certificate for past coverage, talk to your new plan administrator.

You can add up any creditable coverage you have, including the coverage shown on this certificate. However, if at any time you went for 63 days or more without any coverage (called a break in coverage) a plan may not have to count the coverage you had before the break.

Therefore, once your coverage ends, you should try to obtain alternative coverage as soon as possible to avoid a 63-day break. You may use this certificate as evidence of your creditable coverage to reduce the length of any pre-existing condition exclusion if you enroll in another plan.

Right to get special enrollment in another plan. Under HIPAA, if you lose your group health plan coverage, you may be able to get into another group health plan for which you are eligible (such as a spouse's plan), even if the plan generally does not accept late enrollees, if you request enrollment within 30 days. (Additional special enrollment rights are triggered by marriage, birth, adoption, and placement for adoption.)

→   Therefore, once your coverage ends, if you are eligible for coverage in another plan (such as a spouse's plan), you should request special enrollment as soon as possible.

Prohibition against discrimination based on a health factor. Under HIPAA, a group health plan may not keep you (or your dependents) out of the plan based on anything related to your health. Also, a group health plan may not charge you (or your dependents) more for coverage, based on health, than the amount charged a similarly situated individual.

Right to individual health coverage. Under HIPAA, if you are an "eligible individual," you have a right to buy certain individual health policies (or in some states, to buy coverage through a high-risk pool) without a preexisting condition exclusion. To be an eligible individual, you must meet the following requirements:

■ You have had coverage for at least 18 months without a break in coverage of 63 days or more;

■ Your most recent coverage was under a group health plan (which can be shown by this certificate);

- Your group coverage was not terminated because of fraud or nonpayment of premiums;

- You are not eligible for COBRA continuation coverage or you have exhausted your COBRA benefits (or continuation coverage under a similar state provision); and

- You are not eligible for another group health plan, Medicare, or Medicaid, and do not have any other health insurance coverage.

The right to buy individual coverage is the same whether you are laid off, fired, or quit your job.

→ Therefore, if you are interested in obtaining individual coverage and you meet the other criteria to be an eligible individual, you should apply for this coverage as soon as possible to avoid losing your eligible individual status due to a 63-day break.

State flexibility. This certificate describes minimum HIPAA protections under federal law. States may require insurers and HMOs to provide additional protections to individuals in that state.

For more information. If you have questions about your HIPAA rights, you may contact your state insurance department or the U.S. Department of Labor, Employee Benefits Security Administration (EBSA) toll-free at 1-866-444-3272 (for free HIPAA publications ask for publications concerning changes in health care laws). You may also contact the CMS publication hotline at 1-800-633-4227 (ask for "Protecting Your Health Insurance Coverage"). These publications and other useful information are also available on the Internet at: http://www.dol.gov/ebsa, the DOL's interactive web pages—Health *E*laws, or http://www.cms.hhs.gov/hipaa1.

This model form is available on the Department of Labor Web site at http://dol.gov/ebsa/hipaamodelnotice.doc.

SECTION L
WARN Notices

When applicable to a mass layoff or plant closing, the Worker Adjustment and Retraining Notification (WARN) Act requires certain information to be provided to certain persons by certain deadlines. To determine the situations in which WARN applies and the deadlines for providing notice, refer to Chapter2.

If WARN applies, the forms in this section can be used to make sure that the right types of information are given to several parties: affected employees, the representative of affected employees (union), and government officials.

Sample L.1.1   WARN Act Notice to Affected Employees

To: [Name and Address of Affected Employee]

Re: Notice pursuant to Worker Adjustment and Retraining Notification ("WARN") Act, 20 C.F.R., Section 639.7

Date: [Insert date]

Pursuant to the WARN Act, [Company] regrets to inform you that [Company] anticipates conducting a [plant closing] [mass layoff] as described below.

Name and Address of Affected Employment Site

The name and address of the employment site where the [plant closing] [mass layoff] will occur is _____.

Duration and Scope of Action

The [plant closing] [mass layoff] is expected to be [temporary] [permanent]. The entire plant [will] [will not] be closed.

When Job Separations Will Begin, and Your Last Day of Employment

[Company] expects the date of the first separation from employment to be _____ [date]. The [Company] anticipates that your last day of employment will be _____ [date].

"Bumping Rights"

"Bumping rights" [do] [do not] exist under your collective bargaining agreement with [Company]. "Bumping rights" are the rights of senior employees who are scheduled to be laid off to displace or "bump" less senior employees. Please refer to your collective bargaining agreement as to the scope of such bumping rights, and any conditions or limitations on their operation.

Whom to Contact for Further Information

The name and telephone number of the [Company] official to contact for further information is _____.

Sample L.2.1 WARN Act Notice to Representative of Affected Employees

To: [Name and Address of Employee Representative]

Re: Notice pursuant to Worker Adjustment and Retraining Notification ("WARN") Act, 20 CFR, Section 639.7

Date: [Insert date]

Pursuant to the WARN Act, [Company] regrets to inform you that [Company] anticipates conducting a [plant closing] [mass layoff] as described below.

Name and Address of Affected Employment Site

The name and address of the employment site where the [plant closing] [mass layoff] will occur is _____.

Whom to Contact for Further Information

The name and telephone number of the [Company] official to contact for further information is _____.

Duration and Scope of Action

The [plant closing] [mass layoff] is expected to be [temporary] [permanent]. The entire plant [will] [will not] be closed.

When Job Separations Will Begin and Separation Schedule

[Company] expects the date of the first separation from employment to be _____ [date]. The anticipated schedule for making separations is: _____ [describe or insert schedule].

Affected Job Titles and Individual Employees

The job titles of the affected positions, and the names of the persons currently holding the affected jobs, are:

Job Titles	Persons Currently Holding Affected Jobs

Sample L.3.1   WARN Act Notice to Government (Standard Form)

To: [Name and Address of State Dislocated Worker Unit]

And

[Name and Address of Chief Elected Official of Local Government]

Re: Notice pursuant to Worker Adjustment and Retraining Notification ("WARN") Act, 20 CFR, Section 639.7

Date: [Insert date]

Pursuant to the WARN Act, [Company] regrets to inform you that [Company] anticipates conducting a [plant closing] [mass layoff] as described below.

Name and Address of Affected Employment Site

The name and address of the employment site where the [plant closing] [mass layoff] will occur is _____.

Duration and Scope of Action

The [plant closing] [mass layoff] is expected to be [temporary] [permanent]. The entire plant [will] [will not] be closed.

When Job Separations Will Begin and Separation Schedule

[Company] expects the date of the first separation from employment to be _____ [date]. The anticipated schedule for making separations is: _____ [describe or insert schedule].

"Bumping Rights"

"Bumping rights" [do] [do not] exist under one or more collective bargaining agreements with [Company].

Affected Job Titles and Number of Affected Employees in Each Job Classification

The job titles of the affected positions, and the number of affected employees in each job classification are:

Job Titles	Number of Affected Employees in Job Class

Names of Each Union Representing Affected Employees, and Contact Information for Chief Elected Officer Thereof

The name(s) of each union representing affected employees, and the contact information for the Chief Elected Officer thereof [is] [are]:

Union Name	Name and Address of Chief Elected Officer of Union

Whom to Contact for Further Information

The name and telephone number of the [Company] official to contact for further information is _____.

Sample L.3.2 **WARN Act Notice to Government (Short Form)**

To: [Name and Address of State Dislocated Worker Unit]

And

[Name and Address of Chief Elected Official of Local Government]

Re: Notice pursuant to Worker Adjustment and Retraining Notification ("WARN") Act, 20 CFR, Section 639.7

Date: [Insert date]

Pursuant to the WARN Act, [Company] regrets to inform you that [Company] anticipates conducting a [plant closing] [mass layoff] as described below.

Name and Address of Affected Employment Site

The name and address of the employment site where the [plant closing] [mass layoff] will occur is _____.

Whom to Contact for Further Information

The name and telephone number of the [Company] official to contact for further information is _____.

When Job Separations Will Begin

[Company] expects the date of the first separation from employment to be _____ [date].

Number of Affected Employees

[Company] expects number of affected employees to be _____ [number].

Additional Information

The following additional information is available and readily accessible on the plant site:

■ The anticipated schedule for making separations.

■ Whether the [plant closing] [mass layoff] is expected to be temporary or permanent.

■ Whether the plant will or will not be closed.

■ Whether "bumping rights" exist under one or more collective bargaining agreements with [Company].

■ The job titles of the affected positions, and the number of affected employees in each job classification.

■ The name(s) of each union representing affected employees, and the name and address of the Chief Elected Officer thereof.

Endnotes

1. Barrier, Michael, "EPLI Providers Turn Up the Heat," HR Magazine, May 2002, p. 48.

2. "Jury Awards 85-Year-Old Doctor in Age Discrimination Case," www.nbc4.tv/news/4746709/detail.html, retrieved July 22, 2005.

3. Ballard, Wade, "Lawyers' Bad Acts Upon Leaving Firm Tainted Their Hiring of Co-Workers," www.shrm.org/hrnews_published/archives/CMS_009661.asp, retrieved February 12, 2005.

4. Presser, Jay, "Competing While Still Employed Breaches Duty of Loyalty," www.shrm.org/hrnews_published/archives/CMS_012609.asp, retrieved August 17, 2005.

5. "The Mind of a Killer," USA Today, July 15, 2004, p. 2A.

6. SHRM Workplace Violence Survey (2004), p. 6.

7. Kübler-Ross, Elisabeth, On Death and Dying (New York: MacMillan Publishing Co., Inc., 1969).

8. Employers should consult resources dealing specifically with HIPAA issues to determine the full scope of their responsibilities under the Act. A useful publication is the HIPAA Privacy Source Book: A Collection of Practical Samples, by William S. Hubbartt, SPHR, CCP (SHRM, 2004). The U.S. Department of Labor publishes frequently asked questions about HIPAA (www.dol.gov/ebsa/faqs/faq_compliance_hipaa.html).

9. The full implications of ERISA go far beyond the scope of this book. Employers that have policies, plans, or practices that could be subject to ERISA should consult ERISA-specific sources, as well as employment attorneys experienced with ERISA compliance.

10. If the employee is a member of a union, the "due process" afforded in such a "trial" must include the so-called "Weingarten right." This is the right, established by the U.S. Supreme Court in NLRB v. J. Weingarten Inc., 420 U.S. 251 (1975), to have a union representative with the employee during a workplace investigatory interview that might lead to discipline by the employer.

11. HR Briefing, October 10, 1998.

12. HR Briefing, October 10, 1998.

13. SHRM Workplace Violence Survey (2004), p. v.

14. Id., p. 5.

15. Barrier, Michael, "Protecting Trade Secrets," HR Magazine (May 2004), p. 54.

16. Id., p. 55.

17. SHRM Reference and Background Checking Survey Report (2004), p. 19.

Index

Note: italicized page numbers indicate figures

About the Authors

Wendy Bliss, J.D., SPHR

Wendy Bliss's professional background includes experience as a human resource executive, attorney, senior editor, and professional speaker. Since 1994, she has provided human resource consulting, corporate training and coaching services nationally through her Colorado Springs-based firm, Bliss & Associates. Her clients include diverse organizations in many industries, from small-family owned businesses to *Fortune 500* companies.

Wendy is the author of *Legal, Effective References: How to Give and Get Them,* the HR Series Adviser for the *Business Literacy for Human Resource Professionals* series co-published by Harvard Business School Press and the Society for Human Resource Management (SHRM). She has written numerous articles for publications including *HR Magazine, Employment Management Today, HR Matters* and the *Denver University Law Review* and conducted seminars throughout the United States for SHRM and the American Management Association.

National media including the *ABC News "20/20"* show, *Time* magazine, the *New York Times,* the *Associated Press,* the *Washington Post, USAToday.com,* and *HR Magazine* have used Wendy as an expert source on workplace issues.

Wendy is a certified Senior Professional in Human Resources (SPHR). She graduated from the University of Kansas, and received her Juris Doctor degree from the University of Denver College of Law. She has served as an officer or member of non-profit boards and panels, including as President of SHRM's Consultants Forum, President of the Pikes Peak chapter of the American Society for Training and Development, and a member of SHRM's Special Expertise Panels for Employee Relations and HR Consulting/Outsourcing.

Gene R. Thornton, Esq., PHR

Gene R. Thornton is a business litigation attorney specializing in the prevention, investigation, and litigation of employment claims for both employers and employees. Gene has handled numerous investigations, lawsuits, and arbitrations under federal and state laws, including matters of termination, discrimination and harassment, wage and hour compliance, family and medical leave, and non-compete and trade secrets, as well as common law claims of all types. He also has significant experience as an independent fact-finder and has served as an arbitrator for the National Association of Securities Dealers, Inc. ("NASD") since 1989.

Gene has published over fifty articles on employment law issues and has presented numerous seminars to employers and other attorneys.

Currently a solo law practitioner in Colorado Springs, He formerly was a shareholder and director of the Denver law firm of Hopper & Kanouff, P.C. where he was responsible for human resource matters. His undergraduate degree is from Northwestern University in Communication Studies, and his Juris Doctor is from the University of Denver. After graduating from law school, Gene served a judicial clerkship on the Colorado Court of Appeals. He is also a graduate of the National Institute for Trial Advocacy ("NITA") and has been certified as a Professional in Human Resources (PHR) from the Human Resource Certification Institute

Selected Additional Titles from the Society for Human Resource Management (SHRM®)

Building Profit through Building People: Making Your Workforce the Strongest Link in the Value-Profit Chain
  By Ken Carrig and Patrick M. Wright

The Comprehensive, All-in-One HR Operating Guide: 539 ready-to-adapt human resource letters, memos, procedures, practices, forms...and more
  By R.J. Landry

Diverse Teams at Work: Capitalizing on the Power of Diversity
  By Lee Gardenswartz and Anita Rowe

Harvard/SHRM Series on Business Literacy for HR Professionals
Series Advisor Wendy Bliss, J.D., SPHR
Essentials of Corporate Communication
Essentials of Finance and Budgeting
Essentials of Managing Change and Transition
Essentials of Negotiation
Essentials of Power, Influence, and Persuasion

HR Source Book Series
Performance Appraisal Source Book
  By Mike Deblieux
HIPAA Privacy Source Book
  By William S. Hubbartt, SPHR, CCP
Hiring Source Book
  By Cathy Fyock, CAP, SPHR
Trainer's Diversity Source Book
  By Jonamay Lambert, M.A. and Selma Myers, M.A.
Human Resource Essentials: Your Guide to Starting and Running the HR Function
  By Lin Grensing-Pophal, SPHR

The Future of Human Resource Management: 64 thought leaders explore the critical HR issues of today and tomorrow
  Edited by Mike Losey, Sue Meisinger, and Dave Ulrich

Outsourcing Human Resources Functions: How, Why, When, and When Not to Contract for HR Services
  By Mary F. Cook and Scott R. Gildner

Practical HR Series
Legal, Effective References: How to Give and Get Them
  By Wendy Bliss, J.D., SPHR
Investigating Workplace Harassment: How to Be Fair, Thorough, and Legal
  By Amy Oppenheimer, J.D., and Craig Pratt, MSW, SPHR
Proving the Value of HR: How and Why to Measure ROI
  By Jack J. Phillips, Ph.D. and Patricia Pulliam Phillips, Ph.D.

Supervisor's Guide to Labor Relations
  By T.O. Collier, Jr.

Understanding the Federal Wage & Hour Laws: What Employers Must Know about FLSA and its Overtime Regulations
  By Seyfarth Shaw LLP

TO ORDER SHRM BOOKS

SHRM offers a member discount on all books that it publishes or sells. To order this or any other book published by the Society, contact the SHRMStore.®

ONLINE: www.shrm.org/shrmstore

BY PHONE: 800-444-5006 (option #1); or 770-442-8633 (ext. 362); or TDD 703-548-6999

BY FAX: 770-442-9742

BY MAIL: SHRM Distribution Center
             P.O. Box 930132
             Atlanta, GA 31193-0132
             USA

Using the Accompanying CD-ROM

The materials on the accompanying CD-ROM are readable on a PC and are in two formats: Portable Document Format (PDF) and Rich Text Format (RTF).

Portable Document Format (PDF) Files

To open the PDF files, all you need is the free Adobe® Reader®. The PDF files on this disc are compatible with Reader versions 7.0 and higher. Adobe Reader or the full version of Acrobat is required. You can download the latest version of Adobe Reader for free at http://www.adobe.com/products/acrobat/readstep2.html. See "Getting Started," below.

Rich Text Form (RTF) Files

The RTF files can be opened in many word-processing programs. You will be given the option to download these files. See "Getting Started," below. **NOTE:** The RTF files are "read only." To adapt them for your use, open a file and safe it under a different name. You will be able to edit that new file.

Getting Started

To access the files on the CD-ROM, insert the CD-ROM into your compact disk drive. The disk will AutoRun and open a preliminary screen; click "Next" to proceed. You will see an information screen "Using the Accompanying CD-ROM." Click "Next." The disk will give you the option to either open the PDF files or install the RTF files. If you select the PDF files, the disk will either open those files OR will tell you that you need to get Adobe Reader. Follow the directions on your screen.

STOP!

Please read the following before opening the CD-ROM accompanying this book.

By opening the CD-ROM package, you are agreeing to be bound by the following agreement:

Once you open the seal on the software package, this book and the CD-ROM are nonrefundable. (With the seal unbroken, the book and CD-ROM are refundable only under the terms generally allowed by the seller.)

This software product is protected by copyright and all rights are reserved by the Society for Human Resource Management (SHRM®) and its licensors. Purchasers of the book may use the materials on the CD-ROM as part of their own work providing that that include the full crediting.

Copying the software to another medium or format for use on a single computer is permitted and therefore does not violate the U.S. Copyright Law. Copying the software for any other purposes is not permitted and is therefore a violation of the U.S. Copyright Law.

This software product is sold as is without warranty of an kind, either express or implied, including but not limited to the implied warranty of merchantability and fitness for a particular purpose. Neither SHRM nor its dealers or distributors assumes any liability for any alleged or actual damage arising from the use of or the inability to use this software. (Some states to now allow the exclusion of implied warranties, so the exclusion may not apply to you if you receive this product in such a state.)